THE TRUTH
ABOUT
THE TRUTH

For books written by the editor, see the last page of this book.

A NEW CONSCIOUSNESS READER

This New Consciousness Reader is part of a new series of original and classic writing by renowed experts on leading-edge concepts in personal development, psychology, spiritual growth, and healing. Other books in this series include:

The Awakened Warrior
EDITED BY RICK FIELDS

Dreamtime and Dreamwork
EDITED BY STANLEY KRIPPNER, PH.D.

The Erotic Impulse
EDITED BY DAVID STEINBERG

Fathers, Sons, and Daughters
EDITED BY CHARLES SCULL, PH.D.

Healers on Healing
EDITED BY RICHARD CARLSON, PH.D., AND BENJAMIN SHIELD

In the Company of Others
EDITED BY CLAUDE WHITMYER

Meeting the Shadow
EDITED BY CONNIE ZWEIG AND JEREMIAH ABRAMS

Mirrors of the Self
EDITED BY CHRISTINE DOWNING

The New Paradigm in Business
EDITED BY MICHAEL RAY
AND ALAN RINZLER FOR THE WORLD BUSINESS ACADEMY

Paths Beyond Ego
EDITED BY ROGER WALSH, M.D., PH.D., AND FRANCES VAUGHAN, PH.D.

Reclaiming the Inner Child
EDITED BY JEREMIAH ABRAMS

Spiritual Emergency
EDITED BY STANISLAV GROF, M.D., AND CHRISTINA GROF

To Be a Man
EDITED BY KEITH THOMPSON

To Be a Woman
EDITED BY CONNIE ZWEIG

The Truth About the Truth
EDITED BY WALTER TRUETT

What Survives?
EDITED BY GARY DOORE, PH.D.

Who am I?
EDITED BY ROBERT FRAGER, PH.D.

FOUNDING SERIES EDITOR: CONNIE ZWEIG, PH.D.

To Be a Man
EDITED BY KEITH THOMPSON

To Be a Woman
EDITED BY CONNIE ZWEIG

What Survives?
EDITED BY GARY DOORE, PH.D.

Who Am I?
EDITED BY ROBERT FRAGER

THE TRUTH

ABOUT

THE TRUTH

De-Confusing and Re-Constructing the Postmodern World

Edited by

WALTER TRUETT ANDERSON

Jeremy P. Tarcher/Penguin
a member of
Penguin Group (USA) Inc.
New York

Most Tarcher/Penguin books are available at special quantity
discounts for bulk purchase for sales promotions, premiums,
fund-raising, and educational needs. Special books or book excerpts
also can be created to fit specific needs.
For details, write Penguin Group (USA) Inc.
Special Markets, 375 Hudson Street
New York, NY 10014

Permissions appear on page 253.

Jeremy P. Tarcher/Penguin
a member of
Penguin Group (USA) Inc.
375 Hudson Street
New York, NY 10014
www.penguin.com

Library of Congress Cataloging-in-Publication Data

The truth about the truth : deconfusing and re-constructing the postmodern world /
edited by Walter Truett Anderson.
p.   cm.
"A Jeremy P. Tarcher/Putnam book."
Includes bibliographical references.
ISBN 0-87477-801-8 (acid-free paper)
1. Postmodernism.   I. Anderson, Walt, date.
B831.2.T77   1995   95-5537 CIP
149—dc20

Design by Books Unbound
Cover design by Susan Shankin

Printed in the United States of America
21 22 23 24 25

This book is printed on acid-free paper. ∞

IN MEMORY OF ROLLO MAY,
1909–1994,
PHILOSOPHER AND FRIEND

CONTENTS

INTRODUCTION: What's Going On Here?   1

PART ONE. IN AND OUT OF THE GRAND HOTEL

THEMES AND DEFINITIONS

1. STEINAR KVALE Themes of Postmodernity   18
2. CHARLES JENCKS What Is Post-Modernism?   26
3. UMBERTO ECO "I Love You Madly," He Said Self-consciously   31

THE CONSTRUCTION OF REALITY

4. ERNEST BECKER The Fragile Fiction   34
5. PETER L. BERGER AND THOMAS LUCKMANN
   The Dehumanized World   36
6. MICHEL FOUCAULT Strategies of Power   40

THREE USEFUL INVENTIONS

7. ISAIAH BERLIN The Idea of Pluralism   46
8. ROY WAGNER The Idea of Culture   53
9. WERNER SOLLORS The Idea of Ethnicity   58

PART TWO. ALL THAT IS SOLID MELTS INTO AIR

SYMBOLS AT WORK AND PLAY

10. RICHARD SHWEDER Santa Claus on the Cross   72
11. JEAN BAUDRILLARD The Map Precedes the Territory   79
12. ERNEST STERNBERG The Economy of Icons   82
13. JACQUES DERRIDA The Play of Substitution   86
14. STEPHEN KATZ How to Speak and Write Postmodern   92

DIFFERENT KINDS OF DIFFERENCE

15. JAMES DAVISON HUNTER The Orthodox and the Progressive   96
16. RICHARD RORTY Ironists and Metaphysicians   100
17. PAULINE MARIE ROSENAU Affirmatives and Skeptics   107
18. WALTER TRUETT ANDERSON Four Different Ways
    to Be Absolutely Right   110
19. BELL HOOKS Postmodern Blackness   117

PART THREE. SELF, SEX AND SANITY

THE PLURALISTIC PERSON, THE DISAPPEARING SELF

20. ROBERT JAY LIFTON The Protean Style 130
21. KENNETH J. GERGEN The Healthy, Happy Human Being
Wears Many Masks 136
22. CONNIE ZWEIG The Death of the Self
in the Postmodern World 145

SEX AND GENDER

23. MAUREEN O'HARA Constructing Emancipatory Realities 151
24. WILLIAM SIMON The Postmodernization of Sex and Gender 156

RECONSTRUCTING PSYCHOLOGY

25. STANLEY KRIPPNER AND MICHAEL WINKLER
Studying Consciousness in the Postmodern Age 161
26. MAUREEN O'HARA AND WALTER TRUETT ANDERSON
Psychotherapy's Own Identity Crisis 170

PART FOUR. FAITH AND FREEDOM

SCIENCE WITHOUT SCIENTISM

27. HOWARD GARDNER Gifted Worldmakers 182
28. THOMAS KUHN Scientists and Their Worldviews 189
29. PAUL FEYERABEND Anything Goes 199

RELIGION IN THE AGE OF DISBELIEF

30. HUSTON SMITH Postmodernism and the World's Religions 204
31. MARTIN MARTY Religio-Secular Society 215
32. ARTHUR SCHLESINGER, JR. The Opening
of the American Mind 224
33. VÁCLAV HAVEL The Search for Meaning
in a Global Civilization 232

EPILOGUE: The End and Beginning of Enlightenment 239

Notes 245
Contributors 257

Introduction: What's Going On Here?

Some postmodern news items:

An American anthropologist visited Japan during the Christmas season and noticed that the retail merchants there had begun to take a great interest in the symbolism of Christmas. When he wandered into a large department store in Tokyo, he saw a striking example of this: a Christmas display that prominently featured Santa Claus nailed to a cross.[1]

The Lapps of northern Finland have almost abandoned their traditional form of chanting, called "yoiking." But now some young Lapps are reviving it, learning the songs from the old people and holding public concerts. In the process, they experiment and improvise. One group put on a concert with a rock band, combining yoiking with hard rock. They are also developing an electronically augmented form, called "techno-yoik."[2]

Fashion editors say "the religious look" is hot: clothes that resemble monastic robes, jumpers with giant crosses stitched into the design, rosary necklaces. A jewelry designer reports a strong demand for Stars of David, but also a brisk trade in "basic crosses," Russian Orthodox crosses, Maltese crosses and ankhs. A fashion show in Germany unveiled a collection inspired by nuns' habits. An Italian collection featured the "Hasidic look," with female models wearing long side curls and wide-brimmed felt hats.[3]

In the 1990 census, almost 10 million Americans created a giant statistical headache by refusing to identify themselves in terms of any of the standard categories. They insisted on being listed as "other race." Some of the dissenters were of highly mixed backgrounds, some just didn't like to be pigeonholed. An official said the whole system will probably have to change: "Basically what you're asking is a person's judgment of their race or ethnicity. And people's perceptions of themselves and their answers can change from census to census."[4]

What is it that is going on here—here and everywhere—that produces such a burst of cultural chaos and creativity, such rampant pluralism? What gives so many people a feeling of permission to tinker with the hallowed symbolic heritage of societies—mixing rituals and traditions like greens in a salad, inventing new personal identities, revising old political ideologies, picking and choosing what to believe and what not to believe? Is there a pattern that links such diverse events as the collapse of Communism, the information/communications revolution, the doctrinal civil wars within organized religions and the restless spiritual and cultural wanderings of the educated and affluent?

The message of this book is that there is—that we are in the midst of a great, confusing, stressful and enormously promising historical transition, and it has to do with a change not so much in *what* we believe as in *how* we believe.

People rarely understand or even notice great historical transitions as they take place; it is said that Louis XVI, at the end of the day the Bastille fell, wrote in his diary *Rien*, "Nothing happened." Revolutions of belief are even more elusive, because they take place within human minds. You don't always know what's going on, even when it is your own mind that has been the scene of the upheaval. It's quite possible, for example, to go from seeing science as absolute and final truth to seeing it as an ever-changing body of ideas—a bigtime shift, any philosopher will tell you—without feeling that anything special has happened, without losing all confidence in scientific facts: For all practical purposes the speed of light remains 186,000 miles per second, gravity still makes water run downhill, and ontogeny goes right on recapitulating phylogeny. It's equally possible to move from seeing a religion as timeless truth to seeing it as the product of a certain culture—and still happily worship at your church or temple.

People all over the world are now making such shifts in belief—to be more precise, shifts in belief about belief. They are not, of course, always doing it effortlessly. It's true that some people scarcely notice the difference when they cease to regard their society's beliefs as absolutely the last word, but that same change feels to many like a great liberation, and to many others like a grievous loss. It can be profoundly troubling, or it can be painfully threatening. However it feels, it happens. It happens because we are charging headlong into a new era: a time of rethinking and rebuilding in which beliefs about belief are shaken as never before, a time in which issues once left to the philosophers—such as the nature of truth—become matters of vital everyday importance to ordinary people. When you think about your personal beliefs and values, when you make decisions about your religious life, when you worry about whether or not to conform to the customs of your society or community—even when you consult your most fundamental sense of who and what you are—you are taking an active part in this transition.

LOOKING BACK, LOOKING AHEAD

The word commonly used to describe this era is "postmodern"—a puzzling, uppity term, seeming to imply that the modern era, which we have always equated with all that is new and progressive, has reached the age of retirement. I first noticed it in Stephen Toulmin's book *The Return to Cosmology*. Toulmin said:

> We must reconcile ourselves to a paradoxical-sounding thought: namely, the thought that *we no longer live in the "modern" world.* The "modern" world is now a thing of the past. Our own natural science today is no longer "modern" science. Instead . . . it is rapidly engaged in becoming "post-modern" science: the science of the "postmodern" world, of "postnational-ist" politics and "postindustrial" society—the world that has not yet discovered how to define itself in terms of what it *is,* but only in terms of what it has *just-now ceased to be.*[5]

Postmodern is a makeshift word we use until we have decided what to name the baby. It is a word of looking back. But what is it, exactly, that we are looking back *at*? What is it that the world has just now ceased to be?

One of the best answers was offered by David Harvey of Oxford University in his book *The Condition of Postmodernity.* Harvey defined postmodernity as the situation in which the world finds itself after the breakdown of the "Enlightenment project," which lasted from the latter part of the eighteenth century until well into the twentieth. That was the project aimed at getting all the world's diverse peoples to see things the same way—the rational way. The thinkers of the Enlightenment, Harvey said, "took it as axiomatic that there was only one possible answer to any question. From this it followed that the world could be controlled and rationally ordered if we could only picture and represent it rightly. But this presumed that there existed a single correct mode of representation which, if we could uncover it (and this was what scientific and mathematical endeavors were all about), would provide the means to Enlightenment ends." The Enlightenment—and the twentieth-century scientific rationalism that grew out of it—was not only a philosophical effort, then, but an ideology of progress: a belief in "linear progress, absolute truths, and rational planning of ideal social orders."[6]

Another book you're likely to hear quoted wherever anybody tries to define postmodern is Jean-Francois Lyotard's *The Postmodern Condition*. Lyotard, a French philosopher, was commissioned by the Council of Universities of Quebec in the late 1970s to do a study on the state of knowledge in the Western world. He said in his report that all modern systems of knowledge, including science, had been supported by some "metanarrative" or "grand discourse" about the main direction of history.

A metanarrative is a *story* of mythic proportions, a story big enough and meaningful enough to pull together philosophy and research and politics and art, relate them to one another, and—above all—give them a unifying sense of direction. Lyotard cited as examples the Christian religious story of God's will being worked out on Earth, the Marxist political story of class conflict and revolution, and the Enlightenment's intellectual story of rational progress. (For Americans, Manifest Destiny was once a great metanarrative; for colonial powers, the theme of taking up "the white man's burden" served a similar purpose.) He proceeded to define the postmodern era as a time of "incredulity toward metanarratives"—all of them.

Lyotard didn't mean that all people have ceased to believe in all stories, but rather that the stories aren't working so well anymore—in part because there are too many, and we all know it. He took Yeats' famous "the centre cannot hold" a step farther: He said there are a lot of centers, and none of them holds. Instead, we are exposed to a babble of diverse and contradictory fragments of stories, and the arts and sciences go their various ways.[7]

Lyotard's argument was in some ways a subtle and difficult one, but it is not hard to get a sense of what a multistoried world looks and sounds like. All you have to do is turn on your nearest television set and flip randomly from channel to channel: Listen to the religious prophecies, the political messages, the forecasts of ecological and/or economic doom just a commercial break away from cheerful promises of brighter tomorrows. Notice that with each channel you briefly enter the subculture of another ethnic group, another age level, another profession or interest or lifestyle. Consider the impact of a similar array of messages being beamed to every part of the world—people everywhere being bombarded by the sermons, the commercials, the vivid images of other people living quite different kinds of lives.

You get a better perspective on the present situation by contrasting it not only to the just-ending modern era, but also to the premodern—to life in isolated tribes, small villages, early city-states. In premodern societies, most people lived within the context of a single coherent cultural package. Premodern societies weren't necessarily simple or primitive, but people in them were relatively free from the "culture shock" experience of coming into contact with other people with entirely different values and beliefs—the kind of experience that, in contemporary urban life, you're likely to have a couple of times before lunch.

The long march out of premodernity was a series of culture shocks—another step taken each time somebody made the unsettling discovery that the same world could contain multiple world*views*. Different people have done quite different things when they made that discovery: Conquerors frequently tried to kill off the wrong thinkers. Missionaries tried to persuade or force them to convert to the correct view of reality. Philosophers tried to create systems of understanding so profound—so super-human—that they might be offered to the world as more than just another culturally-based set of beliefs. Some people place the roots of modernism as far back as the time of Socrates and Plato, who were engaged in just such a project of searching for essential truths, deeper and more durable than those embodied in the myths of their tribal gods.

Over the past few centuries, various great belief-systems—philosophical, religious, political and combinations thereof—have flexed their muscles in the world. The modern era has been a time of battles between religions, between religion and science, between political ideologies. And although each of these had its own inventory of essential truths, none has been able to gain universal agreement that those truths were all that true.

It doesn't look like we are about to become all Christians, all Marxists, all Muslims, all cool modern rationalists.

I'd sum it all up this way: People in premodern, traditional societies had an experience of universality but no concept of it. They could get through their days and lives without encountering other people with entirely different worldviews—and, consequently, they didn't have to worry a lot about how to deal with pluralism. People in modern civilization have had a concept of universality—based on the hope (or fear) that some genius, messiah or tyrant would figure out how to get everybody on the same page— but no experience of it. Instead, every war, every trade mission, every migration brought more culture shocks. Now, in the postmodern era, the very concept of universality is, as the deconstructionists say, "put into question." The old strategies of conquest, repression and conversion are still being strenuously applied in many places—labeled now by nifty euphemisms like "ethnic cleansing"—but they aren't very effective. It begins to look like we're all going to have to get used to a world of multiple realities.

Postmodernity, then, is the age of over-exposure to otherness— because, in traveling, you put yourself into a different reality; because, as a result of immigration, a different reality comes to you; because, with no physical movement at all, only the relentless and ever-increasing flow of information, cultures interpenetrate. It becomes harder and harder to live out a life within the premodern condition of an undisturbed traditional society or even within the modern condition of a strong and well-organized belief system. All the major-league belief systems are still around, but all of them are in some kind of postmodern trouble: internal civil wars. Believers commuting in and out. Innovators creating strange new variations—free-market Communism, feminist Christianity, New Age science.

We are living in a new world, a world that does not know how to define itself by what it is, but only by what it has just-now ceased to be.

AN "ISM" FOR OUR TIME

And, although it seems a bit nitpicky, I think it's useful to make a distinction between postmodernity and postmodernism—the first being the time (or condition) in which we find ourselves, the second being the various schools and movements it has produced. So far, I have been talking mostly about postmodernity.

I have noticed, over the years that I have been traveling and discussing these matters with various groups, that it's a lot easier to get agreement about the -ity than the -ism. The word "postmodernism" is floating around rather freely these days, and it means different things to different people. To some, it means funny architecture; to others, French intellectuals you can't understand; to still others, anything weird, campy, trendy or high-tech. Some people equate it with the idea that all values and beliefs are equal.

Postmodernisms—their way paved by the psychedelic, academic, racial and political upheavals of the 1960s—began to catch the attention of culture-watchers in the early 1970s. America was being invaded at about that time by the works of French intellectuals such as Michel Foucault, whose "archaeological" studies showed how earlier civilizations had constructed new concepts—about madness, for example—that also gave rise to new systems of power. Through the 1980s and 1990s more and more people have become familiar with some form of postmodernism—either by taking the high road through academia, where its ideas are endlessly pondered in the lecture halls and the dormitories; or by taking the low road through popular culture, where they are reflected in movies, music and fiction. Currently, postmodern thought is entering into a new growth phase linked to the explosion of information and communications technologies, the global mass-media economy of images, the ever-increasing determination of many men and women to reconstruct traditional ideas about sex and gender.

Many people fervently hope that postmodernism—whatever they mean by it—will go away. And a lot of them are going to get their wish: Styles will change, of course. Some of the intellectual movements that have landed at the top of the academic pecking order will be deposed; this appears to be happening to deconstruction already. The radical relativism of the sort I described earlier doesn't have to go away, because it was never here. Nobody really believes that everything is equal, because the human mind doesn't work that way; whatever else it is doing, it is always tirelessly, relentlessly evaluating.

Postmodernisms will come and go, but postmodernity—the postmodern condition—will still be here. It is a major transition in human history, a time of rebuilding all the foundations of civilization, and the world is going to be occupied with it for a long time to come. And, although it touches different people in vastly different ways, it is happening to us all. We are all emerging from out of the security of our tribes, traditions, religions and worldviews into a global civilization that is dazzlingly, overwhelmingly pluralistic.

Surrounded by so many truths, we can't help but revise our concept of truth itself: our beliefs about belief. More and more people become acquainted with the idea that, as philosopher Richard Rorty puts it, truth is made rather than found.[8] This idea itself is not exactly new. It came into the Eastern world with Buddhism about 2,500 years ago, and into the Western world at about the same time with Heraclitus. It has been the message of various mystics and philosophers over the centuries. It is like a minor theme in a symphony that is heard at first faintly in the background and eventually swells into dominance.

Seeing truth as made, not found—seeing reality as socially constructed—doesn't mean deciding there is nothing "out there." It means understanding that all our stories about what's out there—all our scientific facts, our religious teachings, our society's beliefs, even our personal perceptions—are the products of a highly creative interaction between human minds and the cosmos. The cosmos may be found; but the ideas we form about it, and the things we say about it, are made. One of the main themes of postmodern thought is that language is deeply involved in the social construction of reality. Rorty says: "We need to make a distinction between the claim that the world is out there and the claim that truth is out there. To say that the world is out there, that it is not our creation, is to say, with common sense, that most things in space and time are the effects of causes which do not include human mental states. To say that truth is not out there is simply to say that where there are no sentences there is no truth, that sentences are elements of human languages, and that human languages are human creations."[9]

Postmodern thought is closely linked to the "linguistic turn" in philosophy—the growing consensus that ideas cannot be understood apart from the language systems that produced them—and to recent research on the human brain and nervous system. No serious postmodern thinker believes that reality is constructed by an effortless whim: It is a complex and in many ways still mysterious process. It involves minds and bodies, cool thoughts and hot passions, personal experiences and the collective history of humanity. It is very closely related to the activities we call play, art, craft, poetry, theater. But—whatever you emphasize—we come to see that no truths in the world are, so to speak, untouched by human hands.

So we find all kinds of men and women at work—some flying a "postmodernist" flag and some not—trying to define the present situation, explain it, exploit it, make it go away or figure out what we should do about it.

Some people study the reality-construction process: Cognitive scientists and neuroscientists analyze the workings of the individual brain/mind as it assembles the chaotic raw data of sensory perception into meaningful experience. Anthropologists and sociologists learn how different societies create different values and beliefs, myths and rituals, laws and institutions.

Psychologists such as Kenneth Gergen focus on postmodern experience—on how it *feels* to live amid such a rich, often contradictory barrage of cultural stimuli; what it does to us and what kind of people we become. They say the postmodern individual is a member of many communities and networks, a participant in many discourses, an audience to messages from everybody and everywhere—messages that present conflicting ideals and norms and images of the world. Gergen believes that this condition (he calls it *multiphrenia*) is the major psychological problem of our time—but also possibly the birth-pangs of a new kind of human being.[10]

In literature and the arts, we have critical theorists who insist that when you experience a work of art you don't simply take in the artist's intention, but actively participate in creating whatever meaning or message you find. You are also the artist.

In the world of religion—or, to be more accurate, in the many worlds of religion—people are overhauling doctrines right and left. How could it be otherwise? If you regard the various truths and practices of a religion as socially constructed—created by certain human beings according to the needs (as they perceived them) of certain times—you are likely to feel free to reconstruct them according to the needs (as you perceive them) of the present time. This may mean ordaining gays, creating ecological rituals, declaring God to be female or going ahead and making up a whole new religion. It may also mean quietly and privately deciding to override certain teachings such as prohibitions against birth control. Other religions are similarly troubled: there are Islamic futurists and feminists, new variations of Hinduism and Buddhism—and, in each religion, fundamentalists who are desperately striving to keep the old faith.

And so it goes through every field of human knowledge, though high culture and low. We see postmodernity on the streets in the behavior of people who are learning to live multiethnic lifestyles; we see it in the wild diversity of pop culture. We see it in politics in many ways—one of them being a striking shift from conflict *between* belief systems to conflict *within* belief systems: between innovators and traditionalists in the organized religions, between revisionists and Marxist reactionaries in the post-Communist world.

FOUR CORNERS OF THE POSTMODERN WORLD

This is a huge transition—one that I think has barely begun—and it doesn't lend itself to simple summaries. But as an introduction to this book I will point out four main dimensions of it:

1. *Self-concept.* Instead of forming our ideas of who and what we are on the basis of the "found" identity fixed by social role or tradition, we begin to understand ourselves in terms of the "made" identity that is constructed (and frequently reconstructed) out of many cultural sources.

2. *Moral and ethical discourse.* We move from the "found" morality of a single cultural and/or religious heritage to the "made" morality forged out of dialogue and choice. We don't become relativists of the sort that are supposed to make no judgments. Instead, we become the kind of relativists—described by contributors to this book as constructivists, ironists or postmodern humanists—who know that when we do make our judgments we're standing on the ever-shifting ground of our own socially constructed cultural worldviews.

3. *Art and culture.* No style dominates. Instead we have endless improvisations and variations on themes; parody and playfulness. Postmodern architects are unabashedly eclectic and call attention to it. People everywhere similarly combine traditions, borrow rituals and myths. All the world's cultural symbols are now in the public domain, and Santa Claus is on the cross.

4. *Globalization.* For the first time in human history we have a truly global civilization. It is a civilization of rapid information exchange and unprecedented mobility. We shouldn't be surprised that, in it, many people begin to see their various tribal ways for what they are, and take them a bit less seriously. Nor should we be surprised that they also want to hold onto their tribal ways if they find them satisfying—and maybe grab a few of some other tribe's ways while they're at it. It is a civilization continually changing form, with unstable boundaries. People now see borders of all kinds as social constructions of reality and feel free to cross them, erase them, reconstruct them.

The selections in this book are all, in one way or another, about the postmodern world. They aren't all in agreement, of course, and they don't always speak the same language. You will encounter some splendid examples of postmodernist jargon. You will find some selections by people who write about the postmodern world without ever using the term "postmodern." You will find some strong critiques of various aspects of postmodernism.

Whatever their bias, they are all contributions to one of the most painfully challenging and yet absolutely essential tasks of human life— trying to understand our time while we are in it.

This time is, for all its jangle, complexity and dissonance, a moment of great beauty and opportunity. We glimpse new ways of thinking about ourselves, new possibilities for coexisting with others—even profoundly different others. We begin to feel a sense of ownership of our worldviews and identities. My own feeling about this time is a hopeful one. I believe that such works as these, taken together, do more than describe the world in terms of what it has just now ceased to be. They also help us understand the world in terms of what it is struggling to become.

PART ONE

IN AND OUT OF THE GRAND HOTEL

There wouldn't be any discussions of the postmodern world—in fact there wouldn't be a postmodern world—without the idea of *culture*. Premodern people, who lived in their cultures as a fish lives in water, had no need for such a notion. Modern people invented it, and postmodern people couldn't live without it. The idea of culture is a conceptual tool that we all use constantly; a thread that runs through public discourse about all kinds of issues—political, moral, religious, psychological. It is inseparable from the idea that there are lots of cultures—cultures, subcultures, counter-cultures.

And of course it means different things to different people. An older meaning of culture, the one I grew up with, referred to all those things that your schoolteachers said was good for you: the art and literature and music of past eras, a great body of dull respectability. If you had those things, you had culture, maybe even Culture. That meaning is still around, but it has become much less important. Nowadays when we use the word we are more likely to be using it in the way evolutionary theorists use it, to refer to something uniquely human. The great biologist Theodosius Dobzhansky, one of the people who helped invent this newer meaning, wrote:

> The appearance of culture signified the beginning of a hitherto non-existent type of evolutionary development. . . . Biological heredity is transmitted by genes; consequently it is handed down exclusively from parents to their children and other direct descendants. Culture is transmitted by teaching and learning. At least in principle, "the social legacy" can be transmitted by anyone to anyone, regardless of biological descent. Man may be said to have two heredities, a biological one and a cultural one; all other species have only the biological one.[1]

This idea of culture as a sort of symbolic DNA—which probably strikes most readers as boringly obvious—was one of the great, radical intellectual products of the modern era. It came partly out of Darwinian evolutionary thinking, partly out of the discoveries of anthropologists who were forced to keep inventing the idea of culture in the course of work that took them deeply into societies where people had entirely different ways of thinking and acting. Anthropologists saw that human beings—biologically pretty much the same everywhere—became quite different as they grew up within different cultures. This discovery was a blow to prevailing ideas about "human nature."

Clifford Geertz, one of our best contemporary anthropologists, declares that there simply "is no such thing as a human nature independent of culture. We are . . . incomplete or unfinished animals who complete or finish ourselves through culture—and not through culture in general but through highly particular forms of it. . . ."[2]

The anthropologists' gift to the world is the idea that human beings create different kinds of cultures, which in turn create different kinds of human beings. Cultures aren't created out of nothing—the genes have their say, the environment has its influence—but they are still creations. This is a fundamentally subversive idea, because if you absorb it and accept it at all, you are likely to begin to (a) notice that you live in a culture, (b) think of it as something that was created by human beings, (c) wonder who created it and for what purpose, (d) wonder what it does to you and (e) think about making some choices and/or changes. And the more people there are working their way through some such inner thought process, the more culturally diverse, complex and unstable a society is likely to be.

Which brings us back to the world we live in.

Jim Collins, in his book *Uncommon Cultures*, says that, although people customarily talk about "the culture" as if it were some tangible object out there on the landscape, there is no such thing—no such single thing. Rather there are all kinds of cultures—discourses is the favorite postmodern term for them—and none of them is particularly able to pull rank on the others. High culture, capital-C Culture, no longer holds its privileged place:

> We need to see popular culture and Post-Modernism as a continuum because both reflect and produce the same cultural perspective—that "culture" no longer can be conceived as a Grand Hotel, as a totalizable system that somehow orchestrates all cultural production and reception according to one master system. Both insist, implicitly or explicitly, that what we consider "our culture" has become *discourse-sensitive*, that how we conceptualize that culture depends upon discourses which construct it in conflicting, often contradictory ways. . . .[3]

So you can—I think with some accuracy—look at the postmodern world as a kind of jailbreak from the Grand Hotel, with people charging in all directions while anxious conservatives try to round them up and get them back inside. But the situation is a bit trickier than that because the symbolic environment is still all around us and within us. What's happening now is that we are all becoming increasingly aware of it; we are (quick change of metaphors here) like fish who are beginning to figure out that we live in the water.

As we become aware that we live in a symbolic environment—which is what the idea of culture enables us to do—we make choices about it. Some people choose grunge rock over *Parsifal,* or Native American sweat ceremonies over High Mass. Others wander in and out of cultures high and low, sampling and improvising, creating new forms, sometimes reinhabiting the Grand Hotel but with a new sense of ownership.

The essence of postmodernity, as the Canadian futurist Ruben Nelson puts it, is that "culture does not simply happen to us anymore." Increasingly, we also happen to it. This is a major transition in the way human beings relate to their symbolic environments, and thus another step—a large one— along the evolutionary path that began with the appearance of language.

In the following readings we look first at some overviews of postmodernism—essays in which different writers survey the whole postmodern territory and tell us what they see out there. After that we explore one of the most important ideas of the postmodern era—the social construction of reality. Then we look at some of the realities that have been constructed in our time—important cultural inventions like pluralism, ethnicity and the idea of culture itself.

I

Themes of Postmodernity

STEINAR KVALE

*Steiner Kvale's survey of postmodern thought shows it going in many
directions, its themes not always compatible with one another.
Among these themes:*

> *A doubt that any human truth is a simple objective represen-
> tation of reality.*
> *A focus on the way societies use language to construct their
> own realities.*
> *A preference for the local and specific over the universal and
> abstract.*
> *A renewed interest in narrative and story-telling.*
> *Acceptance that different descriptions of reality can't always
> be measured against one another in any final—i.e., objective
> and nonhuman—way.*
> *A willingness to accept things as they are on the surface rather
> than to search (à la Freud or Marx) for Deeper Meanings.*

*Most of these themes seem to fit together, and yet a certain
tension typifies the postmodern condition: on the one hand the tendency toward fragmentation, on the other a search for a larger
framework of meaning. Kvale talks about an "expansion of rationality," a belief that reason appears in many guises. This has the*

makings of another Enlightenment project, a search for the floor plan
to a much more spacious Grand Hotel.

It is debatable whether postmodernity is actually a break with modernity, or merely its continuation. Postmodern writers may prefer to write history so that their own ideas appear radically new. Postmodern themes were present in the romanticism of the last century, in Nietzsche's philosophy at the turn of the century, with the surrealists and in literature, for instance in Blixen and Borges. What is new today is the pervasiveness of postmodern themes in culture at large.

"Postmodern" does not designate a systematic theory or a comprehensive philosophy, but rather diverse diagnoses and interpretations of the current culture, a depiction of a multitude of interrelated phenomena.

Postmodern thought is characterized by a loss of belief in an objective world and an incredulity towards meta-narratives of legitimation. With a delegitimation of global systems of thought, there is no foundation to secure a universal and objective *reality*. There is today a growing public acknowledgement that "Reality isn't what is used to be."

In philosophy there is a departure from the belief in one true reality—subjectively copied in our heads by perception or objectively represented in scientific models.[1] There exists no pure, uninterpreted datum; all facts embody theory. In science the notion of an objective reality is an interesting hypothesis, but is not necessary for carrying out scientific work.[2] Knowledge becomes the ability to perform effective actions.

The focus is on the social and linguistic construction of a perspectival reality. In society the development of technology, in particular the electronic media, opens up an increased exposure to a multiplicity of perspectives, undermining any belief in one objective reality.[3] In a world of media, the contrast between reality and fantasy breaks down and is replaced by a hyperreality, a world of self-referential signs.[4] What remains is signs referring to other signs, texts referring to other texts.

A critique of *legitimation* is central in Lyotard's analysis of the postmodern condition. Legitimacy involves the question of what is valid, what is legal, the issue of whether an action is correct and justifiable. Habermas brought the issue to the fore in his book *Legitimation Crisis*,[5] depicting a general loss of faith in tradition and authority, with a resulting relativity of values.

Lyotard identifies "*postmodern* as incredulity towards meta-narratives," as a "paganism," where we pass judgement on truth, beauty and justice without criteria for the judgements. In a comment on the debate between Lyotard and Habermas, Rorty interprets Lyotard as saying that "the trouble with Habermas is not so much that he provides a narrative of emancipation as that he feels the need to legitimize, that he is not content to let the narratives which hold all culture together do their stuff. He is scratching where it does not itch."[6] Rather than continuing the Cartesian attempts of "self-grounding," Rorty advocates a Baconian approach of "self-assertion."

A further theme of modernity is the dichotomy of the *universal and the individual,* between society and the unique person, whereby the rootedness of human activity and language in a given social and historical context is overlooked. In modernity the person is an object for a universal will, or for general laws of history or nature. Or the person is overburdened; man has become the centre of the world, the individual self-feeling being the cornerstone of modern thought, a self stretched out between what it is and what it ought to be.

If we abstract a human from his or her context, we are trapped between the poles of the universal and the individual—the way out is to study humans in their cultural and social context. With the collapse of the universal meta-narratives, the local narratives come into prominence. The particular, heterogeneous and changing language games replace the global horizon of meaning. With a pervasive decentralization, communal interaction and local knowledge become important in their own right. Even such concepts as nation and tradition are becoming rehabilitated in a postmodern age.

The emphasis upon the local surpasses the modern polarity of the universal and the individual, of the objective and the subjective. The local interaction, the communal network, is the point of departure; universal laws and unique individual selves are seen as abstractions from man's being in the world. Rather than equating universal laws with the objective and the individual with the subjective and relative, valid interpretations of meaning and truth are made by people who share decisions and the consequence of their decisions.[7] Instead of a subjective nihilism, we may here talk of a contextual relativism where legitimation of action occurs through linguistic practice and communicative action.

With the collapse of the universal systems of meaning or meta-narratives, a re-narrativization of the culture takes place, emphasizing communication and the impact of a message upon the audience. There is today an interest in *narratives,* on the telling of stories. In contrast to an extrinsic legitimation through appeal to meta-discourses, or Utopia, Lyotard advocates an intrinsic legitimation through a narrative knowledge which "does not give priority to the question of its own legitimation, and . . . certifies itself in the pragmatics of its own transmission without having recourse to argumentation and proof."[8] Narratives themselves contain the criteria of competence and illustrate how they ought to be applied; they are legitimated by the simple fact that they do what they do. A narrative is not merely a transmission of information. In the very act of telling a story the position of the storyteller and the listener, and their place in the social order, is constituted; the story creates and maintains social bonds. The narratives of a community contribute to uphold the values and the social order of that community.

Postmodern thought focuses on *heterogeneous* language games, on the non-commensurable, on the instabilities, the breaks and the conflicts. Rather than regarding a conversation as a dialogue between partners, it is seen as a game, a confrontation between adversaries. A universal consensus of meaning is no ideal; the continual effort after meaning is no longer a big deal. The reply to the modern global sense-makers is simply "just let it be" or "stop making sense."

There exists no standard method for measuring and comparing knowledge within different language games and paradigms; they are incommensurable. A postmodern world is characterized by a continual change of perspectives, with no underlying common frame of reference, but rather a manifold of changing horizons. Rock music videos capture a world of continually changing perspectives and overlapping contexts.

Language and knowledge do not copy reality. Rather, language constitutes reality, each language constructing specific aspects of reality in its own way. The focus is on the linguistic and social construction of reality, on interpretation and negotiation of the meaning of the lived world.

Human language is neither universal nor individual, but each language is rooted in a specific culture, as dialects or as national languages. Current philosophy has undergone a linguistic turn, focusing on language games, speech acts, hermeneutic interpretation, textual and linguistic analysis. The language games take place in local communities; they are heterogeneous and incommensurable. Highly refined expressions in one language, such as poetry, cannot be translated into another language without change of meaning. There exists no universal meta-language, no universal commensurability.

The focus on language implies a decentralization of the subject. The self no longer uses language to express itself; rather the language speaks through the person. The individual self becomes a medium for the culture and its language. The unique self loses prominence; the author is today less an original genius than a gifted craftsman and mediator of the culture through his or her mastery of language.

In postmodern thought there has taken place an *expansion of rationality*. It is not just a "momentary lapse of reason," but a going beyond the cognitive and scientific domain to include also the ethical and aesthetic domains of life in reason. "Modern times" involved a restricted concept of rationality, with a dominance of a technical means-ends rationality. There has been an emphasis on plans and programmes, on calculation, prediction and control. Reason and science have been overburdened with visions of Utopia where all human problems would be solved in the long run by the methods of science and technology.

When the presupposed rationality is seldom found in the given reality, another deeper, more essential reality is constructed to account for the disorder we observe in the world around us. The overstressed conception of a rationality has, in its turn, fostered sceptical reactions in the form of romanticist and irrationalist movements.

Postmodern thought goes beyond a Kantian split of modern culture into science, morality and art, and involves a rehabilitation of the ethical and aesthetic domains. The positivists' split of facts and values is no longer axiomatic; science is a value-constituted and value-constituting enterprise. Appeals to formal logic recede before a rehabilitated rhetoric of persuasion. With the loss of general systems of legitimation, when actions are not justified by appeal to some higher system or idea of progress, the values and the ethical responsibility of the interacting persons become central.

Art is not merely an aesthetic experience, but a way of knowing the world. Rationalist thought has abhorred the non-linear, the imprecise, the unpredictable, and has separated art from science. Mathematicians have been more open to an affinity of science and art, emphasizing the elegance and beauty of models as criteria of truth, cf. for instance *The Beauty of Fractals.*[9]

Postmodern art is characterized by *pastiche* and collage. Art in a post-modern world does not belong to a unitary frame of reference, nor to a project or a Utopia. The plurality of perspectives leads to a fragmentation of experience, the collage becoming a key artistic technique of our time. Styles from different periods and cultures are put together; in postmodern art high-tech may exist side by side with antique columns and romantic ornamenta-tion, the effects being shocking and fascinating. In contrast to modern architecture, tradition is not rejected; nor is it worshipped as in the new classicism. Elements from other epochs are selected and put together in an often ironical recycling of what is usable as decorum. In literature there are collages of texts put together from other texts; the author's individuality and originality are lost in a pervasive use of and references to other texts. Eco's medieval detective novel *The Name of the Rose,* which may be read as a postmodern caricature of the modern meaning hunters, is thus filled with hidden quotes and allusions to other texts.

The reaction against modern rationality and functionalism was visible at an early stage in *architecture.* There was a protest against the functional, against straight lines and square blocks, against the cold logic and boredom of a modern architecture where function preceded form. Postmodern archi-tecture is a reaction against what the painter Hundertwasser has called "the tyranny of the straight line." In the new architecture there is an emphasis on the curvilinear, on the unpredictable, on ornamentation and pastiche and on a non-functional beauty. Reflecting surfaces and labyrinths have become main elements.

On one side there is a return to the medieval village, with its tight-knit community and complex webs of buildings and places. The atriums of the Hyatt Regency Hotels appear as secularized cathedrals with quiet, closed and labyrinthine internal space, with an ornamentation of mixed styles. On the other side there is the Las Vegas trend of architecture, going to the extreme of learning from the most extravagant expressions of current architecture, as expressed in Venturi et al.'s *Learning from Las Vegas*.[10] There is a collage of styles, as in Caesars Palace with its antique statues and parking valets dressed as Roman legionaries. Here there is dominance of the surface, the immense lighted billboards attracting the customer to the less spectacular interior labyrinths of gambling tables and slot machines.

Postmodern thought focuses on the *surface,* with a refined sensibility to what appears, a differentiation of what is perceived. The relation of sign and signified is breaking down; the reference to a reality beyond the sign recedes. In the media, texts and images refer less to an external world beyond the signs than to a chain of signifiers, to other texts and images. A dichotomy of fantasy and reality breaks down or loses interest. There is an intertextuality where texts mainly point to other texts. The TV series *Miami Vice* may refer less to the vice in Miami than to other TV series, imitating and parodying for example the car chases, playing up to the viewer's expectations of a cops-and-robbers series. The image, the appearance, is everything; the appearance has become the essence.

The interest in surface, in what manifestly appears, is in contrast to a debunking attitude where nothing is what it seems to be. This hermeneutics of suspicion, inherent in much modern thought, was carried to its extremes in some versions of psychoanalytic and Marxist thought. An action may never be what it appears to be; rather it is an expression of some deeper, more real reality, a symptom of more basic sexual or economic forces. There is a continual hunt for the underlying plan or rationale, the hidden plot or curriculum, to explain the vicissitudes and disorder of what manifestly appears.

The modern quest for a unitary meaning, where there may be none, has as its pathological extreme the suspicion of paranoia. The debunking attitude may lead to conspiracy theories seeking for the mastermind plot; or, less extreme, to a continual search for an underlying order, constructing a deeper rationality where none is visible.

A postmodern *attitude* involves a suspicion of suspicion, and a refined sensibility to the surface, an openness to the differences and nuances of what appears. It relates to what is given, rather than what has been or what could be—"be cool," "it is no big deal," "no future." The fervent critical attitude of the 1960s and 1970s—as anti-authoritarianism and anti-capitalism—has dissolved. The idea of progress and development, be it the progress of mankind or the individual pilgrim's progress towards salvation of his or her soul, is out. An attitude of tolerant indifference has replaced the involvement and engagement in the social movements and the inner journeys of the 1960s and 1970s. What is left is a liberating nihilism, a living with the here and now, a weariness and a playful irony. Fascination may take the place of reflection; seduction may replace argumentation. There is an oscillation of an intense sensuous fascination by the media and a cool, ironical distance to what appears.

To the existentialists, the discovery of a world without meaning was the point of departure; today a loss of unitary meaning is merely accepted; that is just the way the world is. Postmodern man has stopped waiting for Godot. The absurd is not met with despair; rather it is a living with what is, a making the best of it, a relief from the burden of finding yourself as the goal of life; what remains may be a happy nihilism. With the death of the Utopias, the local and personal responsibility for actions here and now becomes crucial.

2

What Is Post-Modernism?

CHARLES JENCKS

*Most of us are reluctant to identify a time when the postmodern era
began—we prefer to mumble apologetically that it's more a state of
mind than a distinct historical event—but Charles Jencks is not so
diffident: He has written that, in architecture, the modern era ended
promptly at 3:32 P.M. on July 15, 1972, when the Pruitt-Igoe housing
development in St. Louis—once called a perfect modern "machine
for living"—was dynamited as an uninhabitable environment for
the low-income people it had housed. That collapse coincided with
the collapse of doctrinaire "high modernism" and its tendencies
toward standardization.[1]*

    It's clear—although maybe not quite that clear*—that ex-
plicitly "postmodernist" schools and movements were rapidly becoming part of the cultural buzz in the 1970s. Jencks—who is not only an
architect and architectural critic, but also a major theorist of postmodernity (architects use the hyphen)—offers his own description of
the main themes and voices.*

The Modern Age, which sounds as if it would last forever, is fast becoming a thing of the past. Industrialisation is quickly giving way to Post-

Industrialisation, factory labour to home and office work and, in the arts, the Tradition of the New is leading to the combination of many traditions. Even those who still call themselves Modern artists and architects are looking backwards and sideways to decide which styles and values they will continue.

The Post-Modern Age is a time of incessant choosing. It's an era when no orthodoxy can be adopted without self-consciousness and irony, because all traditions seem to have some validity. This is partly a consequence of what is called the information explosion, the advent of organised knowledge, world communication and cybernetics. It is not only the rich who become collectors, eclectic travellers in time with a superabundance of choice, but almost every urban dweller. Pluralism, the "ism" of our time, is both the great problem and the great opportunity: where Everyman becomes a Cosmopolite and Everywoman a Liberated Individual, confusion and anxiety become ruling states of mind and ersatz a common form of mass-culture. This is the price we pay for a Post-Modern Age, as heavy in its way as the monotony, dogmatism and poverty of the Modern epoch. But, in spite of many attempts in Iran and elsewhere, it is impossible to return to a previous culture and industrial form, impose a fundamentalist religion or even a Modernist orthodoxy. Once a world communication system and form of cybernetic production have emerged they create their own necessities and they are, barring a nuclear war, irreversible.

The challenge for a Post-Modern Hamlet, confronted by an *embarras de richesses,* is to choose and combine traditions selectively, to *eclect* (as the verb of eclecticism would have it) those aspects from the past and present which appear most relevant for the job at hand. The resultant creation, if successful, will be a striking synthesis of traditions; if unsuccessful, a smorgasbord. Between inventive combination and confused parody the Post-Modernist sails, often getting lost and coming to grief, but occasionally realising the great promise of a plural culture with its many freedoms. Post-Modernism is fundamentally the eclectic mixture of any tradition with that of the immediate past: it is both the continuation of Modernism and its transcendence. Its best works are characteristically doubly-coded and ironic, making a feature of the wide choice, conflict and discontinuity of traditions, because this heterogeneity most clearly captures our pluralism. Its hybrid style is opposed to the minimalism of Late-Modern ideology and all revivals which are based on an exclusive dogma or taste.

This, at least, is what I take Post-Modernism to be as a cultural movement and historical epoch. But, as the reader will discover, the word and concept have changed over fifty years and have only reached such a clarification in the last ten. Seen as progressive in some quarters, it is damned as reactionary and nostalgic in others; supported for its social and technological realism, it is also accused of escapism. Even, at times, when it is being condemned for its schizophrenia this "failing" is turned by its defenders into a virtue. Some writers define it negatively, concentrating on aspects of inflation, the runaway growth typified by a multiplying economy.[2] But a critical reading of the evidence will show that fast-track production and consumption beset all areas of contemporary life and are not the monopoly of any movement.

Virtually the first positive use of the prefix "post" was by the writer Leslie Fiedler in 1965 when he repeated it like an incantation and tied it to current radical trends which made up the counter-culture: "post-humanist, post-male, post-white, post-heroic . . . post-Jewish."[3] These anarchic and creative departures from orthodoxy, these attacks on Modernist elitism, academicism and puritanical repression, do indeed represent the first stirrings of Post-Modern culture as Andreas Huyssen later pointed out in 1984, although Fiedler and others in the 1960s were never to put this argument as such and conceptualise the tradition.[4] This had to wait until the 1970s and the writings of Ihab Hassan, by which time the radical movements which Fiedler celebrated were, ironically, out of fashion, reactionary, or dead.

Ihab Hassan became by the mid-1970s the self-proclaimed spokesman for the Postmodern (the term is conventionally elided in literary criticism) and he tied this label to the ideas of experimentalism in the arts and ultra-technology in architecture—William Burroughs and Buckminster Fuller, "Anarchy, Exhaustion/Silence . . . Decreation/Deconstruction/Antithesis . . . Intertext . . ." —in short those trends which I, with others, would later characterise as Late-Modern. In literature and then in philosophy, because of the writings of Jean-François Lyotard (1979) and a tendency to elide Deconstruction with the Post-Modern, the term has often kept its associations with what Hassan calls "discontinuity, indeterminancy, immanence."[5] Mark C. Taylor's curiously titled *ERRING, A Postmodern A/Theology* is characteristic of this genre which springs from Derrida and Deconstruction.[6] There is also a tendency among philosophers to discuss all Post-Positivist thinkers together as Post-Modern whether or not they have anything more in common than a rejection of Modern Logical Positivism. Thus there are two quite different meanings to the term and a general confusion which is not confined to the public. This and the pretext of several recent conferences on the subject has led to this little tract: "What is Post-Modernism?" It *is* a question, as well as the answer I will give, and one must see that its continual growth and movement mean that no definitive answer is possible—at least not until it stops moving.

In its infancy in the 1960s Post-Modern culture was radical and critical, a minority position established, for instance, by Pop artists and theorists against the reduced view of Modern art, the aestheticism reigning in such institutes as the Museum of Modern Art. In architecture, Team Ten, Jane Jacobs, Robert Venturi and the Advocacy Planners attacked "orthodox Modern architecture" for its elitism, urban destruction, bureaucracy and simplified language. By the 1970s, as these traditions grew in strength and changed and Post-Modernism was now coined as a term for a variety of trends, the movement became more conservative, rational and academic. Many protagonists of the 1960s, such as Andy Warhol, lost their critical function altogether as they were assimilated into the art market or commercial practice. In the 1980s the situation changed again. Post-Modernism was finally accepted by the professions, academies and society at large. It became as much part of the establishment as its parent, Modernism, and rival brother, Late-Modernism, and in literary criticism it shifted closer in meaning to the architectural and art traditions.

John Barth (1980) and Umberto Eco (1983), among many other authors, now define it as a writing which may use traditional forms in ironic or displaced ways to treat perennial themes.[7] It acknowledges the validity of Modernism—the change in the world view brought on by Nietzsche, Einstein, Freud et al.—but, as John Barth says, it hopes to go beyond the limited means and audience which characterise Modernist fiction: "My ideal postmodernist author neither merely repudiates nor merely imitates either his twentieth-century Modernist parents or his nineteenth-century pre-modernist grandparents. He has the first half of our century under his belt, but not on his back. Without lapsing into moral or artistic simplism, shoddy craftsmanship, Madison Avenue venality, or either false or real naiveté, he nevertheless aspires to a fiction more democratic in its appeal than such late-modernist marvels (by my definition and in my judgement) as Beckett's *Stories and Texts for Nothing* or Nabokov's *Pale Fire*. He may not hope to reach and move the devotees of James Michener and Irving Wallace—not to mention the lobotomized mass-media illiterates. But he *should* hope to reach and delight, at least part of the time, beyond the circle of what Mann used to call the Early Christians: professional devotees of high art."[8] This search for a wider audience than the Early Christians also distinguishes Post-Modern architects and artists from their Late-Modern counterparts and from the more hermetic concerns that Ihab Hassan defined in the 1970s. There are of course many other specific goals on the agenda which give Post-Modernism a direction.

But because its meaning and tradition change, one must not only define the concept but give its dates and specific context. To reiterate, I term Post-Modernism that paradoxical dualism, or double coding, which its hybrid name entails: the continuation of Modernism and its transcendence. Hassan's "postmodern" is, according to this logic, mostly Late-Modern, the continuation of Modernism in its ultra or exaggerated form. Some writers and critics, such as Barth and Eco, would agree with this definition, while just as many, including Hassan and Lyotard, would disagree. In this agreement and disagreement, understanding and dispute, there is the same snake-like dialectic which the movement has always shown and one suspects that there will be several more surprising twists of the coil before it is finished. Of one thing we can be sure: the announcement of death is, until the other Modernisms disappear, premature.

3

"I Love You Madly," He Said Self-consciously

UMBERTO ECO

Umberto Eco's best-selling novel The Name of the Rose *is often cited as an example of postmodern literature. It transcends the boundary between popular and serious literature, between low culture and high, and it parodies another genre (the detective novel), the great expression of the modern era's search for certainty. In a postscript to his novel, Eco presents his own idea about the postmodern attitude—finds in it a kind of transcendence, and a kind of parody, of our own experiences of life.*

Unfortunately, "postmodern" is a term *bon à tout faire*. I have the impression that it is applied today to anything the user of the term happens to like. Further, there seems to be an attempt to make it increasingly retroactive: first it was apparently applied to certain writers or artists active in the last twenty years, then gradually it reached the beginning of the century, then still further back. And this reverse procedure continues; soon the postmodern category will include Homer.

Actually, I believe that postmodernism is not a trend to be chronologically defined, but, rather, an ideal category—or, better still, a *Kunstwollen*, a way of operating. We could say that every period has its own postmodernism, just as every period would have its own mannerism (and, in fact, I wonder if postmodernism is not the modern name for mannerism as metahistorical category). I believe that in every period there are moments of crisis like those described by Nietzsche in his *Thoughts out of Season,* in which he wrote about the harm done by historical studies. The past conditions us, harries us, blackmails us. The historic avant-garde (but here I would also consider avant-garde a metahistorical category) tries to settle scores with the past. "Down with moonlight"—a futurist slogan—is a platform typical of every avant-garde; you have only to replace "moonlight" with whatever noun is suitable. The avant-garde destroys, defaces the past: *Les Demoiselles d'Avignon* is a typical avant-garde act. Then the avant-garde goes further, destroys the figure, cancels it, arrives at the abstract, the informal, the white canvas, the slashed canvas, the charred canvas. In architecture and the visual arts, it will be the curtain wall, the building as stele, pure parallelepiped, minimal art; in literature, the destruction of the flow of discourse, the Burroughs-like collage, silence, the white page; in music, the passage from atonality to noise to absolute silence (in this sense, the early Cage is modern).

But the moment comes when the avant-garde (the modern) can go no further; because it has produced a metalanguage that speaks of its impossible texts (conceptual art). The postmodern reply to the modern consists of recognizing that the past, since it cannot really be destroyed, because its destruction leads to silence, must be revisited: but with irony, not innocently. I think of the postmodern attitude as that of a man who loves a very cultivated woman and knows he cannot say to her, "I love you madly," because he knows that she knows (and that she knows that he knows) that these words have already been written by Barbara Cartland. Still, there is a solution. He can say, "As Barbara Cartland would put it, I love you madly." At this point, having avoided false innocence, having said clearly that it is no longer possible to speak innocently, he will nevertheless have said what he wanted to say to the woman: that he loves her, but he loves her in an age of lost innocence. If the woman goes along with this, she will have received a declaration of love all the same. Neither of the two speakers will feel innocent, both will have accepted the challenge of the past, of the already said, which cannot be eliminated; both will consciously and with pleasure play the game of irony. . . . But both will have succeeded, once again, in speaking of love.

Irony, metalinguistic play, enunciation squared. Thus, with the modern, anyone who does not understand the game can only reject it, but with the postmodern, it is possible not to understand the game and yet to take it seriously. Which is, after all, the quality (the risk) of irony. There is always someone who takes ironic discourse seriously. I think that the collages of Picasso, Juan Gris, and Braque were modern: this is why normal people would not accept them. On the other hand, the collages of Max Ernst, who pasted together bits of nineteenth-century engravings, were postmodern: they can be read as fantastic stories, as the telling of dreams, without any awareness that they amount to a discussion of the nature of engraving, and perhaps even of collage. If "postmodern" means this, it is clear why Sterne and Rabelais were postmodern, why Borges surely is, and why in the same artist the modern moment and the postmodern moment can coexist, or alternate, or follow each other closely. Look at Joyce. The *Portrait* is the story of an attempt at the modern. *Dubliners*, even if it comes before, is more modern than *Portrait*. *Ulysses* is on the borderline. *Finnegans Wake* is already postmodern, or at least it initiates the postmodern discourse: it demands, in order to be understood, not the negation of the already said, but its ironic rethinking.

4

The Fragile Fiction

ERNEST BECKER

Ernest Becker is best known for his powerful The Denial of Death, *which was awarded a Pulitzer Prize for general nonfiction. He also wrote* The Birth and Death of Meaning, *a wide-ranging study of the evolution of the human mind. It contained the following remarkable passage, which summarizes the postmodern condition—this moment in which the symbolic environment becomes visible—better than any single statement I have ever read.*

The world of human aspiration is largely fictitious, and if we do not understand this we understand nothing about man. It is a largely symbolic creation by an ego-controlled animal that permits action in a psychological world, a symbolic-behavioral world removed from the boundness of the present moment, from the immediate stimuli which enslave all lower organisms. Man's freedom is a fabricated freedom, and he pays a price for it. He must at all times *defend the utter fragility of his delicately constituted fiction, deny its artificiality.* That's why we can speak of "joint theatrical staging," "ritual formulas for social ceremonial," and "enhancing of cultural meaning," with utmost seriousness. There is no cynicism implied here, no derision, nor any pity. We must realize simply that this is how *this* animal must act if he is to function as *this* animal. Man's fictions are not superfluous creations that could be "put aside" so that the "more serious" business of life could continue. The flesh-and-blood action of lower animals is no more infused with seriousness than is the ethereal symbolic conduct with which man organizes his dominion over nature. We may deal with flimsier coin, but, like the abstractness of high finance, the business is even the more serious for it.

The most astonishing thing of all, about man's fictions, is not that they have from prehistoric times hung like a flimsy canopy over his social world, but that he should have come to discover them at all. It is one of the most remarkable achievements of thought, of self-scrutiny, that the most anxiety-prone animal of all could come to *see through himself* and discover the fictional nature of his action world. Future historians will probably record it as one of the great, liberating breakthroughs of all time, and it happened in ours.

5

The Dehumanized World

PETER L. BERGER AND THOMAS LUCKMANN

Peter L. Berger and Thomas Luckmann are eminent practitioners of the sub-discipline called the sociology of knowledge—the study of how people go about the business of creating their cultures. In their now-classic book The Social Construction of Reality—*first published in 1966 and enormously influential on the thinking of our time—they pointed out that there is something people routinely do* after *they have created a ritual, a belief, a myth, a social role or a law: They forget they created it, and live in a world they never knew they made.*

To what extent is an institutional order, or any part of it, apprehended as a non-human facticity? This is the question of the reification of social reality.

Reification is the apprehension of human phenomena as if they were things, that is, in non-human or possibly suprahuman terms. Another way of saying this is that reification is the apprehension of the products of human activity *as if* they were something else than human products—such as facts of nature, results of cosmic laws, or manifestations of divine will. Reification implies that man is capable of forgetting his own authorship of the human world, and further, that the dialectic between man, the producer, and his products is lost to consciousness. The reified world is, by definition, a dehumanized world. It is experienced by man as a strange facticity, an *opus alienum* over which he has no control rather than as the *opus proprium* of his own productive activity.

As soon as an objective social world is established, the possibility of reification is never far away. The objectivity of the social world means that it confronts man as something outside of himself. The decisive question is whether he still retains the awareness that, however objectivated, the social world was made by men—and, therefore, can be remade by them. In other words, reification can be described as an extreme step in the process of objectivation, whereby the objectivated world loses its comprehensibility as a human enterprise and becomes fixated as a non-human, non-humanizable, inert facticity. Typically, the real relationship between man and his world is reversed in consciousness. Man, the producer of a world, is apprehended as its product, and human activity as an epiphenomenon of non-human processes. Human meanings are no longer understood as world-producing but as being, in their turn, products of the "nature of things." It must be emphasized that reification is a modality of consciousness, more precisely, a modality of man's objectification of the human world. Even while apprehending the world in reified terms, man continues to produce it. That is, man is capable paradoxically of producing a reality that denies him.

Reification is possible on both the pretheoretical and theoretical levels of consciousness. Complex theoretical systems can be described as reifications, though presumably they have their roots in pretheoretical reifications established in this or that social situation. Thus it would be an error to limit the concept of reification to the mental constructions of intellectuals. Reification exists in the consciousness of the man in the street and, indeed, the latter presence is more practically significant. It would also be a mistake to look at reification as a perversion of an originally non-reified apprehension of the social world, a sort of cognitive fall from grace. On the contrary, the available ethnological and psychological evidence seems to indicate the opposite, namely, that the original apprehension of the social world is highly reified both phylogenetically and ontogenetically. This implies that an apprehension of reification *as* a modality of consciousness is dependent upon an at least relative *de*reification of consciousness, which is a comparatively late development in history and in any individual biography.

Both the institutional order as a whole and segments of it may be apprehended in reified terms. For example, the entire order of society may be conceived of as a microcosm reflecting the macrocosm of the total universe as made by the gods. Whatever happens "here below" is but a pale reflection of what takes place "up above." Particular institutions may be apprehended in similar ways. The basic "recipe" for the reification of institutions is to bestow on them an ontological status independent of human activity and signification. Specific reifications are variations on this general theme. Marriage, for instance, may be reified as an imitation of divine acts of creativity, as a universal mandate of natural law, as the necessary consequence of biological or psychological forces, or, for that matter, as a functional imperative of the social system. What all these reifications have in common is their obfuscation of marriage as an ongoing human production. As can be readily seen in this example, the reification may occur both theoretically and pretheoretically. Thus the mystagogue can concoct a highly sophisticated theory reaching out from the concrete human event to the farthest corners of the divine cosmos, but an illiterate peasant couple being married may apprehend the event with a similarly reifying shudder of metaphysical dread. Through reification, the world of institutions appears to merge with the world of nature. It becomes necessity and fate, and is lived through as such, happily *or* unhappily as the case may be.

Roles may be reified in the same manner as institutions. The sector of self-consciousness that has been objectified in the role is then also apprehended as an inevitable fate, for which the individual may disclaim responsibility. The paradigmatic formula for this kind of reification is the statement "I have no choice in the matter, I have to act this way because of my position"—as husband, father, general, archbishop, chairman of the board, gangster, or hangman, as the case may be. This means that the reification of roles narrows the subjective distance that the individual may establish between himself and his role-playing. The distance implied in all objectification remains, of course, but the distance brought about by disidentification shrinks to the vanishing point. Finally, identity itself (the total self, if one prefers) may be reified, both one's own and that of others. There is then a total identification of the individual with his socially assigned typifications. He is apprehended as *nothing but* that type. This apprehension may be positively or negatively accented in terms of values or emotions. The identification of "Jew" may be equally reifying for the anti-Semite and the Jew himself, except that the latter will accent the identification positively and the former negatively. Both reifications bestow an ontological and total status on a typification that is humanly produced and that, even as it is internalized, objectifies but a segment of the self. Once more, such reifications may range from the pretheoretical level of "what everybody knows about Jews" to the most complex theories of Jewishness as a manifestation of biology ("Jewish blood"), psychology ("the Jewish soul") or metaphysics ("the mystery of Israel").

6

Strategies of Power

MICHEL FOUCAULT

Michel Foucault carved out a special position in the postmodern conversation as the explorer of the power relationships that are invariably involved in the reality-construction process, so that every human culture brings forth methods—sometimes extremely subtle ones—for regulating the behavior of its members. His contribution to the scholarship of postmodernism was to show how, at certain times and places in the past, specific realities had been constructed— attitudes toward poverty and classifications of disease as well as ideas about mental and sexual deviance. Foucault also contributed to the style of postmodernism. He was cryptic, subversive, unwilling to be identified as a member of any discipline or movement—unwilling to be identified at all. "Do not ask me who I am and do not ask me to remain the same," he remarked once. "Leave it to the bureaucrats to see that our papers are in order."[1]

Here, in an interview with the French magazine L'Express, he reflects on his work and on the subject of truth as a form of power.

P.B. We now come to your latest book, *La volonté de savoir*, which is the first volume in a huge project—a "history of sexuality." How is this research into sexuality related to your previous work?

FOUCAULT In my studies of madness or the prison, it seemed to me that the question at the center of everything was: what is power? And, to be more specific: how is it exercised, what exactly happens when someone exercises power over another? It seemed to me then that sexuality, in so far as it is, in every society, and in ours in particular, heavily regulated, was a good area to test what the mechanisms of power actually were. Especially as the analyses that were current during the 1960s defined power in terms of prohibition: power, it was said, is what prohibits, what prevents people doing something. It seemed to me that power was something much more complex than that.

P.B. In order to analyze power, one must not link it *a priori* to repression . . .

FOUCAULT Exactly . . .

P.B. In an interview you had with Gilles Deleuze in 1972, you said this: "It's the great unknown at present: who exercises power? And where does he exercise it? Nowadays we know more or less who exploits, where the profit goes, into whose hands it goes and where it is reinvested. But power . . . we know very well that it is not those who govern who hold power. But the notion of 'ruling class' is neither very clear nor very highly developed."[2] Could you explain this analysis of power to me in greater detail?

FOUCAULT It would be bold of me indeed if I were to tell you that my ideas on this subject are clearer now than at that time. I still believe, then, that the way in which power is exercised and functions in a society like ours is little understood. Of course, there are sociological studies that show us who the bosses of industry are at present, how politicians are formed and where they come from; but there are also more general studies, usually inspired by Marxism, concerning the domination of the bourgeois class in our societies. But, under this general umbrella, things seem to me to be much more complex. In the Western industrialized societies, the questions "Who exercises power? How? On whom?" are certainly the questions that people feel most strongly about. The problem of poverty, which haunted the nineteenth century, is no longer, for our Western societies, of primary importance. On the other hand: Who makes decisions for me? Who is preventing me from doing this and telling me to do that? Who is programming my movements and activities? Who is forcing me to live in a particular place when I work in another? How are these decisions on which my life is completely articulated taken? All these questions seem to me to be fundamental ones today. And I don't believe that this question of "who exercises power?" can be resolved unless that other question "how does it happen?" is resolved at the same time. Of course we have to show who those in charge are, we know that we have to turn, let us say, to deputies, ministers, principal private secretaries, etc., etc. But this is not the important issue, for we know perfectly well that even if we reach the point of designating exactly all those people, all those "decision-makers," we will still not really know why and how the decision was made, how it came to be accepted by everybody, and how it is that it hurts a particular category of person, etc.

P.B.   So we can't study power without what you call the "strategies of power" . . .

FOUCAULT   Yes, the strategies, the networks, the mechanisms, all those techniques by which a decision is accepted and by which that decision could not but be taken in the way it was.

P.B.   All your analyses tend to show that there is power everywhere, even in the fibers of our bodies, for example, in sexuality. Marxism has been criticized for analyzing everything in terms of economics and even of reducing everything, in the final analysis, to an economic problem. Can you, too, not be criticized for seeing power everywhere and, in the final analysis, of reducing everything to power?

FOUCAULT   That's an important question. For me, power is the problem that has to be resolved. Take an example like the prisons. I want to study the way in which people set about using—and late on in history—imprisonment, rather than banishment or torture, as a punitive method. That's the problem. There have been excellent German historians and sociologists of the Frankfurt School who, after studying it, have drawn the following conclusion: in a bourgeois, capitalist, industrial society, in which labor is the essential value, it was considered that people found guilty of crimes could not be condemned to a more useful penalty than to be forced to work. And how were they forced to work? By locking them up in a prison and forcing them to work so many hours a day. This, in brief, is the explanation of the problem posed by those German historians and sociologists. It is an explanation of an economist type. Though I'm not entirely convinced by this reasoning, for the excellent reason . . . that people have never worked in prisons! The profitability of work done in the prisons has always been negligible—it was work for the sake of work. But let's look at the problem more closely. In reality, when we examine how, in the late eighteenth century, it was decided to choose imprisonment as the essential mode of punishment, one sees that it was after all a long elaboration of various techniques that made it possible to locate people, to fix them in precise places, to constrict them to a certain number of gestures and habits— in short, it was a form of "dressage." Thus we see the appearance of garrisons of a type that didn't exist before the end of the seventeenth century; we see the appearance of the great boarding schools, of the Jesuit type, which still did not exist in the seventeenth century; in the eighteenth century, we see the appearance of the great workshops employing hundreds of workers. What developed, then, was a whole technique of human dressage by location, confinement, surveillance, the perpetual supervision of behavior and tasks, in short, a whole technique of "management" of which the prison was merely one manifestation or its transposition into the penal domain. Now what do all these new techniques used to train individuals amount to? I state it very clearly in *Surveiller et punir:* in the case of the workshops, these new techniques did of course respond to the economic necessities of production; in the case of the barracks, they are bound up with problems of both a practical and political kind, with the development of a professional army, which had to perform fairly difficult tasks (knowing how to fire a cannon, for example); and in the case of the schools, with problems of a political and economic character. I say all this in my book. But what I also try to bring out is that, from the eighteenth century onwards, there has been a specific reflection on the way in which these procedures for training and exercising power over individuals could be extended, generalized, and improved. In other words, I constantly show the economic or political origin of these methods; but, while refraining from seeing power everywhere, I also think there is a specificity in these new techniques of training. I believe that the methods used, right down to the way of conditioning individuals' behavior, have a logic, obey a type of rationality, and are all based on one another to form a sort of specific stratum.

P.B. From a certain point on, then, the "specific techniques of power," as you call them, appear to have functioned of themselves, without any economic justification?

FOUCAULT There was no really "rational" economic reason to force prisoners to work in prisons. Economically, it served no purpose and yet it was done. There is a whole series of similar ways of exercising power that, while having no economic justification, were nevertheless transposed into the judicial institution.

P.B. One of your theses is that the strategies of power actually produce knowledge. Contrary to the received idea, there seems to be no incompatibility between power and knowledge.

FOUCAULT Philosophers or even, more generally, intellectuals justify and mark out their identity by trying to establish an almost uncrossable line between the domain of knowledge, seen as that of truth and freedom, and the domain of the exercise of power. What struck me, in observing the human sciences, was that the development of all these branches of knowledge can in no way be dissociated from the exercise of power. Of course, you will always find psychological or sociological theories that are independent of power. But, generally speaking, the fact that societies can become the object of scientific observation, that human behavior became, from a certain point on, a problem to be analyzed and resolved, all that is bound up, I believe, with mechanisms of power—which, at a given moment, indeed, analyzed that object (society, man, etc.) and presented it as a problem to be resolved. So the birth of the human sciences goes hand in hand with the installation of new mechanisms of power.

P.B. Your analysis of the relations between knowledge and power takes place in the area of the human sciences. It does not concern the exact sciences, does it?

FOUCAULT Oh no, not at all! I would not make such a claim for myself. And, anyway, you know, I'm an empiricist: I don't try to advance things without seeing whether they are applicable. Having said that, to reply to your question, I would say this: it has often been stressed that the development of chemistry, for example, could not be understood without the development of industrial needs. That is true and has been demonstrated. But what seems to me to be more interesting to analyze is how science, in Europe, has become institutionalized as a power. It is not enough to say that science is a set of procedures by which propositions may be falsified, errors demonstrated, myths demystified, etc. Science also exercises power: it is, literally, a power that forces you to say certain things, if you are not to be disqualified not only as being wrong, but, more seriously than that, as being a charlatan. Science has become institutionalized as a power through a university system and through its own constricting apparatus of laboratories and experiments.

P.B.   Doesn't science produce "truths" to which we submit?

FOUCAULT   Of course. Indeed, truth is no doubt a form of power. And in saying that, I am only taking up one of the fundamental problems of Western philosophy when it poses these questions: Why, in fact, are we attached to the truth? Why the truth rather than lies? Why the truth rather than myth? Why the truth rather than illusion? And I think that, instead of trying to find out what truth, as opposed to error, is, it might be more interesting to take up the problem posed by Nietzsche: how is it that, in our societies, "the truth" has been given this value, thus placing us absolutely under its thrall?

7

The Idea of Pluralism

ISAIAH BERLIN

Giambattista Vico, writing in the early 1700s, held views that were far ahead of his time. He proposed that different peoples of different times and places had fundamentally different realities. "As God's truth is what God comes to know as he creates and assembles it," Vico wrote, "so human truth is what man comes to know as he builds it, shaping it by his actions."[1] That was a revolutionary idea, and so was his follow-up proposition that there really wasn't any objective way to stand outside of all cultures and say that one society's art or poetry was better than another's. Most people assumed, in Vico's day, that you could pass final judgment about whether the creations of ancient Greece and Rome were superior to the efforts of their contemporaries. They argued about that passionately—and, of course, inconclusively.

Sir Isaiah Berlin recollects his experience as a university student, when his reading of philosophers such as Vico, Niccolò Machiavelli, and Johann Gottfried Herder led him to rethink his assumptions about what philosophy could accomplish. He had come to Oxford as a child of the Enlightenment, sure that philosophy was a way to find truth that would be the same for all people in all times and places. In moving beyond that assumption he gained another kind of wisdom, and a deeper appreciation of human diversity. And he always remained a great admirer of Vico, whom he called "the true father both of the modern concept of culture and of what one might call cultural pluralism."[2]

When I became a student at the University of Oxford, I began to read the works of the great philosophers. . . . Socrates thought that if certainty could be established in our knowledge of the external world by rational methods (had not Anaxagoras arrived at the truth that the moon was many times larger than the Peloponnese, however small it looked in the sky?) the same methods would surely yield equal certainty in the field of human behaviour—how to live, what to be. This could be achieved by rational argument. Plato thought that an élite of sages who arrived at such certainty should be given the power of governing others intellectually less well endowed, in obedience to patterns dictated by the correct solutions to personal and social problems. The Stoics thought that the attainment of these solutions was in the power of any man who set himself to live according to reason. Jews, Christians, Muslims (I knew too little about Buddhism) believed that the true answers had been revealed by God to his chosen prophets and saints, and accepted the interpretation of these revealed truths by qualified teachers and the traditions to which they belonged.

The rationalists of the seventeenth century thought that the answers could be found by a species of metaphysical insight, a special application of the light of reason with which all men were endowed. The empiricists of the eighteenth century, impressed by the vast new realms of knowledge opened by the natural sciences based on mathematical techniques, which had driven out so much error, superstition, dogmatic nonsense, asked themselves, like Socrates, why the same methods should not succeed in establishing similar irrefutable laws in the realm of human affairs. With the new methods discovered by natural science, order could be introduced into the social sphere as well—uniformities could be observed, hypotheses formulated and tested by experiment; laws could be based on them, and then laws in specific regions of experience could be seen to be entailed by wider laws; and these in turn to be entailed by still wider laws, and so on upwards, until a great harmonious system, connected by unbreakable logical links and capable of being formulated in precise—that is, mathematical—terms, could be established.

The rational reorganisation of society would put an end to spiritual and intellectual confusion, the reign of prejudice and superstition, blind obedience to unexamined dogmas, and the stupidities and cruelties of the oppressive regimes which such intellectual darkness bred and promoted. All that was wanted was the identification of the principal human needs and discovery of the means of satisfying them. This would create the happy, free, just, virtuous, harmonious world which Condorcet so movingly predicted in his prison cell in 1794. This view lay at the basis of all progressive thought in the nineteenth century, and was at the heart of much of the critical empiricism which I imbibed in Oxford as a student.

At some point I realised that what all these views had in common was a Platonic ideal: in the first place, that, as in the sciences, all genuine questions must have one true answer and one only, all the rest being necessarily errors; in the second place, that there must be a dependable path towards the discovery of these truths; in the third place, that the true answers, when found, must necessarily be compatible with one another and form a single whole, for one truth cannot be incompatible with another—that we knew *a priori*. This kind of omniscience was the solution of the cosmic jigsaw puzzle. In the case of morals, we could then conceive what the perfect life must be, founded as it would be on a correct understanding of the rules that governed the universe.

True, we might never get to this condition of perfect knowledge—we may be too feeble-witted, or too weak or corrupt or sinful, to achieve this. The obstacles, both intellectual and those of external nature, may be too many. Moreover, opinions, as I said, had widely differed about the right path to pursue—some found it in churches, some in laboratories; some believed in intuition, others in experiment, or in mystical visions, or in mathematical calculation. But even if we could not ourselves reach these true answers, or indeed, the final system that interweaves them all, the answers must exist— else the questions were not real. The answers must be known to someone: perhaps Adam in Paradise knew; perhaps we shall only reach them at the end of days; if men cannot know them, perhaps the angels know; and if not the angels, then God knows. These timeless truths must in principle be knowable.

Some nineteenth-century thinkers—Hegel, Marx—thought it was not quite so simple. There were no timeless truths. There was historical development, continuous change; human horizons altered with each new step in the evolutionary ladder; history was a drama with many acts; it was moved by conflicts of forces in the realms of both ideas and reality, sometimes called dialectical, which took the form of wars, revolutions, violent upheavals of nations, classes, cultures, movements. Yet after inevitable setbacks, failures, relapses, returns to barbarism, Condorcet's dream would come true. The drama would have a happy ending—man's reason had achieved triumphs in the past, it could not be held back for ever. Men would no longer be victims of nature or of their own largely irrational societies: reason would triumph; universal harmonious cooperation, true history, would at last begin.

For if this was not so, do the ideas of progress, of history, have any meaning? Is there not a movement, however tortuous, from ignorance to knowledge, from mythical thought and childish fantasies to perception of reality face to face, to knowledge of true goals, true values as well as truths of fact? Can history be a mere purposeless succession of events, caused by a mixture of material factors and the play of random selection, a tale full of sound and fury signifying nothing? This was unthinkable. The day would dawn when men and women would take their lives in their own hands and not be self-seeking beings or the playthings of blind forces that they did not understand. It was, at the very least, not impossible to conceive what such an earthly paradise could be; and if conceivable we could, at any rate, try to march towards it. That has been at the centre of ethical thought from the Greeks to the Christian visionaries of the Middle Ages, from the Renaissance to progressive thought in the last century; and indeed, is believed by many to this day.

At a certain stage in my reading, I naturally met with the principal works of Machiavelli. They made a deep and lasting impression upon me, and shook my earlier faith. I derived from them not the most obvious teachings—on how to acquire and retain political power, or by what force or guile rulers must act if they are to regenerate their societies, or protect themselves and their states from enemies within or without, or what the principal qualities of rulers on the one hand, and of citizens on the other, must be, if their states are to flourish—but something else. Machiavelli was not a historicist: he thought it possible to restore something like the Roman Republic or Rome of the early Principate. He believed that to do this one needed a ruling class of brave, resourceful, intelligent, gifted men who knew how to seize opportunities and use them, and citizens who were adequately protected, patriotic, proud of their state, epitomes of manly, pagan virtues. That is how Rome rose to power and conquered the world, and it is the absence of this kind of wisdom and vitality and courage in adversity, of the qualities of both lions and foxes, that in the end brought it down. Decadent states were conquered by vigorous invaders who retained these virtues.

But Machiavelli also sets, side by side with this, the notion of Christian virtues—humility, acceptance of suffering, unworldliness, the hope of salvation in an afterlife—and he remarks that if, as he plainly himself favours, a state of a Roman type is to be established, these qualities will not promote it: those who live by the precepts of Christian morality are bound to be trampled on by the ruthless pursuit of power by men who alone can re-create and dominate the republic which he wants to see. He does not condemn Christian virtues. He merely points out that the two moralities are incompatible, and he does not recognise any overarching criterion whereby we are enabled to decide the right life for men. The combination of *virtù* and Christian values is for him an impossibility. He simply leaves you to choose—he knows which he himself prefers.

The idea that this planted in my mind was the realisation, which came as something of a shock, that not all the supreme values pursued by mankind now and in the past were necessarily compatible with one another. It undermined my earlier assumption, based on the *philosophia perennis,* that there could be no conflict between true ends, true answers to the central problems of life.

Then I came across Giambattista Vico's *La scienza nuova.* Scarcely anyone in Oxford had then heard of Vico, but there was one philosopher, Robin Collingwood, who had translated Croce's book on Vico, and he urged me to read it. This opened my eyes to something new. Vico seemed to be concerned with the succession of human cultures—every society had, for him, its own vision of reality, of the world in which it lived, and of itself and of its relations to its own past, to nature, to what it strove for. This vision of a society is conveyed by everything that its members do and think and feel— expressed and embodied in the kinds of words, the forms of language that they use, the images, the metaphors, the forms of worship, the institutions that they generate, which embody and convey their image of reality and of their place in it; by which they live. These visions differ with each successive social whole—each has its own gifts, values, modes of creation, incommensurable with one another: each must be understood in its own terms— understood, not necessarily evaluated.

The Homeric Greeks, the master class, Vico tells us, were cruel, barbarous, mean, oppressive to the weak; but they created the *Iliad* and the *Odyssey*, something we cannot do in our more enlightened day. Their great creative masterpieces belong to them, and once the vision of the world changes, the possibility of that type of creation disappears also. We, for our part, have our sciences, our thinkers, our poets, but there is no ladder of ascent from the ancients to the moderns. If this is so, it must be absurd to say that Racine is a better poet than Sophocles, that Bach is a rudimentary Beethoven, that, let us say, the Impressionist painters are the peak to which the painters of Florence aspired but did not reach. The values of these cultures are different, and they are not necessarily compatible with one another. Voltaire, who thought that the values and ideals of the enlightened exceptions in a sea of darkness—of classical Athens, of Florence of the Renaissance, of France in the *grand siècle* and of his own time—were almost identical, was mistaken. Machiavelli's Rome did not, in fact, exist. For Vico there is a plurality of civilisations (repetitive cycles of them, but that is unimportant), each with its own unique pattern. Machiavelli conveyed the idea of two incompatible outlooks; and here were societies the cultures of which were shaped by values, not means to ends but ultimate ends, ends in themselves, which differed, not in all respects—for they were all human—but in some profound, irreconcilable ways, not combinable in any final synthesis.

After this I naturally turned to the German eighteenth-century thinker Johann Gottfried Herder. Vico thought of a succession of civilisations, Herder went further and compared national cultures in many lands and periods, and held that every society had what he called its own centre of gravity, which differed from that of others. If, as he wished, we are to understand Scandinavian sagas or the poetry of the Bible, we must not apply to them the aesthetic criteria of the critics of eighteenth-century Paris. The ways in which men live, think, feel, speak to one another, the clothes they wear, the songs they sing, the gods they worship, the food they eat, the assumptions, customs, habits which are intrinsic to them—it is this that creates communities, each of which has its own "life-style." Communities may resemble each other in many respects, but the Greeks differ from Lutheran Germans, the Chinese differ from both; what they strive after and what they fear or worship are scarcely ever similar.

This view has been called cultural or moral relativism—this is what that great scholar, my friend Arnaldo Momigliano, whom I greatly admired, supposed both about Vico and about Herder. He was mistaken. It is not relativism. Members of one culture can, by the force of imaginative insight, understand (what Vico called *entrare*) the values, the ideals, the forms of life of another culture or society, even those remote in time or space. They may find these values unacceptable, but if they open their minds sufficiently they can grasp how one might be a full human being, with whom one could communicate, and at the same time live in the light of values widely different from one's own, but which nevertheless one can see to be values, ends of life, by the realisation of which men could be fulfilled.

"I prefer coffee, you prefer champagne. We have different tastes. There is no more to be said." That is relativism. But Herder's view, and Vico's, is not that: it is what I should describe as pluralism—that is, the conception that there are many different ends that men may seek and still be fully rational, fully men, capable of understanding each other and sympathising and deriving light from each other, as we derive it from reading Plato or the novels of medieval Japan—worlds, outlooks, very remote from our own. Of course, if we did not have any values in common with these distant figures, each civilisation would be enclosed in its own impenetrable bubble, and we could not understand them at all; this is what Spengler's typology amounts to. Intercommunication between cultures in time and space is only possible because what makes men human is common to them, and acts as a bridge between them. But our values are ours, and theirs are theirs. We are free to criticise the values of other cultures, to condemn them, but we cannot pretend not to understand them at all, or to regard them simply as subjective, the products of creatures in different circumstances with different tastes from our own, which do not speak to us at all.

8

The Idea of Culture

ROY WAGNER

*If any single occupational group deserves the credit—or the blame—
for bringing us into the postmodern era, it is the anthropologists. They
created a new profession out of the study of otherness, and their
findings have made it impossible for any literate person to believe that
there is only one way of seeing the world.*

*Anthropologists are scientists of a sort, whose paradoxical work
has been to study culture objectively, and at the same time to understand that we always approach other cultures with the biases of our
own. Do anthropologists find the truth about culture or do they make
it? Roy Wagner believes they do a bit of both—that by inventing the
concept of culture, they are then able to study other human beings,
and in the process to learn something about themselves.*

Anthropology studies the phenomenon of man, not simply man's mind, his
body, evolution, origins, tools, art, or groups alone, but as parts or aspects of
a general pattern, or whole. To emphasize this fact and make it a part of their
ongoing effort, anthropologists have brought a general word into widespread
use to stand for the phenomenon, and that word is *culture*. When they speak

as if there were only one culture, as in "human culture," this refers very broadly to the phenomenon of man; otherwise, in speaking of "a culture" or "the cultures of Africa," the reference is to specific historical and geographical traditions, special cases of the phenomenon of man. Thus culture has become a way of talking about man, and about particular instances of man, when viewed from a certain perspective. Of course the word "culture" has other connotations as well, and important ambiguities which we shall examine presently.

By and large, though, the concept of culture has come to be so completely associated with anthropological thinking that if we should ever want to, we could define an anthropologist as someone who uses the word "culture" habitually. Or else, since the process of coming to depend on this concept is generally something of a "conversion experience," we might want to amend this somewhat and say that an anthropologist is someone who uses the word "culture" with hope—or even with faith.

The perspective of the anthropologist is an especially grand and far-reaching one, for the phenomenon of man implies a comparison with the other phenomena of the universe, with animal societies and living species, with the fact of life, matter and space, and so forth. The term "culture," too, in its broadest sense, attempts to bring man's actions and meanings down to the most basic level of significance, to examine them in universal terms in an attempt to understand them. When we speak of people belonging to different cultures, then, we are referring to a very basic kind of difference between them, suggesting that there are specific varieties of the phenomenon of man. Although there has been much "inflation" of the word "culture," it is in this "strong" sense that I will use it here.

The fact that anthropology chooses to study man in terms that are at the same time so broad and so basic, to understand both man's uniqueness and his diversity through the notion of culture, poses a peculiar situation for the science. Like the epistemologist, who considers "the meaning of meaning," or like the psychologist, who thinks about how people think, the anthropologist is forced to include himself and his own way of life in his subject matter, and study himself. More accurately, since we speak of a person's total capability as "culture," the anthropologist uses his own culture to study others, and to study culture in general.

Thus the awareness of culture brings about an important qualification

of the anthropologist's aims and viewpoint as a scientist: the classical rationalist's pretense of absolute objectivity must be given up in favor of a relative
objectivity based on the characteristics of one's own culture. It is necessary,
of course, for a research worker to be as unbiased as possible insofar as he is
aware of his assumptions, but we often take our culture's more basic assumptions so much for granted that we are not even aware of them. Relative
objectivity can be achieved through discovering what these tendencies are,
the ways in which one's culture allows one to comprehend another, and the
limitations it places on this comprehension. "Absolute" objectivity would
require that the anthropologist have no biases, and hence no culture at all.

The idea of culture, in other words, places the researcher in a position
of equality with his subjects: each "belongs to a culture." Because every
culture can be understood as a specific manifestation, or example, of the
phenomenon of man, and because no infallible method has ever been
discovered for "grading" different cultures and sorting them into their
natural types, we assume that every culture, as such, is equivalent to every
other one. This assumption is called "cultural relativity."

The combination of these two implications of the idea of culture, the
fact that we ourselves belong to a culture (relative objectivity), and that we
must assume all cultures to be equivalent (cultural relativity), leads to a
general proposition concerning the study of culture. As the repetition of
the stem "relative" suggests, the understanding of another culture involves
the relationship between two varieties of the human phenomenon; it aims
at the creation of an intellectual relation between them, an understanding
that includes both of them. The idea of "relationship" is important here
because it is more appropriate to the bringing together of two equivalent
entities, or viewpoints, than notions like "analysis" or "examination," with
their pretensions of absolute objectivity.

Let us take a closer look at the way in which this relation is achieved.
An anthropologist *experiences,* in one way or another, the subject of his study;
he does so through the world of his own meanings, and then uses this
meaningful experience to communicate an understanding to those of his
own culture. He can only communicate this understanding if his account
makes sense in the terms of his culture. And yet if these theories and
discoveries represent uncontrolled fantasies, like many of the anecdotes of
Herodotus, or the travelers' tales of the Middle Ages, we can scarcely speak of

a proper relating of cultures. An "anthropology" which never leaves the boundaries of its own conventions, which disdains to invest its imagination in a world of experience, must always remain more an ideology than a science.

But here the question arises of how much experience is necessary. Must the anthropologist be adopted into a tribe, get on familiar terms with chiefs and kings, or marry into an average family? Need he only view slides, study maps, and interview captives? Optimally, of course, one would want to know as much as possible about one's subjects, but in practice the answer to this question depends upon how much time and money are available, and on the scope and intentions of the undertaking. For the quantitative researcher, the archeologist dealing with evidences of a culture, or the sociologist measuring its effects, the problem is one of obtaining an adequate *sample*, finding enough evidential material so that one's estimates are not too far off. But the cultural or social anthropologist, although he may at times be concerned with sampling, is committed to a different kind of thoroughness—one based on the depth and comprehensiveness of his insight into the subject culture.

If the thing that anthropologists call "culture" is as all-encompassing as we have assumed, then this obsession on the part of the fieldworker is not misplaced, for the subject culture is as much a separate world of thought and action as his own. The only way in which a researcher could possibly go about the job of creating a relation between such entities would be to simultaneously *know* both of them, to realize the relative character of his own culture through the concrete formulation of another. Thus gradually, in the course of fieldwork, he himself becomes the link between cultures through his living in both of them, and it is this "knowledge" and competence that he draws upon in describing and explaining the subject culture. "Culture" in this sense draws an invisible equal sign between the knower (who comes to know himself) and the known (who are a community of knowers).

We might actually say that an anthropologist "invents" the culture he believes himself to be studying, that the relation is more "real" for being his particular acts and experiences than the things it "relates." Yet this explanation is only justified if we understand the invention to take place objectively, along the lines of observing and learning, and not as a kind of free fantasy. In experiencing a new culture, the fieldworker comes to realize new potentialities and possibilities for the living of life, and may in fact undergo a personality change himself. The subject culture becomes "visible," and then "believable" to him, he apprehends it first as a distinct entity, a way of doing things, and then secondly as a way in which he could be doing things. Thus he comprehends for the first time, through the intimacy of his own mistakes and triumphs, what anthropologists speak of when they use the word "culture." Before this he had no culture, as we might say, since the culture in which one grows up is never really "visible"—it is taken for granted, and its assumptions are felt to be self-evident. It is only through "invention" of this kind that the abstract significance of culture (and of many another concept) can be grasped, and only through the experienced contrast that his own culture becomes "visible." In the act of inventing another culture, the anthropologist invents his own, and in fact he reinvents the notion of culture itself.

9

The Idea of Ethnicity

WERNER SOLLORS

Postmodernists reject "essentialist" ideas about familiar matters such as race, in favor of "constructivist" ideas that take those things to be inventions—truths not found, but made. Here, a professor of African-American studies shows how this leads to a truly radical perspective about much of what is going on in the world today.

On all sides, right and left, people are strenuously defending ethnicities. Conservatives and fundamentalists around the world are fretting about the dilution of their ancient ethnic cultures—and expressing their concerns in white supremacist movements, anti-immigration policies, neo-fascist political parties, ethnic cleansing warfare. At the same time, earnest liberals rally to the support of "indigenous peoples," enlist in "cultural preservation" efforts to maintain other ethnic groups in their "original state." All of these are biased in favor of an idea of the naturalness and timelessness of those cultures, blinkered against recognizing them as inventions that have been turned into things by the process of reification.

This essay implies that the work ahead for the post-postmodern world is (a) to go fully into the recognition that some of our most cherished concepts of human solidarity are inventions, and (b) to invent some new concepts.

If the titles of some publications of the past two decades and the arguments made recently by scholars in various disciplines are at all representative of a larger trend, the word "invention" has become a central term for our understanding of the universe. "Invention" is no longer reserved for accounts of technological advances such as the telegraph, or limited to neo-Aristotelian discussions of the relationship of poetry and history or of originality and plagiarism. Even a casual glance at publications since the 1960s and at recent critical interventions reveals that a variety of voices now use the word in order to describe, analyze, or criticize such diverse phenomena as the invention of culture; of literary history; of narrative; of childhood as well as the loss of childhood; of adolescence; of motherhood; of kinship; of the self; of America; of New England; of Billy the Kid and the West; of the Negro; of the Indian; of the Jew; of Jesus and Christianity; of Athens; of the modern hospital; of the museum of science; of the 1920s in Paris; of our ability to "see" photographic pictures; of the vision of the outlaw in America; or of the American way of death. In view of such evidence, Jacques Derrida's observation—made in 1986 in a memorial address honoring Paul de Man—that "invention" has become a rather popular category in intellectual discourse seems, if anything, an understatement.

The term "invention" is, however, not just part of a fad; and we would not be better off without this buzzword, which, after all, offers an adequate description of a profound change in modes of perception. The interpretation of previously "essentialist" categories (childhood, generations, romantic love, mental health, gender, region, history, biography, and so on) as "inventions" has resulted in the recognition of the general cultural constructedness of the modern world. What were the givens in intellectual pursuits until very recently have now become the problematic issues. At this juncture the category of "invention" has been stressed in order to emphasize not so much originality and innovation as the importance of *language* in the social construction of reality. Some postmodern discourse has gone so far as to let "reality" disappear behind an inventive language that dissembles it. Michel Foucault's attack upon the faith in value-neutral language for the human sciences has intensified the perception among humanists that, as Hayden White put it, "the very constitution of their field of study [is] a *poetic* act, a genuine 'making' or 'invention' of a domain of inquiry."[1] Whereas the Renaissance Aristotelians used "invention" to clarify and define the dividing line between history and literature and to assert individual ingenuity, post-modernists speak of "invention" in order to lay bare the textual strategies in the construction of the "individual" and to show the dependence of historiography upon the rhetorical devices of literature; they thus portray biography and historiography as forms of "fiction-making."[2] To use an example from another discipline, in *Writing Culture* the anthropologist James Clifford invokes Michel Foucault, Michel de Certeau, Gerard Genette, Hayden White, and Terry Eagleton, reminds ethnographers of the rhetorical tradition of viewing texts as "composed of inventions rather than observed facts," and stresses the meaning of "inventing" as "making up . . . things not actually real."[3] Clifford places his enterprise into a "post-anthropological" and "post-literary" context, in which he may regard ethnographies, too, as fictions.

What is one to do after such knowledge? In some disciplines reactions have set in that resemble Monsieur Jourdain's sudden recognition in Molière's *Le Bourgeois Gentilhomme* that he had been speaking *prose* all along, without knowing it. If language and rhetoric become productive forces that constitute the ideological terms which then appear to be the "natural" signposts in our universe, this results in a strengthened emphasis on linguistics in all disciplines. Instead of old-style "factual" studies, self-conscious exercises in describing all the world as a text and everything in it as "signs" are on the rise. Similarly, "authors" and "individuals" are, at times, replaced by neo-essentialist battles between rhetorical categories such as metaphor and metonymy. Is it possible to take the postmodern assault seriously and yet to adhere to some notion of history and of individual and collective life in the modern world? Can one speak of invention in such contexts?

The forces of modern life embodied by such terms as "ethnicity," "nationalism," or "race" can indeed be meaningfully discussed as "inventions." Of course, this usage is meant not to evoke a conspiratorial interpretation of a manipulative inventor who single-handedly makes ethnics out of unsuspecting subjects, but to suggest widely shared, though intensely debated, collective fictions that are continually reinvented. The anthropologist Michael Fischer recently argued in his contribution to *Writing Culture:* "What the newer works [of American ethnic literature] bring home forcefully is . . . the paradoxical sense that ethnicity is something reinvented and reinterpreted in each generation by each individual and that it is often something quite puzzling to the individual, something over which he or she lacks control."⁴ Even more suggestively, the political scientist Benedict Anderson has, in *Imagined Communities*, reflected upon the conditions under which modern national and ethnic groups have been invented (or "imagined").⁵

Anderson invokes Ernest Gellner's memorable argument: "Nationalism is not the awakening of nations to self-consciousness; it *invents* nations where they do not exist." It is this understanding of nationalism that could be helpful toward an interpretation of ethnicity, too. The invention of nationalisms and ethnicities must have been peaking in the eighteenth and nineteenth centuries, in a period of very dramatic changes. Technological inventions such as the steamboat, the railroad, the Gatling gun, and, especially, the advances in printing techniques had a direct bearing on ethnic migrations and confrontations. As Anderson argues, the European aristocratic order, based on directly related families, was challenged by the American and French revolutions and increasingly replaced by various national bourgeois systems, which relied on the more *imaginary* ways of connectedness that the new technologies provided. In the wake of this development the idea that nation, nationality, or ethnic belonging mattered a great deal for people became more and more widespread. Though the revolutionary ideals of *egalité* or the Declaration of Independence provided the popular slogans for the termination of aristocratic systems, new hierarchies immediately emerged, often in the name of ethnicity. The nation-state was viewed as an ideal, and ethnic homogeneity or racial purity was advocated by thinkers like Louis Agassiz and Arthur Gobineau. In the era of these new hierarchies, however, communities needed to create a sense of cohesion by what Benedict Anderson has termed "reverberation." The immediate connectedness of the aristocracy was replaced by a mediated form of cohesion that depended, among other things, on literacy and "national" (and ethnic) literatures. Communities by reverberation relied, as Anderson stresses, on texts and on words; and in this sense, they were "invented" communities. Nationalism needed a literature to be spread. With Anderson, who mentions Benjamin Franklin as the crucial founding father *and* printer, one might speak of a double quest for literacy and nationalism in the modern world. One may also say that nationalism and ethnicity may be the most successfully exported items from Revolutionary America and from Napoleonic and post-

Napoleonic Europe—as, indeed, ethnocentrism may ironically have become one of the universals around the globe.

The book that may be seen as a model collection for applying the concept of "invention" to a critical, yet eminently historical, study of nationalisms is Eric Hobsbawm and Terence Ranger's volume *The Invention of Tradition*, which focuses on the invention and diffusion of modern cultural symbols—not just such texts as "folk" ballads and anthems but also such nonverbal symbols as flags and imperial pageantry—in the name of supposedly ancient national and ethnic traditions. The various contributors to *The Invention of Tradition* emphasize the very recent (and highly inauthentic) emergence of such cultural features as the Scottish tartan and kilt or the Welsh love for music.[6] Many traditions turn out to be "neo-traditions" that are made up in order to make more palatable breaks with actual traditions or to substantiate politically motivated feelings of peoplehood.

By calling ethnicity—that is, belonging and being perceived by others as belonging to an ethnic group—an "invention," one signals an interpretation in a modern and postmodern context. There is a certain, previously unrecognized, semantic legitimacy in insisting on this context. After all (as far as I know), the word "postmodern" first appeared in print in 1916 as part of Randolph Bourne's *ethnic* reflections on "Trans-National America"; and, tellingly, the word "ethnicity" first saw print in 1941, in a book by W. Lloyd Warner that had the adjective "modern" in its title.[7] Ethnicity would thus seem to make a perfect subject for a modern approach that utilizes the decoding techniques familiar from the scholarship of "invention." Yet by and large, studies tend less to set out to explore its construction than to take it for granted as a relatively fixed or, at least, a known and self-evident category. The traditional way of looking at ethnicity therefore still dominates. It rests on certain premises:

Ethnic groups are typically imagined as if they were natural, real, eternal, stable, and static units. They seem to be always already in existence. As a subject of study, each group yields an essential continuum of certain myths and traits, or of human capital. The focus is on the group's preservation and survival, which appear threatened. Conflicts generally seem to emerge from the world outside of the particular ethnic group investigated. Assimilation is the foe of ethnicity; hence there are numerous polemics against the blandness of melting pot, mainstream, and majority culture (even though these polemics themselves surely must have cultural dominance at this moment in history). The studies that result from such premises typically lead to an isolationist, group-by-group approach that emphasizes "authenticity" and cultural heritage within the individual, somewhat idealized group—at the expense of more widely shared historical conditions and cultural features, of dynamic interaction and syncretism. Some challenges to this view may be expressed in the following set of questions:

Is not the ability of ethnicity to present (or invent) itself as a "natural" and timeless category the problem to be tackled? Are not ethnic groups part of the historical process, tied to the history of modern nationalism? Though they may pretend to be eternal and essential, are they not of rather recent origin and eminently pliable and unstable? Is not modernism an important *source* of ethnicity? Do not new ethnic groups continually emerge? Even where they exist over long time spans, do not ethnic groups constantly change and redefine themselves? What is the active contribution literature makes, as a productive force, to the emergence and maintenance of communities by reverberation and of ethnic distinctions? Are not the formulas of "originality" and "authenticity" in ethnic discourse a palpable legacy of European romanticism? How is the illusion of ethnic "authenticity" stylistically created in a text? Despite all the diatribes, is not the opposition between "pluralism" and "assimilation" a false one? Does not any "ethnic" system rely on an opposition to something "non-ethnic," and is not this very antithesis more important than the interchangeable content (of flags, anthems, and the applicable vernacular)?

Such questions are inspired by some newer anthropological, sociological, and historical thinking, according to which ethnicity is not so much an ancient and deep-seated force surviving from the historical past, but rather the modern and modernizing feature of a contrasting strategy that may be shared far beyond the boundaries within which it is claimed. It marks an acquired modern sense of belonging that replaces visible, concrete communities whose kinship symbolism ethnicity may yet mobilize in order to appear more natural. The trick that it passes itself off as blood, as "thicker than water," should not mislead interpreters to take it at face value. It is not a thing but a process—and it requires constant detective work from readers, not a settling on a fixed encyclopedia of supposed cultural essentials.

Since the "vernacular" (a category that, of course, goes back to the replacement of Latin by local modern languages in European literature) has recently been placed in the foreground of some approaches to American ethnicity, let me offer an Afro-American illustration here. Zora Neale Hurston uses the beautiful phrase "percolate on down the avenue" in a short story that has both a precise sense of the idiom and an openness toward the modern context within which any vernacular articulates itself: " 'But baby!' Jelly gasped. 'Dat shape you got on you! I bet the Coca-Cola Company is paying you good money for the patent!' "[8] Hurston, who accompanies her text with a six-page glossary, undoubtedly manages to suggest a unique and very specific cultural timbre, and the title "Story in Harlem Slang" (first published in 1942) is fully justified. Yet it deserves notice that her effect of "authenticity" is achieved not by some purist, archival, or preservationist attitude toward a fixed past but by a remarkable openness toward the ability of a specific idiom to interact with "outside" signals and to incorporate them. In that way elements of a widely shared everyday life, like a humanized soft drink bottle, or a verbalized "percolator" (not exactly a traditional cultural staple, many past "coffee" associations and Bessie Smith's "brand new coffee grinder" notwithstanding), become "natural" and even central elements in the vernacular. It is the ethnic text's ability to generate the sense of difference out of a shared cultural context of coffeemakers and Coca-Cola bottles that makes this example representative.

It is not any a priori cultural *difference* that makes ethnicity. "The Chinese laundryman does not learn his trade in China; there are no laundries in China." This the Chinese immigrant Lee Chew asserts in Hamilton Holt's *Life Stories of Undistinguished Americans* (1906).[9] One can hardly explain the prevalence of Chinese-American laundries by going back to Chinese history proper. It is always the specificity of power relations at a given historical moment and in a particular place that triggers off a strategy of pseudo-historical explanations that camouflage the inventive act itself.

This is true not only for mild forms of symbolic ethnic identification, but also for those virulent types of ethnocentrism which manifested themselves as racism. For example, when Henry W. Grady mapped out the essentials of the white Southerners' creed in 1885, he invoked a supposed two-thousand-year-old "race instinct" that militates against social mingling across racial boundaries—an instinct that he felt was "deeper than prejudice or pride, and bred in the bone and the blood." Yet since his political purpose lay in the justification of the modern legalization of racial segregation as the defeated white Southerners' self-defense against Northerners, Grady paradoxically also had to grant that he was speaking of this supposedly permanent "race instinct" as a modern political scheme invented to prevent "amalgamation." He tellingly defined the "race instinct" with the following anecdote:

> [Milhaud], in voting in the French Convention for the beheading of Louis XVI, said: "If death did not exist, it would be necessary to-day to invent it." So of this instinct. It is the pledge of the integrity of each race, and of peace between the races. Without it, there might be a breaking down of all lines of division and a thorough intermingling of whites and blacks.[10]

This line of reasoning—modeled upon an attempt at passing off an execution as a natural part of the life cycle—reveals that what is advocated in the name of immutable instincts belongs not to the realm of biology but to that of political history, especially of the period since the French Revolution.

Afro-American writers have been particularly astute in detecting the sinister implications of the invention of ethnic purity, passed off as natural. For example, Charles W. Chesnutt, the highly acclaimed author of such books as *The Conjure Woman* and *The Wife of His Youth*, observed in 1905: "We are told that we must glory in our color and zealously guard it as a priceless heritage." Yet he did not endorse this admonition, and his comment deserves to be quoted at length:

> Frankly, I take no stock in this doctrine. It seems to me a modern invention of the white people to perpetute the color line. It is they who preach it, and it is their racial integrity which they wish to preserve: they have never been unduly careful of the purity of the black race. . . . Why should a man be proud any more than he should be ashamed of a thing for which he is not at all responsible? . . . Are we to help the white people to build up walls between themselves and us to fence in a gloomy back yard for our descendents to play in?[11]

PART TWO

ALL THAT IS SOLID MELTS INTO AIR

Karl Marx's denunciation of bourgeois modernism—"All that is solid melts into the air, all that is holy is profaned"—seems even more on target as a charge against postmodernity.[1] There is something about postmodern ideas with their talk of socially constructed reality that can have a dizzying, vertiginous effect—a feeling of having no place left to stand, nothing in which to believe in.

And, indeed, a deep and probably permanent change is taking place in our time—a breakdown of confidence in symbols. The ancient philosophical discourse about the connection between symbols and the things they stand for has come back to life with a vengeance.

Premodern people knew there was a profound connection between a word and its referent. That was what made magic possible: A sorcerer could utter a word—such as the name of a person being cursed—and have an effect upon the thing it stood for. Visual symbols had the same kind of power. That was what made idolatry possible: People found it perfectly logical to worship statues of gods as if they were gods themselves.

Moderns, particularly in this century, became increasingly doubtful about that connection. If you were an anthropologist, you heard about the Sapir-Whorf hypothesis. Linguists Edward Sapir and Benjamin Whorf claimed that languages don't simply serve as neutral tools that people use to report what's "out there"—but rather that they set the ground rules for what people see, understand, and talk about. Every language is its own set of blueprints for constructing reality, deciding what will be noticed and what overlooked, establishing the rules for communication. In learning a language, they said, a person "channels his reasoning and builds the house of his consciousness."[2]

That idea is now part of the common understanding. I don't know how many times I have been informed that Eskimos have many words for snow, and that this linguistic richness enables them to see and understand snow variations that would be invisible to the rest of us. People used to say, "If I hadn't seen it I never would have believed it." The postmod switcheroo, which you hear often these days, is, "If I hadn't believed it, I never would have seen it." Such slogans, the mere fact that they are floating around in the social atmosphere, reveal postmodern consciousness at work and sometimes at play, because many postmoderns appear to feel free to *play around* with symbols—verbal and visual. Umberto Eco has already touched on this in his description of how people now play the game of irony: When they say something, they may mean it—but they mean it in different ways. Their ironic play expresses their awareness that symbols have an existence of their own, are not merely road maps to some objective nonhuman reality.

The first group of essays in this section look at different aspects of this situation. Richard Shweder points out that symbols of all sorts—such as Santa Claus—easily detach from their familiar cultures, float freely in the wind like dandelion seeds, and grow up in strange new varieties in other places. He also proposes a positive and sane way of living in this world, which he calls "postmodern humanism." Jean Baudrillard claims that signs have gone through a series of evolutions, so that now they have no relationship to any reality whatever. Ernest Sternberg talks about the "economy of icons" that arises as we become increasingly occupied with the making, buying and selling of symbols. And the homely notion that words simply report reality is severely mauled by Jacques Derrida, who "deconstructs" writing to show that what words really relate to is—other words.

But postmodernism, for all its talk of play, is often monumentally pompous, and for a change of pace we follow Derrida's deconstruction of Jean-Jacques Rousseau with Steven Katz's deconstruction of postmodernist prose—a refreshing prod into the windbag tendencies of our own time.

We also consider the deep differences that the postmodern condition brings forth—not only the kinds of difference we call pluralism, but also strong differences of opinion about how damn much difference we can put up with. Clearly, not everybody wants to be a postmodern humanist. Every age produces its own polarizations. The postmodern era does this, at the same time that it retains some of the old polarizations. We still have conflicts between black and white, young and old, rich and poor—all the old favorites—and now we also have the kind of conflicts that James Davison Hunter calls culture wars: on one side the people who feel comfortable "re-symbolizing" old belief systems such as religions, and on the other those who want to keep matters as they were, with the symbols firmly linked to universal truth. Conservatives prefer to believe that the symbols of the faith—such as the words in the Bible—represent a truth beyond words and culture. These are serious conflicts, and not always playful; conservatives don't think symbols are playthings.

The polarization that Hunter describes is one way of comprehending the landscape of the postmodern world, and in subsequent essays in this section we look at other ways that people comprehend the present situation, channel their reasoning and build their houses of consciousness on this uncertain new terrain.

IO

Santa Claus on the Cross

RICHARD SHWEDER

The word "anthropology" means the study of human beings, but modern anthropologists had a narrower mandate: It was to go off someplace and study premodern societies—the more pristinely premodern the better. The anthropologists did their work so well, found so many different cultures and worldviews, that they helped bring the modern era tumbling to its conclusion. Now, as the times change, so does the work of anthropologists: They look at a world in which all the cultures are flowing together in most curious ways, and symbols have become world travelers. And they are asked to explain.

There is no single best place to be raised, but one of the really good places to be raised is any place where you learn that there is no single best place to be raised. I call that place "postmodern humanism."

Perhaps there was a time in the mythic past when the anthropological "other" was pristine, unitary, alien, and lived very far away. If so, things have changed. In the postmodern world that commerce has helped to create, the anthropological "other" is sophisticated, multiplex, near at hand, and deeply embedded in the bureaucratic institutions of the world system. Anthropology is no longer the discipline that adduces good reasons for the customs of others, which they cannot adduce for themselves. United Airlines, CNN, a Visa card, and Western perspectives have usually gotten there first, or are soon to arrive, and encounters between cultures over questions of "authority," "voice," and "paradigm comparisons" more often than not have the feel of a segment from the Monty Python Show.

A few years ago, for example, I heard a story from Clifford Geertz about a visitor to Japan who wandered into a department store in Tokyo, at a time when the Japanese had begun to take a great interest in the symbolism of the Christmas season. And what symbol of the Christmas season did the visitor discover prominently on display in the Tokyo department store? Santa Claus nailed to a cross!

When I first heard that story, I opened a "Santa Claus nailed to a cross" file, which has grown over the years. Some people think that in the postmodern world words have no reference or validity and you can never know quite what you are talking about. When I look at my file, I feel reassured that in our postmodern world truth is still stranger than fiction, even as it has become more difficult to pin things down. Here are some other entries from the file.

There is an entry about a South Asian Indian woman, married to an American, who applied for U.S. citizenship so that her father who had lived all his life in the Third World could join the American Peace Corps. At the final stage of being "naturalized" in New York, the immigration officer said to her, "Do you swear that you will bear arms in defense of the Constitution of the United States?" Compounding the irony of her situation she replied, "No, I won't do that." He asked, "What do you mean?" She said, "I am a pacifist. I don't believe in killing." He said, "Who taught you that?" She said, "Mahatma Gandhi." He said, "Who is he?" She said, "A great Indian religious leader." He said, "Well, you will have to get a note from him." She said, "I can't, he is dead." He said, "Well, get a note from whoever took his place."

There is a parallel entry in my file about an American scholar trained as a "symbolic anthropologist" who sought official research permission to do work among the Maori people of New Zealand. As part of the official procedure he found himself interrogated by a "native," a Maori with an Oxford Ph.D. in anthropology, who was a gatekeeper for the tribe and who had some doubts about the "Chicago school" of symbolism as a way to represent the beliefs and practices of "others."

There is an entry in my file about a prominent member of an East African tribe, a professional philosopher, who had an interest in reviving traditional practices. As it turned out, the old ways and customs had been discarded and forgotten even by the elders of his tribe. The main repository of knowledge about the past was located in ethnographies published in Europe and the United States. He realized he needed a Western anthropologist as a consultant. He had no difficulty finding someone to take the job.

There is an entry in my file about the organizers of a cultural festival in Los Angeles, who lost funding from the Korean government when they decided to "represent" Korea with a performance by indigenous shamans rather than with the ballet company proposed by the Korean government. The Thai community of Los Angeles was also offended because the festival featured a classical dance troupe from Cambodia but only popular street theater from Thailand.[1] The distinction between high and low, primitive and modern is not peculiar to the West. It seems that these days it is largely in the West that people get nervous when the idea of a hierarchy of taste and value is invoked. We prefer to talk about "popular" culture.

There is an entry about all those incredible ethnographic accounts from New Guinea, where in the highlands the men avoid women, and in the lowlands young men inseminate each other in homosexual rites, and here and there married men, loathing the pollution of the sexual act, induce themselves to vomit or bleed their noses after making love to their wives and before returning to the men's hut. Such accounts have had prominence in the lore of anthropology, yet, after a few years of contact with the West, almost everything that was exotic about New Guinea seems to have disappeared. Anthropologists go back to their field sites to discover that no one knows the names for plants anymore or cares very much for the old rituals. Everyone is going to school so that they can have access to jobs, manufactured goods, and T-shirts from the Hard Rock Cafe. The sexual symbolism and avoidance customs of the culture seemed very deep indeed, until they just went away.

And there are many personal entries. In 1982, for example, I was living in what I thought was a relatively remote district of India when television first landed. It immediately became a dowry item in arranged marriages and a basic necessity demanded by women in purdah. I was invited to watch the unveiling of a television set in a traditional household. What was the first image to appear on the tube? An old segment from "I Love Lucy." Lucy was out on a blind date with a duck hunter. I was asked to explain.

Some time later I was in Manhattan watching cable television with a parochial "Westerner." As I flipped stations what did I discover? News from New Delhi and a segment from the Hindu epic *The Ramayana*. I was asked to explain. I flipped channels again. There was a Japanese soap opera, heavily scripted with facial displays of shyness, embarrassment, and self-effacing apologetic dialogue ("I am sorry for dominating our children" and "I am sorry for this and especially sorry for that"). With "public access" to our living rooms, there is more and more to explain, and it is less and less clear how to take a stand on questions of fact and value without seeming hegemonic, dogmatic or prejudiced. It is less and less clear whether prejudgment is always such a bad thing.

My friend the literary critic Anatole Broyard used to tell his writing students, "Hang on to your prejudices, they are the only taste you have got." Almost everyone in the academy these days has heard of the continental dictum that it is our prejudices that make it possible for us to see, which means that in thinking, as in life, if you do not fix a starting point you'll never get started. Broyard, who sensed our postmodern predicament and knew how to express it with grace and wit, formulated the aphorism this way: "Paranoids are the only ones who notice things anymore."[2] Nietzsche-like he understood that any prejudice is better than no prejudice at all, and that in a postmodern world of cable television and metaphysical jet lag, the best one can do is stay on the move, keeping your options for prejudice open while developing some sensibility or at least some good sense.

Unfortunately too many have misunderstood such exciting deconstructive insights. They have drawn the conclusion that the authority of a voice or viewpoint has little to do with what is said and everything to do with who says it. They have overlooked the fact that you do not have to be a Westerner or a male to articulate a Western or masculine perspective, and that most Westerners and most males are not very good at it anyhow. Authoritative voices, one is tempted to say, speak for the muse, and you know such voices speak for the muse not because of who they are, least of all their social designation, but because what they say binds you to a reality.

So, with regard to the problem of "difference," what are the options for prejudice, the starting points, the interpretive moves, the authoritative voices on the current theory scene?

One option, and it is an option with a distinguished pedigree, is to reify the other. That is the approach of most "structuralisms" and other modernist accounts of "otherness." When I visited with Claude Levi-Strauss for the first and only time in Paris in 1990, he told me that he hears the term "postmodern" all the time but does not understand what it means, and that he would have preferred to live before the twentieth century, before the postmodern era. "But where in the world would you have preferred to live in the past?" I asked, thinking of Athens in the fifth century B.C., India at the time of Buddha, and all those famous cultures of the world—the Nuer, the Dani, the Bororo, the Samoans, the Trobriand Islanders—studied by anthropologists. "In France, of course," Levi-Strauss replied. "Why France?" I asked. "Because French subjectivity is the only subjectivity I can ever understand," he replied. "But what about all those other cultures you have studied all your life? Can't you enter into their subjectivity?" I asked. "No," he replied: "I can only understand other cultures as objects, not as subjects."

I had a better understanding of postmodernism after that meeting with Levi-Strauss. If postmodern scholarship has done nothing else, it has reduced the distance between the subjectivity of the anthropologist and his or her anthropological object (or is it "subject"?) and persuaded us to revalue the here and the there, the then and the now, the self and the other as an artful (not "literal" and certainly not "fanciful") product of the human imagination. Within the terms of that artful project there are other options for the representation of self and otherness besides treating the other as a thing.

One option is to treat the other as really very much like the self. There are anthropologists—Roger Keesing of Australia National University is among the most articulate—who believe that the differences between peoples have been exaggerated by anthropologists, that anthropologists "choose the most exotic possible cultural data" as their texts and "give them the most exotic possible readings,"[3] and that there is a kind of primary knowledge of the world shared by all peoples, a common sense that is both common and sensible.

A second option is to treat the other as an unsophisticated version of the self, as the dark age, superstitious and confused predecessor to our enlightenment. Ernest Gellner of the University of Cambridge[4] is a colorful exponent of this developmental point of view, which argues that the world woke up and became good for the first time in the West about three hundred years ago, when magic disappeared and when it was finally realized that sticks and stones can break your bones but words can never harm you. Gellner's view plays rather poorly in the capitals of Western anthropology, where the idea of constituted realities, performative utterances, and other forms of "word magic" are very much in vogue, but rather well in the relatively disenchanted capitals of the Third World, among the Westernized or Westernizing elite.

A third option is to go native or indigenous, as articulated by my University of Chicago colleague McKim Marriott:

> . . . the social sciences used in India today have developed from thought about Western, rather than Indian cultural realities. As a result although they pretend to universal applicability, the Western sciences often do not recognize and therefore cannot deal with the questions to which many Indian institutions are answers.[5]

Marriott went on to argue that "All social sciences develop from thought about what is known to particular cultures and are thus 'cultural' or 'ethno-' social sciences in their origins. All are initially parochial in scope." He proposed for India a new set of social science concepts and ideas derived from the parochial realities known to Indian people.

The irony of Marriott's approach, which has not gone unnoticed in India, is that Marriott is an "outsider" who seems more appreciative of the indigenous perspective of "others" than are many "insiders," who are in fact members of the Westernizing elite. But that is just the beginning of the irony. The "insiders," mostly literati who are somewhat distanced from the traditional cultural realities that Marriott has in mind, disagree with each other about who is really "inside." Do "Indian cultural realities" sum up to a Hindu social science or a Muslim social science? And what about the Jains? Who gets credit for it? And how can Marriott even understand Indian ethnosociology unless he is in some sense an "insider" too? Perhaps the distinction between inside and outside is not so clear, as any respectable Indian ethnotheory ought to assert. Perhaps parochial concepts and ideas can, after all, actually have a more universal appeal.

Indeed, at the end of his essay Marriott himself contrasts "conventional Western social science," which he believes grows out of Western theology, law, and common sense, with "the [Western] findings of current linguistics, of molecular and atomic physics, of ecological biology, and of social systems theory," which he believes are quite compatible with the parochial assumptions of a Hindu social science. In the end—if there is an end—it turns out that the radical relativism of Marriott's ethnotheory agenda is merely apparent, for if we look in the right place, the parochial "other" can be found well within ourselves.

In other words, in this postmodern ironical world that international trade has helped to create in which the inside is out (Coca-Cola is everywhere) and the outside is in (the Japanese own Rockefeller Center), a new kind of humanism has begun to emerge. Going native amounts to traveling abroad or across ethnic boundaries to find some suppressed aspect of the self valued and on public display in another land or neighborhood, which one can then bring back as theoretical or cultural critique. The unity of human beings is no longer to be found in that which makes us common and all the same, but rather in a universal original multiplicity which makes each of us so variegated that "others" become fully accessible and imaginable to us through some aspect or other of our own complex self.

Postmodern humanism—this universalism without the uniformity— challenges us to do several apparently contradictory things. The contradiction is, however, merely apparent because we never do those things all at once, or with the same breath or in the same frame of reference. Postmodern humanism advises us to restrict the scope of our generalizations to local cultural worlds. It grants us permission to cultivate our prejudices so that we can see (there is *something* to be said in favor of "close mindedness," as a limit on nihilism). Yet it also entices us to stay on the move between alternative prejudices, leaving ourselves open to be astonished by the integrity and value of alien things. It seeks to move the human imagination across great divides in cultural tastes, likes, preferences, and sensibilities, to make it possible for us to comprehend and value each other without requiring that we be the same. It still remains to be seen how this postmodern humanism—this universalism without the uniformity—will fully take shape and for which tribes it will be seen as a thing of great worth.

II

The Map Precedes the Territory

JEAN BAUDRILLARD

This oft-quoted passage from Jean Baudrillard is a good example of the provocative, suggestive, disturbing and less-than-lucid Gallic approach to postmodernity. Baudrillard says imagery has evolved through four stages: Once people simply believed that a sign stood for some nonhuman truth. Then they began to suspect that signs were lies, concealing or misrepresenting truth. Then they decided that signs were there to mask the absence of any real truth. Then they got to the stage—this is Baudrillard's version of postmodernity—in which there is no connection whatever between an image and any nonhuman truth. The image, for all practical purposes, is reality.

The simulacrum is never that which conceals the truth—it is the truth which conceals that there is none.
The simulacrum is true.   —ECCLESIASTES

If we were able to take as the finest allegory of simulation the Borges tale where the cartographers of the Empire draw up a map so detailed that it ends up exactly covering the territory (but where the decline of the Empire sees this map become frayed and finally ruined, a few shreds still discernible in the deserts—the metaphysical beauty of this ruined abstraction, bearing witness to an Imperial pride and rotting like a carcass, returning to the substance of the soil, rather as an aging double ends up being confused with the real thing)—then this fable has come full circle for us, and now has nothing but the discrete charm of second-order simulacra.

Abstraction today is no longer that of the map, the double, the mirror or the concept. Simulation is no longer that of a territory, a referential being or a substance. It is the generation by models of a real without origin or reality: a hyperreal. The territory no longer precedes the map, nor survives it. Henceforth, it is the map that precedes the territory—PRECESSION OF SIMULACRA—it is the map that engenders the territory and if we were to revive the fable today, it would be the territory whose shreds are slowly rotting across the map. It is the real, and not the map, whose vestiges subsist here and there, in the deserts which are no longer those of the Empire, but our own.

Outside of medicine and the army, favored terrains of simulation, the affair goes back to religion and the simulacrum of divinity: "I forbad any simulacrum in the temples because the divinity that breathes life into nature cannot be represented."

This was the approach of the Jesuits, who based their politics on the virtual disappearance of God and on the worldly and spectacular manipulation of consciences—the evanescence of God in the epiphany of power—the end of transcendence, which no longer serves as alibi for a strategy completely free of influences and signs. Behind the baroque of images hides the grey eminence of politics.

Thus perhaps at stake has always been the murderous capacity of images, murderers of the real, murderers of their own model as the Byzantine icons could murder the divine identity. To this murderous capacity is opposed the dialectical capacity of representations as a visible and intelligible mediation of the Real. All of Western faith and good faith was engaged in this wager on representation: that a sign could refer to the depth of meaning, that a sign could *exchange* for meaning and that something could guarantee this exchange—God, of course. But what if God himself can be simulated, that is to say, reduced to the signs which attest his existence? Then the whole system becomes weightless, it is no longer anything but a gigantic simulacrum—not unreal, but a simulacrum, never again exchanging for what is real, but exchanging in itself, in an uninterrupted circuit without reference or circumference.

So it is with simulation, insofar as it is opposed to representation. The latter starts from the principle that the sign and the real are equivalent (even if this equivalence is utopian, it is a fundamental axiom). Conversely, simulation starts from the *utopia* of this principle of equivalence, *from the radical negation of the sign as value,* from the sign as reversion and death sentence of every reference. Whereas representation tries to absorb simulation by interpreting it as false representation, simulation envelops the whole edifice of representation as itself a simulacrum.

This would be the successive phases of the image:
—it is the reflection of a basic reality
—it masks and perverts a basic reality
—it masks the *absence* of a basic reality
—it bears no relation to any reality whatever: it is its own pure simulacrum.

In the first case, the image is a *good* appearance—the representation is of the order of sacrament. In the second, it is an *evil* appearance—of the order of malefice. In the third, it *plays at being* an appearance—it is of the order of sorcery. In the fourth, it is no longer in the order of appearance at all, but of simulation.

The transition from signs which dissimulate something to signs which dissimulate that there is nothing, marks the decisive turning point. The first implies a theology of truth and secrecy (to which the notion of ideology still belongs). The second inaugurates an age of simulacra and simulation, in which there is no longer any God to recognise his own, nor any last judgement to separate true from false, the real from its artificial resurrection, since everything is already dead and risen in advance.

When the real is no longer what it used to be, nostalgia assumes its full meaning. There is a proliferation of myths of origin and signs of reality; of second-hand truth, objectivity and authenticity. There is an escalation of the true, of the lived experience; a resurrection of the figurative where the object and substance have disappeared.

12

The Economy of Icons

ERNEST STERNBERG

Postmodern business people may not have read Baudrillard, but they know a thing or two about images. They know that our deepest longings are for immaterial things—the stuff of dreams—and that we will pay good money for products that feed our fantasies. Ernest Sternberg says this has led to a new stage in the development of capitalism—an economy of icons. In this wondrous marketplace we find displayed not only designer clothes, but designer environments, and people with designer personalities.

A century of progress in commercial marketing strategies has now culminated in a momentous transformation of capitalism. Whereas for most of the capitalist era business firms produced goods and services presumed to have identifiable *uses*, the new postmodern firms devote themselves to generating images that appeal to consumers' *desires* and *longings*. These advanced capitalist firms have become producers of presentations—of performances, images, narratives, and phantasms that turn commodities into valuable icons.

Commodities are merely useful, hence easily replicable through alternative technological processes, reducing their market value. Icons attain market value through carefully constructed, proprietary images that evoke the consumer's dreams—dreams of ethnic identity, rebellious youthfulness, close-knit community, or sexual excitation. The icon's status as a food item, vacation, or human persona reveals only its mundane form; its greater economic value arises from carefully crafted significations.

In this iconic economy, the automobile becomes a vehicle for self-liberation; the store containing racks of ready-to-wear garments turns into a boutique for expressing ruggedness, motherhood, or masculinity; and foods that were once depicted as analogs of gastronomic inputs become accessories to carefully designed sensuous nostalgia.

Consider an advertisement that appeared in 1990 on American television, in which a woman photographed in soft-focus sits in a room reminiscent of the United States of the 1940s. She is dressed in a negligee at a table that prominently displays a bottle of ketchup. Suddenly, she perceptibly thrills, because a uniformed man has entered the room, apparently returning from military service. The scene ends with their embrace, set off by the upright ketchup bottle in the foreground. We as viewers immediately understand that the brand of tomato condiment will allow us to partake in such passion.

For the ketchup maker, commercial success comes from the capacity to present the significations that engage the consumer. In a reversal of the modern industrial logic (in which the firm prepares a good and then considers how to market it), the postmodern firm begins with the celebrity, the pop-culture character, logo, or news event—and then asks about the selection of mundane salable items to which it can be attached.

This postmodern capitalist logic applies not only to movable goods but to the full range of economic products. Real-estate developers, for example, have discovered that they do not simply supply containers (houses, buildings) for activity, but entire environments. The profitable developer now designs environments that respond to the shopper's longings for security, community, or escape—whether the "shopper" is a retail customer, a home buyer, or the prospective tenant of a business property, which will in turn attract other shoppers. The designs may suggest foreign exoticism, a quaint fishing village, wilderness hideaway, ethnic festival, or secure rural America.

Tourist destinations—postmodern products of ever-greater importance—now serve the tourists' yearning for experience, of history, techno-

logical wonders, or nature. They may even present slices of "true life"—
native ceremonies, local folklore, traditional material artifacts—though often with negligible ethnographic veracity. As compared to early- and mid-
twentieth century tourism, which sought to provide merely leisure and
recreation, this is designer tourism. Tourism businesses design the hos-
pitality of the reception staff, the behaviors of the native performers, the
cycle and rhythm of tourist activities, the presentation of exhibits, and the
shape of the built or "natural" environment so that each caters to tourists'
desires for evocative experience.

In one of the strangest turns of advanced capitalism, the intent to sell
through images also results in the iconification of the self. Job seekers and
salespersons (and the public relations specialists who advise them) have
learned from media celebrities: They strive for success and profit by shaping
their own personas. As sellers of the self, they adapt their beliefs and conduct
to the consumer's (employer's, client's, viewer's) presumed desire for authority, sexual titillation, human contact, or genuine expertise.

The industries producing iconic goods, sanctuaries, pilgrimage sites,
and personas depend on what has become the most dynamic driving force in
advanced capitalism: a conglomeration of movie and video studios, video-
game designers, television and cable programmers, theme parks and advertising firms, sports and music entrepreneurs, and news-reporting services,
along with several segments of high culture, such as art museums and
theaters. These industries share the ability to generate the story-lines and the
images that entice the consuming public. They also share a finite phantasmagoric inventory, which can accommodate only a limited rate of innovation. In this intensely competitive cultural environment, the core image-
making complex generates the imaginative stock that secondary industries
draw upon for commercially successful icon production.

The rise of iconic capitalism coincided with the intellectual embrace of
postmodernity, but the writings on postmodernity have been much more
likely to examine its consequences for art, philosophy, or criticism than for
the economy. And to the extent that this literature has anything to say about
the economy, it has usually confounded concepts of postmodernity with
postindustrialism.

As most commonly understood, the postindustrial information economy is marked by the ascendance to power of rational calculation, exercised

by a new technocratic and scientific elite, and abetted by computer and communications technologies. But postmodern iconic capitalism has little to do with rational calculation. Indeed, it appears as a bizarre obverse of the information economy.

In the ketchup advertisement, the image as broadcast is certainly composed of "bits" of data. But it conveys no information. Nor is information an issue in the production process. The firm selling the product has put far more managerial effort and expense into investing the ketchup with iconic content than into the biochemistry of tomato processing or the logistics of bottle distribution. For this firm, the tough business problems are not these routine technical matters, but those of situating the product amid the welter of cultural, historical, and sexual representations through which consumers realize their desires.

Therefore, though advanced technologies have indeed led to the rapid transmission of information, what has more profoundly reshaped capitalism is that these technologies have also created the electronic and mechanical capacity to reproduce images. But these technologies themselves came into existence as capitalist firms realized their utility in iconic production. Advanced communications technologies did not create the postmodern economy, but recursively participated in its rise.

As capitalist firms increasingly harnessed these technologies to pursue business advantage in consumer markets, they undermined the firmly founded reality of modern industrialism, until it collapsed into a commercial hyperreality of rampant, disjointed significations. In this economy, investors and corporate elites attain wealth—as postmodern politicians attain prestige—if they succeed in cornering the phantasmagoric resource that elicits viewers' desires and fears.

Conventional economic concepts leave us increasingly unable to make sense of this kind of capitalism. The barometric explanation, in which prices and quantities ascend or descend in response to hydraulic fluctuations in demand and supply, no longer throws much light on the economy. As we make our way into twenty-first-century capitalism, the time has come for a post-dismal economics.

13

The Play of Substitution

JACQUES DERRIDA

Here is Jacques Derrida at work—at work, in this case, deconstruct-
ing one of the icons of the Enlightenment, Jean-Jacques Rousseau.
Deconstruction is not, as it is sometimes taken to be, merely an
attempt to destroy or refute an argument. Nothing so straightfor-
ward. Rather, it is an attempt to show that words are ambiguous,
unsteady on their feet, not to be trusted as dependable representatives
of something "out there." The word under investigation is "supple-
ment," and Derrida explores the various ways Rousseau, in his
Confessions, *talks about substituting one thing for another: kissing a*
bed that belongs to his passionately adored Madame de Warens
instead of kissing her, indulging in masturbation instead of inter-
course (Rousseau calls masturbation "the dangerous supplement,"
and that is the title of the essay from which this excerpt is taken),
living with his mistress Thérèse instead of Madame de Warens.

In the following passage, Derrida's discussion of Rousseau's
supplements metamorphoses into a discussion of language as a supple-
ment for nonhuman reality, of the dubious relationship between a
word and its referent outside the text. In the process, Derrida comes
perilously close to making a clear and concise statement about what
he means by deconstruction. He also makes the much-debated asser-
tion "il n'y a pas de hors-texte," which is sometimes taken to mean

there isn't anything outside the text at all. I don't think he means that: A statement that there isn't anything outside is, after all, a statement about what is outside. I think he means that human experience is inseparably entangled with our descriptions of it.

Ah, my Thérèse! I am only too happy to possess you, modest and healthy, and not to find what I never looked for. [The question is of "maidenhood" (*pucelage*), which Thérèse has just confessed to have lost in innocence and by accident.] At first I had only sought amusement; I now saw that I had found more and gained a companion. A little intimacy with this excellent girl, a little reflection upon my situation, made me feel that, while thinking only of my pleasures, I had done much to promote my happiness. *To supply the place of* my extinguished ambition, I needed a lively sentiment which should *take complete possession of* [literally "fill"—*remplit*] my heart. In a word, I needed a successor to mamma. As I should never live with her again, I wanted someone to live with her pupil, in whom I might find the simplicity and docility of heart which she had found in me. I felt it necessary that the gentle tranquillity of private and domestic life *should make up* to me for the loss of the brilliant career which I was renouncing. When I was quite alone, I felt a void in my heart, which it only needed another heart to *fill*. Destiny had deprived me of, or, at least in part, alienated me from, that heart for which Nature had formed me. From that moment I was alone; for *with me it has always been everything or nothing. I found in Thérèse the substitute* [*supplément*] *that I needed.*[1]

Through this sequence of supplements a necessity is announced: that of an infinite chain, ineluctably multiplying the supplementary mediations that produce the sense of the very thing they defer: the mirage of the thing itself, of immediate presence, of originary perception. Immediacy is derived. That all begins through the intermediary is what is indeed "inconceivable [to reason]."

"For me there has never been an intermediary between everything or nothing." The intermediary is the mid-point and the mediation, the middle term between total absence and the absolute plenitude of presence. It is clear that mediacy is the name of all that Rousseau wanted opinionatedly to efface. This wish is expressed in a deliberate, sharp, thematic way. It does not have to be deciphered. Jean-Jacques recalls it here at the very moment when he is spelling out the supplements that are linked together to replace a mother or a Nature. And here the supplement occupies the middle point between total absence and total presence. The play of substitution fills and marks a determined lack. But Rousseau argues as if the recourse to the supplement—here to Thérèse—was going to appease his impatience when confronted with the intermediary: "From that moment I was alone; for me there has never been an intermediary between everything and nothing. I found in Thérèse the substitute that I needed." The virulence of this concept is thus appeased, as if one were able to *arrest it,* domesticate it, tame it.

This brings up the question of the usage of the word "supplement": of Rousseau's situation within the language and the logic that assures to this word or this concept sufficiently *surprising* resources so that the presumed subject of the sentence might always say, through using the "supplement," more, less, or something other than what he *would mean* [*voudrait dire*]. This question is therefore not only of Rousseau's writing but also of our reading. We should begin by taking rigorous account of this *being held within* [*prise*] or this *surprise:* the writer writes *in* a language and *in* a logic whose proper system, laws, and life his discourse by definition cannot dominate absolutely. He uses them only by letting himself, after a fashion and up to a point, be governed by the system. And the reading must always aim at a certain relationship, unperceived by the writer, between what he commands and what he does not command of the patterns of the language that he uses. This relationship is not a certain quantitative distribution of shadow and light, of weakness or of force, but a signifying structure that critical reading should *produce.*

What does produce mean here? In my attempt to explain that, I would initiate a justification of my principles of reading. A justification, as we shall see, entirely negative, outlining by exclusion a space of reading that I shall not fill here: a task of reading.

To produce this signifying structure obviously cannot consist of repro-ducing, by the effaced and respectful doubling of commentary, the con-scious, voluntary, intentional relationship that the writer institutes in his exchanges with the history to which he belongs thanks to the element of language. This moment of doubling commentary should no doubt have its place in a critical reading. To recognize and respect all its classical exigencies is not easy and requires all the instruments of traditional criticism. Without this recognition and this respect, critical production would risk developing in any direction at all and authorize itself to say almost anything. But this indispensable guardrail has always only *protected*, it has never *opened*, a reading.

Yet if reading must not be content with doubling the text, it cannot legitimately transgress the text toward something other than it, toward a referent (a reality that is metaphysical, historical, psychobiographical, etc.) or toward a signified outside the text whose content could take place, could have taken place outside of language, that is to say, in the sense that we give here to that word, outside of writing in general. That is why the methodological considerations that we risk applying here to an example are closely dependent on general propositions that we have elaborated above; as regards the absence of the referent or the transcendental signified. *There is nothing outside of the text* [there is no outside-text; *il n'y a pas de hors-texte*]. And that is neither because Jean-Jacques' life, or the existence of Mamma or Thérèse *themselves,* is not of prime interest to us, nor because we have access to their so-called "real" existence only in the text and we have neither any means of altering this, nor any right to neglect this limitation. All reasons of this type would already be sufficient, to be sure, but there are more radical reasons. What we have tried to show by following the guiding line of the "dangerous supplement," is that in what one calls the real life of these existences "of flesh and bone," beyond and behind what one believes can be circumscribed as Rousseau's text, there has never been anything but writing; there have never been anything but supplements, substitutive significations which could only come forth in a chain of differential references, the "real" supervening, and being added only while taking on meaning from a trace and from an invocation of the supplement, etc. And thus to infinity, for we have read, *in the text,* that the absolute present, Nature, that which words like "real mother" name, have always already escaped, have never existed; that what opens meaning and language is writing as the disappearance of natural presence.

Although it is not commentary, our reading must be intrinsic and remain within the text. That is why, in spite of certain appearances, the locating of the word *supplement* is here not at all psychoanalytical, if by that we understand an interpretation that takes us outside of the writing toward a psychobiographical signified, or even toward a general psychological structure that could rightly be separated from the signifier. This method has occasionally been opposed to the traditional doubling commentary; it could be shown that it actually comes to terms with it quite easily. *The security with which the commentary considers the self-identity of the text, the confidence with which it carves out its contour, goes hand in hand with the tranquil assurance that leaps over the text toward its presumed content, in the direction of the pure signified.* And in effect, in Rousseau's case, psychoanalytical studies like those of Dr. Laforgue transgress the text only after having read it according to the most current methods. The reading of the literary "symptom" is most banal, most academic, most naive. And once one has thus blinded oneself to the very tissue of the "symptom," to its proper texture, one cheerfully exceeds it toward a psychobiographical signified whose link with the literary signifier then becomes perfectly extrinsic and contingent. One recognizes the other aspect of the same gesture when, in general works on Rousseau, in a package of classical shape that gives itself out to be a synthesis that faithfully restores, through commentary and compilation of themes, the totality of the work and the thought, one encounters a chapter of biographical and psychoanalytical cast on the "problem of sexuality in Rousseau," with a reference in an Appendix to the author's medical case-history.

If it seems to us in principle impossible to separate, through interpretation or commentary, the signified from the signifier, and thus to destroy writing by the writing that is yet reading, we nevertheless believe that this impossibility is historically articulated. It does not limit attempts at deciphering in the same way, to the same degree, and according to the same rules. Here we must take into account the history of the text in general. When we speak of the writer and of the encompassing power of the language to which he is subject, we are not only thinking of the writer in literature. The philosopher, the chronicler, the theoretician in general, and at the limit everyone writing, is thus taken by surprise. But, in each case, the person writing is inscribed in a determined textual system. Even if there is never a pure signified, there are different relationships as to that which, from the signifier, *is presented* as the irreducible stratum of the signified. For example, the philosophical text, although it is in fact always written, includes, precisely as its philosophical specificity, the project of effacing itself in the face of the signified content which it transports and in general teaches. Reading should be aware of this project, even if, in the last analysis, it intends to expose the project's failure. The entire history of texts, and within it the history of literary forms in the West, should be studied from this point of view. With the exception of a thrust or a point of resistance which has only been very lately recognized as such, literary writing has, almost always and almost everywhere, according to some fashions and across very diverse ages, lent itself to this *transcendent* reading, in that search for the signified which we here put in question, not to annul it but to understand it within a system to which such a reading is blind. Philosophical literature is only one example within this history but it is among the most significant. And it interests us particularly in Rousseau's case. Who at the same time and for profound reasons produced a philosophical literature to which belong *The Social Contract* and *La nouvelle Héloise,* and chose to live by literary writing; by a writing which would not be exhausted by the message—philosophical or otherwise—which it could, so to speak, deliver. And what Rousseau has said, as philosopher or as psychologist, of writing in general, cannot be separated from the system of his own writing. We should be aware of this.

14

How to Speak and Write Postmodern

STEPHEN KATZ

The postmodern era has given the world some really good ideas and some really bad writing. From Derrida on down to humble troopers in the trenches of academia, a style that has come to prevail among postmodernists is one of endless complexification and obscurity. The general idea seems to be that the surest way to establish yourself as a profound thinker is to make it very difficult for anybody to under-stand what you are saying. This has the virtue, also, of protecting you against the possible discovery that you have nothing to say whatever. Here Stephen Katz offers instruction on how to play that language game.

Postmodernism has been the buzzword in academia for the last decade. Books, journal articles, conference themes and university courses have re-sounded to the debates about postmodernism that focus on the uniqueness of our times, where computerization, the global economy and the media have irrevocably transformed all forms of social engagement. As a professor of sociology who teaches about culture, I include myself in this environment. Indeed, I have a great interest in postmodernism both as an intellectual movement and as a practical problem. In my experience there seems to be a gulf between those who see the postmodern turn as a neo-conservative reupholstering of the same old corporate trappings, and those who see it as a long overdue break with modernist doctrines in education, aesthetics and politics. Of course there are all kinds of positions in between, depending upon how one sorts out the optimum route into the next millennium.

However, I think the real gulf is not so much positional as linguistic. Posture can be as important as politics when it comes to the intelligentsia. In other words, it may be less important whether or not you like postmodernism than whether or not you can speak and write postmodernism. Perhaps you would like to join in conversation with your local mandarins of cultural theory and all-purpose deep thinking, but you don't know what to say. Or, when you do contribute something you consider relevant, even insightful, you get ignored or looked at with pity. Here is a quick guide, then, to speaking and writing postmodern.

First, you need to remember that plainly expressed language is out of the question. It is too realist, modernist and obvious. Postmodern language requires that one uses play, parody and indeterminacy as critical techniques to point this out. Often this is quite a difficult requirement, so obscurity is a well-acknowledged substitute. For example, let's imagine you want to say something like, "We should listen to the views of people outside of Western society in order to learn about the cultural biases that affect us." This is honest but dull. Take the word "views." Postmodernspeak would change that to "voices," or better, "vocalities," or even better, "multivocalities." Add an adjective like "intertextual," and you're covered. "People outside" is also too plain. How about "postcolonial others"? To speak postmodern properly one must master a bevy of biases besides the familiar racism, sexism, ageism, etc. For example, phallogocentricism (male-centredness combined with rationalistic forms of binary logic).

Finally "affect us" sounds like plaid pajamas. Use more obscure verbs and phrases, like "mediate our identities." So, the final statement should say, "We should listen to the intertextual multivocalities of postcolonial others outside of Western culture in order to learn about the phallogocentric biases that mediate our identities." Now you're talking postmodern!

Sometimes you might be in a hurry and won't have the time to muster even the minimum number of postmodern synonyms and neologisms needed to avoid public disgrace. Remember, saying the wrong thing is acceptable if you say it the right way. This brings me to a second important strategy in speaking postmodern, which is to use as many suffixes, prefixes, hyphens, slashes, underlinings and anything else your computer (an absolute must to write postmodern) can dish out. You can make a quick reference chart to avoid time delays. Make three columns. In column A put your prefixes; post-, hyper-, pre-, de-, dis-, re-, ex-, and counter-. In column B go your suffixes and related endings; -ism, -itis, -iality, -ation, -itivity, and -tricity. In column C add a series of well-respected names that make for impressive adjectives or schools of thought, for example, Barthes (Barthesian), Foucault (Foucauldian, Foucauldianism), Derrida (Derridean, Derrideanism).

Now for the test. You want to say or write something like, "Contemporary buildings are alienating." This is a good thought, but, of course, a nonstarter. You wouldn't even get offered a second round of crackers and cheese at a conference reception with such a line. In fact, after saying this, you might get asked to stay and clean up the crackers and cheese after the reception. Go to your three columns. First, the prefix. Pre- is useful, as is post-, or several prefixes at once is terrific. Rather than "contemporary buildings," be creative. "The Pre/post/spacialities of counter-architectural hyper-contemporaneity" is promising. You would have to drop the weak and dated term "alienating" with some well-suffixed words from column B. How about "antisociality," or be more postmodern and introduce ambiguity with the linked phrase, "antisociality/seductivity."

Now, go to column C and grab a few names whose work everyone will agree is important and hardly anyone has had the time or the inclination to read. Continental European theorists are best when in doubt. I recommend the sociologist Jean Baudrillard since he has written a great deal of difficult material about postmodern space. Don't forget to make some mention of gender. Finally, add a few smoothing-out words to tie the whole garbled mess together and don't forget to pack in the hyphens, slashes and parentheses. What do you get? "Pre/post/spacialities of counter-architectural hyper-contemporaneity (re)commits us to an ambivalent recurrentiality of antisociality/seductivity, one enunciated in a de/gendered-Baudrillardian discourse of granulated subjectivity." You should be able to hear a postindustrial pin drop on the retrocultural floor.

At some point someone may actually ask you what you're talking about. This risk faces all those who would speak postmodern and must be carefully avoided. You must always give the questioner the impression that they have missed the point, and so send another verbose salvo of post-modernspeak in their direction as a "simplification" or "clarification" of your original statement. If that doesn't work, you might be left with the terribly modernist thought, "I don't know." Don't worry. Just say, "The instability of your question leaves me with several contradictorily layered responses whose interconnectivity cannot express the logocentric coherency you seek. I can only say that reality is more uneven and its (mis)representations more untrustworthy than we have time here to explore."

Any more questions? No? Then pass the cheese and crackers.

15

The Orthodox and the Progressive

JAMES DAVISON HUNTER

*There is nothing new about conflict over beliefs, but today we are
seeing new players and new ways of drawing the line between Us and
Them. In the area where I live, there used to be an ecumenical
council that brought together representatives of various religions.
Now there are two ecumenical councils—one leaning right, one
leaning left. Conservative Catholics have decided they can get along
better with conservative Jews, Protestants and Muslims than they can
with the revisionist members of their own faith. Likewise liberal
Catholics, Jews, Protestants and Muslims. This is the new and
typically postmodern kind of conflict—within beliefs, concerning
styles of belief—that James Davison Hunter calls culture war. It has
become a world-wide phenomenon, and I suspect it will be around
for some time to come.*

The cleavages at the heart of the contemporary culture war are created by
what I would like to call *the impulse toward orthodoxy* and *the impulse toward
progressivism.* The terms are imperfect, but each aspires to describe in short-
hand a particular locus and source of moral truth, the fundamental (though

perhaps subconscious) moral allegiances of the actors involved in the culture war as well as their cultural and political dispositions. Though the terms "orthodox" and "progressive" may be familiar to many, they have a particular meaning here that requires some elaboration.

Let me acknowledge, first off, that the words, orthodox and progressive, can describe specific doctrinal creeds or particular religious practices. Take orthodoxy. Within Judaism, orthodoxy is defined mainly by commitment to Torah and the community that upholds it; within Catholicism, orthodoxy is defined largely by loyalty to church teaching—the Roman Magisterium; and within Protestantism, orthodoxy principally means devotion to the complete and final authority of Scripture. Substantively, then, these labels can mean vastly different things within different religious traditions.

But I prefer to use the terms orthodox and progressive as *formal properties* of a belief system or world view. What is common to all three approaches to *orthodoxy,* for example (and what makes orthodoxy more of a formal property), *is the commitment on the part of adherents to an external, definable, and transcendent authority.* Such objective and transcendent authority defines, at least in the abstract, a consistent, unchangeable measure of value, purpose, goodness, and identity, both personal and collective. It tells us what is good, what is true, how we should live, and who we are. It is an authority that is sufficient for all time.

Within cultural progressivism, by contrast, moral authority tends to be defined by the spirit of the modern age, a spirit of rationalism and subjectivism. Progressivist moral ideals tend, that is, to derive from and embody (though rarely exhaust) that spirit. From this standpoint, truth tends to be viewed as a process, as a reality that is ever unfolding. There are many distinctions that need to be made here. For example, what about those progressivists who still identify with a particular religious heritage? For them, one may note a strong tendency to translate the moral ideals of a religious tradition so that they conform to and legitimate the contemporary *zeitgeist.* In other words, what all *progressivist* world views share in common *is the tendency to resymbolize historic faiths according to the prevailing assumptions of contemporary life.*

I have been talking about the contemporary cultural divide in the context of religious communities in order to highlight the historical novelty of the contemporary situation. But what about the growing number of "secularists"? These people range from the vaguely religious to the openly agnostic or atheistic. While they would probably claim no affiliation with a church or religious denomination, they nevertheless hold deep humanistic concerns about the welfare of community and nation.

Like the representatives of religious communities, they too are divided. Yet public opinion surveys show that a decided majority of secularists are drawn toward the progressivist impulse in American culture. For these people religious tradition has no binding address, no opinion-shaping influence. Some secularists, however (particularly many secular conservative and neo-conservative intellectuals), are drawn toward the orthodox impulse. For them, a commitment to natural law or to a high view of nature serves as the functional equivalent of the external and transcendent moral authority revered by their religiously orthodox counterparts.

In sum, the contemporary cultural conflict turns upside down (or perhaps inside out) the way cultural conflict has long been waged. Thus, we see those with apparently similar religious or cultural affiliations battling with one another. The culture war encompasses all Americans, religious and "non-religious," in very novel ways.

It nearly goes without saying that those who embrace the orthodox impulse are almost always cultural conservatives, while those who embrace progressivist moral assumptions tend toward a liberal or libertarian social agenda. Certainly, the associations between foundational moral commitments and social and political agendas is far from absolute; some people and organizations will cross over the lines, taking conservative positions on some issues and liberal views on others. Yet the relationship between foundational moral commitments and social and political agendas is too strong and consistent to be viewed as coincidental. This is true for most Americans (as seen in public opinion surveys), but it is especially true for the organizations engaged in the range of contemporary disputes. For the practical purposes of naming the antagonists in the culture war, then, we can label those on one side cultural conservatives or moral traditionalists, and those on the other side liberals or cultural progressives. These are, after all, the terms that the actors in the culture war use to describe themselves. The danger of using these "political" labels, however, is that one can easily forget that they trace back to prior moral commitments and more basic moral visions. We subtly slip into thinking of the controversies debated as political rather than cultural in nature. On political matters one can compromise; on matters of ultimate moral truth, one cannot. This is why the full range of issues today seems interminable.

The real novelty of the contemporary situation emerges out of the fact that the orthodox and progressivist communities are not fighting isolated battles. Evangelical Protestants, for example, are not locked in an isolated conflict with liberal Protestants. Nor are theologically progressive Catholics struggling in isolation with their theologically conservative counterparts in the Roman hierarchy. The contemporary culture war is much larger and more complicated. *At the heart of the new cultural realignment are the pragmatic alliances being formed across faith traditions.* Because of common points of vision and concern, the orthodox wings of Protestantism, Catholicism, and Judaism are forming associations with each other, as are the progressive wings of each faith community—and each set of alliances takes form in opposition to the influence the other seeks to exert in public culture.

These institutional alliances, it should be noted, are not always influential in terms of the joint power they hold. Some of the groups, after all, are quite small and have few resources. But these institutional alliances are *culturally* significant, for the simple reason that ideological and organizational associations are being generated among groups that have historically been antagonistic toward one another. Had the disagreements in each religious tradition remained simply theological or ecclesiastical in nature, these alliances would have probably never developed. But since the divisions have extended into the broader realm of public morality, the alliances have become the expedient outcome of common concerns. In other words, though these alliances are historically "unnatural," they have become pragmatically necessary. Traditional religio-cultural divisions are superseded—replaced by the overriding differences taking form out of orthodox and progressive moral commitments.

These unlikely alliances are at the center of a fundamental realignment in American culture and, in turn, identify the key actors in an emerging cultural conflict.

16

Ironists and Metaphysicians

RICHARD RORTY

America's most eminent philosopher describes a difference in the ways contemporary people think and talk. His description deepens Hunter's progressive-orthodox classification and makes it clear what is meant by postmodern irony.

All human beings carry about a set of words which they employ to justify their actions, their beliefs, and their lives. These are the words in which we formulate praise of our friends and contempt for our enemies, our long-term projects, our deepest self-doubts and our highest hopes. They are the words in which we tell, sometimes prospectively and sometimes retrospectively, the story of our lives. I shall call these words a person's "final vocabulary."

It is "final" in the sense that if doubt is cast on the worth of these words, their user has no noncircular argumentative recourse. Those words are as far as he can go with language; beyond them there is only helpless passivity or a resort to force. A small part of a final vocabulary is made up of thin, flexible, and ubiquitous terms such as "true," "good," "right," and "beautiful." The larger part contains thicker, more rigid, and more parochial terms, for example, "Christ," "England," "professional standards," "decency," "kindness," "the Revolution," "the Church," "progressive," "rigorous," "creative." The more parochial terms do most of the work.

I shall define an "ironist" as someone who fulfills three conditions: (1) She has radical and continuing doubts about the final vocabulary she currently uses, because she has been impressed by other vocabularies, vocabularies taken as final by people or books she has encountered; (2) she realizes that argument phrased in her present vocabulary can neither underwrite nor dissolve these doubts; (3) insofar as she philosophizes about her situation, she does not think that her vocabulary is closer to reality than others, that it is in touch with a power not herself. Ironists who are inclined to philosophize see the choice between vocabularies as made neither within a neutral and universal metavocabulary nor by an attempt to fight one's way past appearances to the real, but simply by playing the new off against the old.

I call people of this sort "ironists" because their realization that anything can be made to look good or bad by being redescribed, and their renunciation of the attempt to formulate criteria of choice between final vocabularies, puts them in the position which Sartre called "meta-stable": never quite able to take themselves seriously because always aware that the terms in which they describe themselves are subject to change, always aware of the contingency and fragility of their final vocabularies, and thus of their selves.

The opposite of irony is common sense. For that is the watchword of those who unselfconsciously describe everything important in terms of the final vocabulary to which they and those around them are habituated. To be commonsensical is to take for granted that statements formulated in that final vocabulary suffice to describe and judge the beliefs, actions and lives of those who employ alternative final vocabularies.

When common sense is challenged, its adherents respond at first by generalizing and making explicit the rules of the language game they are accustomed to play (as some of the Greek Sophists did, and as Aristotle did in his ethical writings). But if no platitude formulated in the old vocabulary suffices to meet an argumentative challenge, the need to reply produces a willingness to go beyond platitudes. At that point, conversation may go Socratic. The question "What is *x*?" is now asked in such a way that it cannot be answered simply by producing paradigm cases of *x*-hood. So one may demand a definition, an essence.

To make such Socratic demands is not yet, of course, to become an ironist in the sense in which I am using this term. It is only to become a "metaphysician," in a sense of that term which I am adapting from Heidegger. In this sense, the metaphysician is someone who takes the question "What is the intrinsic nature of (e.g., justice, science, knowledge, Being, faith, morality, philosophy)?" at face value. He assumes that the presence of a term in his own final vocabulary ensures that it refers to something which *has* a real essence. The metaphysician is still attached to common sense, in that he does not question the platitudes which encapsulate the use of a given final vocabulary, and in particular the platitude which says there is a single permanent reality to be found behind the many temporary appearances. He does not redescribe but, rather, analyzes old descriptions with the help of other old descriptions.

The ironist, by contrast, is a nominalist and a historicist. She thinks nothing has an intrinsic nature, a real essence. So she thinks that the occurrence of a term like "just" or "scientific" or "rational" in the final vocabulary of the day is no reason to think that Socratic inquiry into the essence of justice or science or rationality will take one much beyond the language games of one's time. The ironist spends her time worrying about the possibility that she has been initiated into the wrong tribe, taught to play the wrong language game. She worries that the process of socialization which turned her into a human being by giving her a language may have given her the wrong language, and so turned her into the wrong kind of human being. But she cannot give a criterion of wrongness. So, the more she is driven to articulate her situation in philosophical terms, the more she reminds herself of her rootlessness by constantly using terms like "Weltanschauung," "perspective," "dialectic," "conceptual framework," "historical epoch," "language game," "redescription," "vocabulary," and "irony."

The metaphysician responds to that sort of talk by calling it "relativistic" and insisting that what matters is not what language is being used but what is *true*. Metaphysicians think that human beings by nature desire to know. They think this because the vocabulary they have inherited, their common sense, provides them with a picture of knowledge as a relation between human beings and "reality," and the idea that we have a need and a duty to enter into this relation. It also tells us that "reality," if properly asked, will help us determine what our final vocabulary should be. So metaphysicians believe that there are, out there in the world, real essences which it is our duty to discover and which are disposed to assist in their own discovery. They do not believe that anything can be made to look good or bad by being redescribed—or, if they do, they deplore this fact and cling to the idea that reality will help us resist such seductions.

By contrast, ironists do not see the search for a final vocabulary as (even in part) a way of getting something distinct from this vocabulary right. They do not take the point of discursive thought to be *knowing*, in any sense that can be explicated by notions like "reality," "real essence," "objective point of view," and "the correspondence of language of reality." They do not think its point is to find a vocabulary which accurately represents something, a transparent medium. For the ironists, "final vocabulary" does not mean "the one which puts all doubts to rest" or "the one which satisfies our criteria of ultimacy, or adequacy, or optimality." They do not think of reflection as being governed by criteria. Criteria, on their view, are never more than the platitudes which contextually define the terms of a final vocabulary currently in use. Ironists agree with Davidson about our inability to step outside our language in order to compare it with something else, and with Heidegger about the contingency and historicity of that language.

This difference leads to a difference in their attitude toward books. Metaphysicians see libraries as divided according to disciplines, correspond-ing to different objects of knowledge. Ironists see them as divided according to traditions, each member of which partially adopts and partially modifies the vocabulary of the writers whom he has read. Ironists take the writings of all the people with poetic gifts, all the original minds who had a talent for redescription—Pythagoras, Plato, Milton, Newton, Goethe, Kant, Kierkegaard, Baudelaire, Darwin, Freud—as grist to be put through the same dialectical mill. The metaphysicians, by contrast, want to start by getting straight about which of these people were poets, which philosophers, and which scientists. They think it essential to get the genres right—to order texts by reference to a previously determined grid, a grid which, whatever else it does, will at least make a clear distinction between knowledge claims and other claims upon our attention. The ironist, by contrast, would like to avoid cooking the books she reads by using *any* such grid (although, with ironic resignation, she realizes that she can hardly help doing so).

For a metaphysician, "philosophy," as defined by reference to the canonical Plato-Kant sequence, is an attempt to know about certain things—quite general and important things. For the ironist, "philosophy," so defined, is the attempt to apply and develop a particular antecedently chosen final vocabulary—one which revolves around the appearance-reality distinction. The issue between them is, once again, about the contingency of our language—about whether what the common sense of our own culture shares with Plato and Kant is a tip-off to the way the world is, or whether it is just the characteristic mark of the discourse of people inhabiting a certain chunk of space-time. The metaphysician assumes that our tradition can raise no problems which it cannot solve—that the vocabulary which the ironist fears may be merely "Greek" or "Western" or "bourgeois" is an instrument which will enable us to get at something universal. The metaphysician agrees with the Platonic Theory of Recollection, in the form in which this theory was restated by Kierkegaard, namely, that we have the truth within us, that we have built-in criteria which enable us to recognize the right final vocabulary when we hear it. The cash value of this theory is that our contemporary final vocabularies are close enough to the right one to let us converge upon it—to formulate premises from which the right conclusions will be reached. The metaphysician thinks that although we may not have all the answers, we have already got criteria for the right answers. So he thinks "right" does not merely mean "suitable for those who speak as we do" but has a stronger sense—the sense of "grasping real essence."

For the ironist, searches for a final vocabulary are not destined to converge. For her, sentences like "All men by nature desire to know" or "Truth is independent of the human mind" are simply platitudes used to inculcate the local final vocabulary, the common sense of the West. She is an ironist just insofar as her own final vocabulary does not contain such notions. Her description of what she is doing when she looks for a better final vocabulary than the one she is currently using is dominated by metaphors of making rather than finding, of diversification and novelty rather than convergence to the antecedently present. She thinks of final vocabularies as poetic achievements rather than as fruits of diligent inquiry according to antecedently formulated criteria.

Because metaphysicians believe that we already possess a lot of the "right" final vocabulary and merely need to think through its implications, they think of philosophical inquiry as a matter of spotting the relations between the various platitudes which provide contextual definitions of the terms of this vocabulary. So they think of refining or clarifying the use of terms as a matter of weaving these platitudes (or, as they would prefer to say, these intuitions) into a perspicuous system. This has two consequences. First, they tend to concentrate on the thinner, more flexible, more ubiquitous items in this vocabulary—words like "true," "good," "person," and "object." For the thinner the term, the more platitudes will employ it. Second, they take the paradigm of philosophical inquiry to be logical argument—that is spotting the inferential relationships between propositions rather than comparing and contrasting vocabularies.

The typical strategy of the metaphysician is to spot an apparent contradiction between two platitudes, two intuitively plausible propositions, and then propose a distinction which will resolve the contradiction. Metaphysicians then go on to embed this distinction within a network of associated distinctions—a philosophical theory—which will take some of the strain off the initial distinction. This sort of theory construction is the same method used by judges to decide hard cases, and by theologians to interpret hard texts. That activity is the metaphysician's paradigm of rationality. He sees philosophical theories as converging—a series of discoveries about the nature of such things as truth and personhood, which get closer and closer to the way they really are, and carry the culture as a whole closer to an accurate representation of reality.

The ironist, however, views the sequence of such theories—such interlocked patterns of novel distinctions—as gradual, tacit substitutions of a new vocabulary for an old one. She calls "platitudes" what the metaphysician calls "intuitions." She is inclined to say that when we surrender an old platitude (e.g., "The number of biological species is fixed" or "Human beings differ from animals because they have sparks of the divine with them" or "Blacks have no rights which whites are bound to respect"), we have made a change rather than discovered a fact. The ironist, observing the sequence of "great philosophers" and the interaction between their thought and its social setting, sees a series of changes in the linguistic and other practices of the Europeans. Whereas the metaphysician sees the modern Europeans as particularly good at discovering how things really are, the ironist sees them as particularly rapid in changing their self-image, in re-creating themselves.

The metaphysician thinks that there is an overriding intellectual duty to present arguments for one's controversial views—arguments which will start from relatively uncontroversial premises. The ironist thinks that such arguments—logical arguments—are all very well in their way, and useful as expository devices, but in the end not much more than ways of getting people to change their practices without admitting they have done so. The ironist's preferred form of argument is dialectical in the sense that she takes the unit of persuasion to be a vocabulary rather than a proposition. Her method is redescription rather than inference. Ironists specialize in redescribing ranges of objects or events in partially neologistic jargon, in the hope of inciting people to adopt and extend that jargon. An ironist hopes that by the time she has finished using old words in new senses, not to mention introducing brand-new words, people will no longer ask questions phrased in the old words. So the ironist thinks of logic as ancillary to dialectic, whereas the metaphysician thinks of dialectic as a species of rhetoric, which in turn is a shoddy substitute for logic.

17

Affirmatives and Skeptics

PAULINE MARIE ROSENAU

According to Professor Rosenau, postmodernists come in many varieties—despairing postmodernists, upbeat postmodernists, and postmodernists who don't like to be called postmodernists.

The cut-and-paste character of post-modernism, its absence of unity, is both a strength and a weakness. Everyone can find something about it with which to agree. But, because it is not an "invisible college",[1] an infinite combination of alternatives allow different and varying ways to put together the elements that constitute post-modernism. No wonder its harmony is disrupted by argument; no wonder it is characterized not by orthodoxy so much as by diversity, competing currents, and continual schism.[2] Whether one reads post-modernism as skeptical and cynical or as affirmative and optimistic, or as something else entirely, depends in part on which authors and traditions inspire one's understanding of it. Post-modernism is stimulating and fascinating; and at the same time it is always on the brink of collapsing into confusion.

The divergent, even contradictory expositions of post-modernism underline the need to distinguish among its various orientations if we are ever to be able to talk about it at all. There are probably as many forms of post-modernism as there are post-modernists.[3] If it were not so clumsy, we could speak of post-modernisms. But within this diversity of post-modern pronouncements, as far as the social sciences are concerned, two broad, general orientations, the *skeptical* post-modernists and the *affirmative* post-modernists, can be delineated.

The skeptical post-modernism (or merely skeptics), offering a pessimistic, negative, gloomy assessment, argue that the post-modern age is one of fragmentation, disintegration, malaise, meaninglessness, a vagueness or even absence of moral parameters and societal chaos.[4] Inspired by Continental European philosophies, especially Heidegger and Nietzsche, this is the dark side of post-modernism, the post-modernism of despair, the post-modernism that speaks of the immediacy of death, the demise of the subject, the end of the author, the impossibility of truth, and the abrogation of the Order of Representation. Post-modernists of this orientation adopt a blasé attitude, as if "they have seen it all" and concluded that nothing really new is possible.[5] They argue that the destructive character of modernity makes the post-modern age one of "radical, unsurpassable uncertainty,"[6] characterized by all that is grim, cruel, alienating, hopeless, tired, and ambiguous. In this period no social or political "project" is worthy of commitment. Ahead lies overpopulation, genocide, atomic destruction, the apocalypse, environmental devastation, the explosion of the sun and the end of the solar system in 4.5 billion years, the death of the universe through entropy. Even where there is room for happiness, farce, parody, pleasure, "joyous affirmation,"[7] these are only temporary, empty meaningless forms of gaiety that merely mark a period of waiting for catastrophe.[8] If, as the skeptics claim, there is no truth, then all that is left is play, the play of words and meaning.

Although the affirmative post-modernists, also referred to as simply the affirmatives, agree with the skeptical post-modernists' critique of modernity, they have a more hopeful, optimistic view of the post-modern age. More indigenous to Anglo-North American culture than to the Continent, the generally optimistic affirmatives are oriented toward process. They are either open to positive political action (struggle and resistance) or content with the recognition of visionary, celebratory personal nondogmatic projects that range from New Age religion to New Wave life-styles and include a whole spectrum of post-modern social movements. Most affirmatives seek a philosophical and ontological intellectual practice that is nondogmatic, tentative, and nonideological. These post-modernists do not, however, shy away from affirming an ethic, making normative choices, and striving to build issue-specific political coalitions. Many affirmatives argue that certain value choices are superior to others, a line of reasoning that would incur the disapproval of the skeptical post-modernists.[9]

There is a range of extreme to moderate versions of both affirmative and skeptical post-modernism, and the two dimensions cross-cut one another. In the case of both the affirmatives and the skeptics, the extremists are distinguished from the moderates primarily by the intensity of their opinion and their willingness to carry their post-modern conviction to its most extravagant, excessive conclusion—no matter what the outcome or consequences. On balance our concern focuses on the skeptics and affirmatives with only an occasional reference to extreme and moderate post-modernism.

There are both advantages and disadvantages to the categories of skeptical post-modern and affirmative post-modern. They overlap at the edges and do not constitute the neat "mutually exclusive, jointly exhaustive" groupings so clearly desired by modern social science.

Because the very term post-modernism has come to represent controversy and criticism, many post-modernists avoid the label. Some argue that the word post-modern promotes a singular view of reality, encourages closure, and denies complexity. So they retreat from it to avoid its pejorative associations as something bizarre and frivolous. They refer to themselves in less contested terms, such as post-contemporary. Or they might suggest their work is merely "interpretative."

18

Four Different Ways to Be Absolutely Right

WALTER TRUETT ANDERSON

This is my own mapping of postmodern society, pointing out a kind of diversity that is often overlooked when people talk about pluralism.

In pluralistic societies such as ours there are lots of differences, and there are also different sorts of differences. You can begin to talk about diversity by making a list of the various races and religions, for example, but that doesn't give you the whole picture. You also have to take note of the differences between men and women, and between the young and the old. And then there are also different worldviews—fundamentally different ways of thinking and talking about truth—that cross-cut all those categories. The progressive-orothodox polarization described by James Davison Hunter is one useful way of getting at this, but a slightly more complex view is called for.

Contemporary Western societies have at least four distinguishable worldviews. People who share one of these communicate fairly well with one another, not so well with people of a different worldview. Each worldview forms a somewhat distinct culture within society—each with its own language of public discourse, its own epistemology.

These four worldviews are (a) the postmodern-ironist, which sees truth as socially constructed; (b) the scientific-rational, in which truth is "found" through methodical, disciplined inquiry; (c) the social-traditional in which truth is found in the heritage of American and Western Civilization; and (d) the neo-romantic in which truth is found either through attaining harmony with nature and/or spiritual exploration of the inner self. Each of these has its own set of truths, and its own ideas about what truth *is*—where and how you look for it, how you test or prove it.

We can picture this multireality society—and get a better idea of what is going on in today's world—with the help of the following diagram. Here the arrows indicate a general line of cultural evolution, from premodernity through modernity to postmodernity:

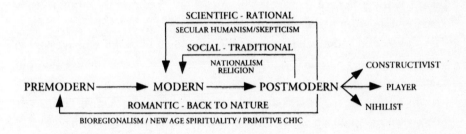

The postmodern-ironist worldview is shown (in three variations) along the leading edge.

The scientific-rational and social-traditional worldviews are conservative attempts to pull back from postmodernity. They seek to hold onto the values of a modern civilization that is now beginning to look kind of shaky.

Neo-romanticism—expressed in many forms of New Age spirituality and radical environmentalism—is even more strongly oriented toward the past: Neo-romantics reject both the postmodern and the modern, and long for a fantasized golden era before the Industrial Revolution and the Enlightenment.

Because life on the front lines of postmodernity is still so varied and so much in flux, postmodernists are not easy to identify as a single group. The diagram shows three subgroups—distinct ways that people are plunging into a world in which truth is not found, but made: These three types of postmodern explorers don't much resemble one another outwardly, but they share a readiness to see reality as social construction.

The first group is composed of people who are actively engaged in thinking through and living a constructivist worldview: Among its leaders are philosophers such as Richard Rorty and Thomas Kuhn; sociologists of knowledge; symbolic anthropologists; constructivist cognitive scientists, psychologists and psychotherapists; constructivist women and feminist scholars; and liberal theologians. You are not likely to recognize any of these people on the street, or to notice anything outrageously postmod about the way they dress or act. In this regard they're like Abraham Maslow's "self-actualizing" subjects, who tended to be outwardly conventional. "The expressed inner attitude," Maslow wrote, "is usually that it is ordinarily of no great consequence which folkways are used, that one set of traffic rules is as good as any other set, that while they make life smoother they do not really matter enough to make a fuss about."[1]

A second and much larger group is composed of people who manage to surf along fairly satisfactorily on the currents of cultural change without taking much interest in abstract ideas or any self-conscious "postmodernism." These are the postmodern players, and their irony is more an attitude or sensibility than an intellectual position. They browse among cultural forms, play mix-and-match with all the pieces of our various heritage. They invent new religious rituals, combine folk music with hard rock, dabble in nostalgia for the 1950s or 1960s. They explore virtual reality, regard clothing as costume, and feel right at home in theme parks.

The third group is made up of the nihilists of the postmodern era, the people who see that there are many conflicting beliefs in the world, and conclude that, since these can't possibly *all* be true, they must all be phoney. A fairly logical position, when you think about it. This new nihilism is most evident in the punk rock subcultures, where the irony is dark and heavy. You can hear it in songs that shout defiance at the conventional pieties and embrace the pleasures or pains of the moment—which are, in their way, at least trustworthy. The nihilists offer a vivid example of what it is that conservatives fear about postmodernity, and predict that it must inevitably lead to: alienation, hedonism, ridicule and contempt for mainstream society.

Scientific-rationalist culture is most strongly entrenched in academia and the sciences, but its representatives are everywhere. You can find its ideas expressed in magazines such as the *Skeptical Enquirer* and *The Humanist*—vigilantly on guard against flaky irrationality in all its forms; anxious to expose the frauds and hucksters among the fundamentalists, the astrologers, the mind readers and the faith healers. For a good scientific rationalist, the main sources of evil in the world are sloppy thinking and lack of respect for hard facts. If you want to see the scientific-rationalist culture in action, drop in sometime at the annual convention of CSICOP, the Committee for Scientific Investigation of Claims of the Para-normal.

If you want to get an eloquent statement of the social-traditional point of view, hunt up Allan Bloom's successful book of a few years back, *The Closing of the American Mind*. Bloom's book is a diatribe against the relativism that, he believes, has taken over the minds of youth and the mainstream of academia. He pleads for a rediscovery of the classic truths to be found in the great literary and philosophical traditions, and, looking back, sees the fifties as an intellectual golden age that was destroyed by the intellectual flakiness of the sixties.[2] Bloom's idea of what we need, however, is not more dry scientific rationalism, but more study of the treasures of Western civilization: the Founding Fathers, the philosophers, Shakespeare, Michelangelo, and—most of all—the wise men of ancient Athens.

The scientific-rational and the social-traditional cultures cling together, in an occasionally quarrelsome coexistence, as the power structure. The official mainstream realities of our time are to be found there. The alliance is weakened by such controversies as the debate between evolution (a keystone of the scientific worldview) and creationism (a stubborn remnant of what was once the central belief of Western civilization)—but, on the whole, scientific rationalism and social traditions support one another. Their alliance formed the twin pillars of modern civilization, and their basic position is that the center can—and damned well better—hold.

So, if you aspire to become President of the United States, you would do well to demonstrate that you are firmly rooted in traditional American culture. Act like a white, middle-class family man and show up in church once in a while. You don't want to be seen as too postmodern or too neo-romantic: Do not say in public that you think truth is socially constructed. If you meditate, keep it a secret. If you want to win an argument, let people know that your side is supported by scientific findings. Numbers are especially good. Even religious fundamentalists use science, whenever possible, to "prove" the truth of their beliefs; it is the *lingua franca* of public discourse, spoken (although in different accents) by all groups.

But although scientific rationalism and social tradition carry a lot of political and social clout, they don't show much vitality or creativity. Modernism, as Jurgen Habermas observed, is dominant but dead. If you want to look for signs of life, you are likely to find it somewhere out on the fringes of postmodernity, or among the neo-romantics.

The growth of the neo-romantic culture in recent years has been nothing short of spectacular. It obviously expresses not only a deep disaffection for modern civilization but also a reluctance to take on the uncertainties of postmodernism. It has most of the features of earlier romanticism—the reverence for nature, the personal-development preoccupation bordering on narcissism, the mystique of the noble savage—but these appear in much-updated forms: environmentalism, spirituality, movies such as *Dances With Wolves*.

The differences among these various cultures become clearer as you examine their ways of thinking about specific issues. Consider, for example, the matter of the self. How do you find your true self? Is there such a thing? For the neo-romantic, there definitely is—and there is no question but that this is an *inner* true self, something that you may be able to discover through meditation or introspection. For a scientific-rationalist, the instructions are exactly the opposite: Look outside yourself to get the truth—the objective facts—about what kind of a person you are; go to an expert, take a bunch of tests, and get the real You—your personality, your intelligence, your aptitudes—on a computer printout.

For a social-traditionalist, the true self is to be found in society, specifically in social roles: You "become somebody" by peforming adequately in the roles that your culture has institutionalized, that great people in the past have modeled for you, and that other people respect and understand: doctor, lawyer, statesman, entrepreneur, husband, wife.

For the postmodernist there is no true self. Whatever you might call by that name is merely the momentary reflection of bodily states, the environment, all the inputs of culture, ideas about what a self might or should be—and the language you are using. The self makes no sense apart from its context. Kenneth Gergen writes: "As the self as a serious reality is laid to rest and the self is constructed and reconstructed in multiple contexts, one enters finally the stage of the *relational self.* One's sense of individual autonomy gives way to a reality of immersed interdependence, in which it is relationship that constructs the self."[3] Constructivists are not terribly interested in conversations about individualism vs. community, because they don't think there is any such thing as an individual, and if you push them far enough you find they're not all that sure there is really any such thing as a community either—if by community you mean a single social context that completely overrides all the other social contexts through which we pass in the course of a day or a lifetime.

Constructivists think roles are good, useful tools for making a society work and giving people a sense of identity, but are likely to remind you that all roles are reified social behaviors. People created them, and sometimes other people need to re-create or even discard them.

Postmodern players base their self-concepts on lifestyle more than social role, and this accounts for some of their changeability. Roles may exist for decades, even centuries, without altering much; but lifestyles come in and out of fashion, and rarely outlive the people who adopt them. Most 1960s hippies, for example, are still around; they just aren't hippies anymore. Meanwhile the punk subculture appears to be growing a bumper crop of new lifestyles, with distinctions and nuances that outsiders do not comprehend and can't even keep track of.

This four-way mapping grew out of numerous workshops I have done with different groups of people, and in the process we have traced many sets of issues—international politics, ideas about nature, ideas about ethics and morality—as they appear to people of different worldviews. We have noted that the culture wars are not a simple polarization between two groups. The skirmish lines cut in different directions on different issues.

The map is a useful construct, but a few reminders are in order: One is that it *is* a construct, a way of looking at the world. The map is not the territory. Another is that the territory—Western civilization in the closing years of the twentieth century—is not standing still. The ground isn't solid under anybody's feet.

By positioning the postmoderns out on the leading edge I indicate that they are the wave of the future, the people you want to study to see where the world is going. This is precisely what I believe and want to communicate, but I don't think this means casually dismissing the values of the other worldviews. In a way we are all postmoderns—all moving into a new and quite different world. And I am coming to believe that the key to survival and success in this world will not merely lie in becoming a good constructivist: It will have to do with an ability to be multilingual. The functioning person in the postmodern world needs to be able to think rationally and understand science, able to appreciate and draw on a social heritage, and able as well to drink from the well of ecological and spiritual feeling that is being tapped by neo-romanticism.

Once, when we were having a discussion about this, somebody said: "What we're looking at here isn't just a map of the culture—it's a map of the mind."

Which, of course, it is. Culture and consciousness always reflect one another, and the mind of every person living in a contemporary society must have some access to each of the four worldviews. The difference is in which one predominates, and how comfortably you can move from one to another. Some people seem to be completely organized around one way of understanding truth, are deeply threatened by the others, and repress their own tendencies to wander into the forbidden worlds of postmodernism or neo-romanticism. Others of us appear to be much more multilingual.

What is happening now, I believe, is not simply that some trendy postmodernism is taking over the world and obliterating the cultures of rationalism, tradition and romanticism. Rather, the inner voice of the postmodern ironist is becoming a part of everybody's psychological makeup. As that happens, people, often without quite noticing it, go about their business in subtly different fashions. If we learn to hear that voice in a constructive (and constructivist) way, it becomes a guide to living in today's multi-worldview world.

19

Postmodern Blackness

BELL HOOKS

The argument against "essentialism" often strikes newcomers to post-modern thought as the driest and most abstract headtrip imaginable. But it takes on a powerful urgency for minorities who must continually struggle to be seen as concrete, particular living beings rather than as handy specimens of some great essential quality—such as blackness.

Here bell hooks offers a well-deserved critique of most post-modern theory—that it is primarily by, for and about comfortable white intellectuals—and suggests an alternative: a passionate engagement with new ideas in popular culture, with black people becoming not only the objects of other people's pronouncements about "blackness," but also major players in the creation of a postmodern society.

Postmodernist discourses are often exclusionary even as they call attention to, appropriate even, the experience of "difference" and "Otherness" to provide oppositional political meaning, legitimacy, and immediacy when they are accused of lacking concrete relevance. Very few African-American intellectuals have talked or written about postmodernism. At a dinner party I talked about trying to grapple with the significance of postmodernism for contemporary black experience. It was one of those social gatherings where only one other black person was present. The setting quickly became a field of contestation. I was told by the other black person that I was wasting my time, that "this stuff does not relate in any way to what's happening with black people." Speaking in the presence of a group of white onlookers, staring at us as though this encounter were staged for their benefit, we engaged in a passionate discussion about black experience. Apparently, no one sympathized with my insistence that racism is perpetuated when blackness is associated solely with concrete gut level experience conceived as either opposing or having no connection to abstract thinking and the production of critical theory. The idea that there is no meaningful connection between black experience and critical thinking about aesthetics or culture must be continually interrogated.

My defense of postmodernism and its relevance to black folks sounded good, but I worried that I lacked conviction, largely because I approach the subject cautiously and with suspicion.

Disturbed not so much by the "sense" of postmodernism but by the conventional language used when it is written or talked about and by those who speak it, I find myself on the outside of the discourse looking in. As a discursive practice it is dominated primarily by the voices of white male intellectuals and/or academic elites who speak to and about one another with coded familiarity. Reading and studying their writing to understand postmodernism in its multiple manifestations, I appreciate it but feel little inclination to ally myself with the academic hierarchy and exclusivity pervasive in the movement today.

Critical of most writing on postmodernism, I perhaps am more conscious of the way in which the focus on "Otherness and difference" that is often alluded to in these works seems to have little concrete impact as an analysis or standpoint that might change the nature and direction of postmodernist theory. Since much of this theory has been constructed in reaction to and against high modernism, there is seldom any mention of black experience or writings by black people in this work, specifically black women (though in more recent work one may see a reference to Cornel West, the black male scholar who has most engaged postmodernist discourse). Even if an aspect of black culture is the subject of postmodern critical writing, the works cited will usually be those of black men.

The failure to recognize a critical black presence in the culture and in most scholarship and writing on postmodernism compels a black reader, particularly a black female reader, to interrogate her interest in a subject where those who discuss and write about it seem not to know black women exist or even to consider the possibility that we might be somewhere writing or saying something that should be listened to, or producing art that should be seen, heard, approached with intellectual seriousness. This is especially the case with works that go on and on about the way in which postmodernist discourse has opened up a theoretical terrain where "difference and Otherness" can be considered legitimate issues in the academy. Confronting both the absence of recognition of black female presence that much postmodernist theory rein- scribes and the resistance on the part of most black folks to hearing about real connection between postmodernism and black experience, I enter a dis- course, a practice, where there may be no ready audience for my words, no clear listener, uncertain then, that my voice can or will be heard.

During the sixties, the black power movement was influenced by per- spectives that could easily be labeled modernist. Certainly many of the ways black folks addressed issues of identity conformed to a modernist universaliz- ing agenda. There was little critique of patriarchy as a master narrative among black militants. Despite the fact that black power ideology reflected a mod- ernist sensibility, these elements were soon rendered irrelevant as militant protest was stifled by a powerful, repressive postmodern state. The period directly after the black power movement was a time when major news magazines carried articles with cocky headlines like "Whatever Happened to Black America?" This response was an ironic reply to the aggressive, unmet demand by decentered, marginalized black subjects who had at least momen- tarily successfully demanded a hearing, who had made it possible for black liberation to be on the national political agenda. In the wake of the black power movement, after so many rebels were slaughtered and lost, many of these voices were silenced by a repressive state; others became inarticulate. It has become necessary to find new avenues to transmit the messages of black liberation struggle, new ways to talk about racism and other politics of domination. Radical postmodernist practice, most powerfully concep- tualized as a "politics of difference," should incorporate the voices of dis- placed, marginalized, exploited, and oppressed black people. It is sadly ironic that the contemporary discourse which talks the most about heterogeneity, the decentered subject, declaring breakthroughs that allow recognition of Otherness, still directs its critical voice primarily to a specialized audience that shares a common language rooted in the very master narratives it claims to challenge. If radical postmodernist thinking is to have a transformative impact, then a critical break with the notion of "authority" as "mastery over" must not simply be a rhetorical device. It must be reflected in habits of being, including styles of writing as well as chosen subject matter. Third world nationals, elites, and white critics who passively absorb white supremacist thinking, and therefore never notice or look at black people on the streets or at their jobs, who render us invisible with their gaze in all areas of daily life, are not likely to produce liberatory theory that will challenge racist domination, or promote a breakdown in traditional ways of seeing and thinking about reality, ways of constructing aesthetic theory and practice.

Without adequate concrete knowledge of and contact with the nonwhite "Other," white theorists may move in discursive theoretical directions that are threatening and potentially disruptive of that critical practice which would support radical liberation struggle.

The postmodern critique of "identity," though relevant for renewed black liberation struggle, is often posed in ways that are problematic. Given a pervasive politic of white supremacy which seeks to prevent the formation of radical black subjectivity, we cannot cavalierly dismiss a concern with identity politics. Any critic exploring the radical potential of postmodernism as it relates to racial difference and racial domination would need to consider the implications of a critique of identity for oppressed groups. Many of us are struggling to find new strategies of resistance. We must engage decolonization as a critical practice if we are to have meaningful chances of survival even as we must simultaneously cope with the loss of political grounding which made radical activism more possible. I am thinking here about the postmodernist critique of essentialism as it pertains to the construction of "identity" as one example.

Postmodern theory that is not seeking to simply appropriate the experience of "Otherness" to enhance the discourse or to be radically chic should not separate the "politics of difference" from the politics of racism. To take racism seriously one must consider the plight of underclass people of color, a vast majority of whom are black. For African-Americans our collective condition prior to the advent of postmodernism and perhaps more tragically expressed under current postmodern conditions has been and is characterized by continued displacement, profound alienation, and despair.

Yearning is the word that best describes a common psychological state shared by many of us, cutting across boundaries of race, class, gender, and sexual practice. Specifically, in relation to the postmodernist deconstruction of "master" narratives, the yearning that wells in the hearts and minds of those whom such narratives have silenced is the longing for critical voice. It is no accident that "rap" has usurped the primary position of rhythm and blues music among young black folks as the most desired sound or that it began as a form of "testimony" for the underclass. It has enabled underclass black youth to develop a critical voice, as a group of young black men told me, a "common literacy." Rap projects a critical voice, explaining, demanding, urging.

Considering that it is as subject one comes to voice, then the postmodernist focus on the critique of identity appears at first glance to threaten and close down the possibility that this discourse and practice will allow those who have suffered the crippling effects of colonization and domination to gain or regain a hearing. Even if this sense of threat and the fear it evokes are based on a misunderstanding of the postmodernist political project, they nevertheless shape responses. It never surprises me when black folks respond to the critique of essentialism, especially when it denies the validity of identity politics, by saying, "Yeah, it's easy to give up identity, when you got one." Should we not be suspicious of postmodern critiques of the "subject" when they surface at a historical moment when many subjugated people feel themselves coming to voice for the first time? Though an apt and oftentimes appropriate comeback, it does not really intervene in the discourse in a way that alters and transforms.

Criticisms of directions in postmodern thinking should not obscure insights it may offer that open up our understanding of African-American experience. The critique of essentialism encouraged by postmodernist thought is useful for African-Americans concerned with reformulating outmoded notions of identity. We have too long had imposed upon us from both the outside and the inside a narrow, constricting notion of blackness. Postmodern critiques of essentialism which challenge notions of universality and static overdetermined identity within mass culture and mass consciousness can open up new possibilities for the construction of self and the assertion of agency.

Employing a critique of essentialism allows African-Americans to acknowledge the way in which class mobility has altered collective black experience so that racism does not necessarily have the same impact on our lives. Such a critique allows us to affirm multiple black identities, varied black experience. It also challenges colonial imperialist paradigms of black identity which represent blackness one-dimensionally in ways that reinforce and sustain white supremacy. This discourse created the idea of the "primitive" and promoted the notion of an "authentic" experience, seeing as "natural" those expressions of black life which conformed to a pre-existing pattern or stereotype. Abandoning essentialist notions would be a serious challenge to racism. Contemporary African-American resistance struggle must be rooted in a process of decolonization that continually opposes reinscribing notions of "authentic" black identity. This critique should not be made synonymous with a dismissal of the struggle of oppressed and exploited peoples to make ourselves subjects. Nor should it deny that in certain circumstances this experience affords us a privileged critical location from which to speak. This is not a reinscription of modernist master narratives of authority which privilege some voices by denying voice to others. Part of our struggle for radical black subjectivity is the quest to find ways to construct self and identity that are oppositional and liberatory. The unwillingness to critique essentialism on the part of many African-Americans is rooted in the fear that it will cause folks to lose sight of the specific history and experience of African-Americans and the unique sensibilities and culture that arise from that experience. An adequate response to this concern is to critique essentialism while emphasizing the significance of "the authority of experience." There is a radical difference between a repudiation of the idea that there is a black "essence" and recognition of the way black identity has been specifically constituted in the experience of exile and struggle.

When black folks critique essentialism, we are empowered to recognize multiple experiences of black identity that are the lived conditions which make diverse cultural productions possible. When this diversity is ignored, it is easy to see black folks as falling into two categories: nationalist or assimilationist, black-identified or white-identified. Coming to terms with the impact of postmodernism for black experience, particularly as it changes our sense of identity, means that we must and can rearticulate the basis for collective bonding. Given the various crises facing African-Americans (economic, spiritual, escalating racial violence, etc.), we are compelled by circumstance to reassess our relationship to popular culture and resistance struggle. Many of us are as reluctant to face this task as many non-black postmodern thinkers who focus theoretically on the issue of "difference" are to confront the issue of race and racism.

Music is the cultural product created by African-Americans that has most attracted postmodern theorists. It is rarely acknowledged that there is far greater censorship and restriction of other forms of cultural production by black folks—literary, critical writing, etc. Attempts on the part of editors and publishing houses to control and manipulate the representation of black culture, as well as the desire to promote the creation of products that will attract the widest audience, limit in a crippling and stifling way the kind of work many black folks feel we can do and still receive recognition. Using myself as an example, that creative writing I do which I consider to be most reflective of a postmodern oppositional sensibility, work that is abstract, fragmented, non-linear narrative, is constantly rejected by editors and publishers. It does not conform to the type of writing they think black women should be doing or the type of writing they believe will sell. Certainly I do not think I am the only black person engaged in forms of cultural production, especially experimental ones, who is constrained by the lack of an audience for certain kinds of work. It is important for postmodern thinkers and theorists to constitute themselves as an audience for such work. To do this they must assert power and privilege within the space of critical writing to open up the field so that it will be more inclusive. To change the exclusionary practice of postmodern critical discourse is to enact a postmodernism of resistance. Part of this intervention entails black intellectual participation in the discourse.

In his essay "Postmodernism and Black America," Cornel West suggests that black intellectuals "are marginal—usually languishing at the interface of black and white cultures or thoroughly ensconced in Euro-American settings." He cannot see this group as potential producers of radical postmodernist thought. While I generally agree with this assessment, black intellectuals must proceed with the understanding that we are not condemned to the margins. The way we work and what we do can determine whether or not what we produce will be meaningful to a wider audience, one that includes all classes of black people. West suggests that black intellectuals lack "any organic link with most of Black life" and that this "diminishes their value to Black resistance." This statement bears traces of essentialism.

Perhaps we need to focus more on those black intellectuals, however rare our presence, who do not feel this lack and whose work is primarily directed towards the enhancement of black critical consciousness and the strengthening of our collective capacity to engage in meaningful resistance struggle. Theoretical ideas and critical thinking need not be transmitted solely in written work or solely in the academy. While I work in a predominantly white institution, I remain intimately and passionately engaged with black community. It's not like I'm going to talk about writing and thinking about postmodernism with other academics and/or intellectuals and not discuss these ideas with underclass nonacademic black folks who are family, friends, and comrades. Since I have not broken the ties that bind me to underclass poor black community, I have seen that knowledge, especially that which enhances daily life and strengthens our capacity to survive, can be shared. It means that critics, writers, and academics have to give the same critical attention to nurturing and cultivating our ties to black community that we give to writing articles, teaching, and lecturing. Here again I am really talking about cultivating habits of being that reinforce awareness that knowledge can be disseminated and shared on a number of fronts. The extent to which knowledge is made available, accessible, etc., depends on the nature of one's political commitments.

Postmodern culture with its decentered subject can be the space where ties are severed or it can provide the occasion for new and varied forms of bonding. To some extent, ruptures, surfaces, contextuality, and a host of other happenings create gaps that make space for oppositional practices which no longer require intellectuals to be confined by narrow separate spheres with no meaningful connection to the world of the everyday. Much postmodern engagement with culture emerges from the yearning to do intellectual work that connects with habits of being, forms of artistic expression, and aesthetics that inform the daily lives of writers and scholars as well as a mass population. On the terrain of culture, one can participate in critical dialogue with the uneducated poor, the black underclass who are thinking about aesthetics. One can talk about what we are seeing, thinking, or listening to; a space is there for critical exchange. It's exciting to think, write, talk about, and create art that reflects passionate engagement with popular cultures, because this may very well be "the" central future location of resistance struggle, a meeting place where new and radical happenings can occur.

PART THREE

SELF, SEX AND SANITY

Postmodernity brings changing ideas, changing styles, changing behaviors—all the things we have surveyed in the foregoing chapters. It brings, above all, a change of *mind*. We are talking about a psychological shift, a deep and unsettling one. It has to do with who you think you are— what we think a human individual is. One of the solid things that melts into air is the modern era's concept of the self.

If you want to find landmarks that show the difference between the modern era and the postmodern, think about the contrast between the psychological literature on "identity problems" written a few decades ago and a contemporary psychologist quoting—with approval—a statement that says: "Identities are highly complex, tension filled, contradictory, and inconsistent entities. Only the one who claims to have a simple, definite, and clear-cut identity has an identity problem."[1] Another psychologist says: "The age of the self is coming to an end. . . . There is a move from the architecture of the 'psyche' to the architecture of current cultural land-scapes."[2]

What does this mean, the age of the self coming to an end? Does it mean we are all going to disappear? That everybody will be the same? Nothing quite so bizarre, although I suspect that human life is going to look (and feel) a lot different as this development unfolds. The various self-concepts that I described in Chapter 18—those rooted in psychological testing, social roles, even romantic certainty of an inner true self—are all, if the postmodern psychologists are right, going to be replaced by a sense of identity based on "a reality of immersed independence, in which it is relationship that constitutes the self."[3] If they are right this is happening already, and our understanding hasn't quite caught up to our experience.

This means an end to individualism as we have known it—the inner-directed, stay-the-course personality that, depending on who you're talking to, is either the great strength or the main problem of modern Western civilization. But it is equally unpromising to the future prospects of the ideal that is so often prescribed as the antidote to individualism—the person deeply rooted in community. The postmodern person is a *multi-community* person, and his or her life as a social being is based on adjusting to shifting contexts and being true to divergent—and occasionally conflicting— commitments.

Much of what was once ordained by cultural tradition is now negotiated. New rules and new roles are being socially constructed—not in the abstract, but by specific people in specific times and places. And sometimes, of course, the negotiation escalates into conflict.

Individuals negotiate (and renegotiate) personal identity, struggling to make internal peace among the multiple components of their selves and the claims of the different communities to which they are connected. Groups of people negotiate (and renegotiate) such matters as gender roles and rules for sexual behavior. In the view of postmodern psychologists and sociologists, our experiences and our realities aren't merely programmed by the genes or projected out of the Freudian unconscious. Rather, they are continually created in collaboration with others, in processes that can't ever be completely detached from the languages we use and the actual situations in which we happen to be. This isn't simply a new round of the old nature-nurture debate, because it is now understood that our genetic heritage and our physical brains provide the equipment for this kind of sociability: We are not, like some animals, genetically instructed to perform specific behaviors; rather, we are genetically instructed to adapt to society. The tricky part is that now we all have to make some choices about what society to adapt to, and how much, and when.

In this group of readings we look first at postmodern ideas about the self, and next at some new perspectives on those all-important badges of identity, gender and sexual behavior.

All women, whether they know it or not, are deeply involved in postmodernity, because it's virtually impossible now to remain isolated from the profound controversies over women's roles that are going on all around us. Relatively few women, however, arrive at what I would call a consciously postmodern stance in relationship to these issues, and the article by Maureen O'Hara gives an idea of what such a stance looks and sounds like. And, as sociologist William Simon points out, changing ideas about sex also affect personal identity, because sexual behavior is always a statement about the self.

You might think that, with belief in the tangible self eroding, the whole enterprise of psychology—conceived as a scientific discipline for studying the tangible, objective psyche—would collapse. And in fact there has been some serious discussion of just that possibility—suggestions that a post-modern psychology may be, as Steinar Kvale puts it, "a contradiction in terms."4 So far there's no sign that psychology is fading away, but clearly there is a lot of rethinking going on. If you look at what is happening in two areas of psychology, consciousness studies and psychotherapy—as we do in the last two selections in Part Three—you can see that all kinds of people are, literally, in the process of changing their minds.

20

The Protean Style

ROBERT JAY LIFTON

People are changing, says psychiatrist Robert Jay Lifton—not only changing, but changing again and again, and sometimes changing back. He sees a new kind of human being emerging amid the uncertainties of our time. He calls it Protean man.

Now, we know from Greek mythology that Proteus was able to change his shape with relative ease from wild boar to lion to dragon to fire to flood. What he found difficult, and would not do unless seized and chained, was to commit himself to a single form, a form most his own, and carry out his function of prophecy. We can say the same of Protean man, but we must keep in mind his possibilities as well as his difficulties.

The Protean style of self-process, then, is characterized by an interminable series of experiments and explorations, some shallow, some profound, each of which can readily be abandoned in favor of still new, psychological quests. This pattern resembles, in many ways, what Erik Erikson has called "identity diffusion" or "identity confusion," and the impaired psychological functioning which these terms suggest can be very much present. But I want to stress that this Protean style is by no means pathological as such, and in fact may be one of the functional patterns necessary to life in our times. I would emphasize that it extends to all areas of human experience—to political as well as to sexual behavior, to the holding and promulgating of ideas, and to the general organization of lives. To grasp this style, then, we must alter our judgments concerning what is psychologically disturbed or pathological, as opposed to adaptive or even innovative.

I would like to suggest a few illustrations of the Protean style, as expressed in America and Europe, drawn both from my own psycho-therapeutic work with patients, and from observations on various forms of literature and art.

One patient of mine, a gifted young teacher, referred to himself as "wearing a number of masks" which he could put on or take off. He asked the question, "Is there, or should there be, one face which should be authentic?" He wasn't really sure, and found parallels to this in literature, in which, he noted, there were representations of "every kind of crime, every kind of sin." And then he added: "For me, there's not a single act I cannot imagine myself committing." He went on to compare himself to an actor on the stage, who, as he put it, "performs with a certain kind of polymorphous versatility," and here he was of course referring, somewhat mockingly, to Freud's well-known phrase, "polymorphous perversity" for diffusely inclu-sive and, in a way also Protean, infantile sexuality. And he went on to ask: "Which is the real person, so far as an actor is concerned? Is he more real when performing on the stage, or when he is at home? I tend to think that for people who have these many, many masks, there is no home. Is it a futile gesture for the actor to try to find his real face?" Here he was asking a very fundamental question, one in fact at issue throughout this chapter. I would add that while he was by no means a happy man, neither was he incapaci-tated. And although he certainly had considerable strain with his "poly-morphous versatility," it could be said that as a teacher and a thinker, and in some ways as a man, he was served rather well by it. In fact, I would claim that polymorphous versatility of one kind or another is becoming increas-ingly prominent in contemporary life.

Protean man has a particular relationship to the holding of ideas, which I think has great significance for the politics, religion, and general intellectual life of the future. Just as elements of the self can be experi-mented with and readily altered, so can idea systems and ideologies be embraced, modified, let go of and reembraced, all with a new ease that stands in sharp contrast to the inner struggle we have in the past associated with these shifts. Until relatively recently, no more than one major ideological shift was likely to occur in a lifetime, and that one would be long remembered as a very significant inner individual turning point accompanied by profound soul-searching and conflict. But today, it is not so unusual to encounter several such shifts accomplished relatively painlessly within a year, or even a month, whether in politics, aesthetic values, or style of living. Among many groups the rarity is the man who has gone through life holding firmly to a single ideological vision.

In one sense, this tendency is related to the "end of ideology" spoken of by Daniel Bell, since Protean man is incapable of maintaining an unquestioning allegiance to the large ideologies and Utopian thought of the nineteenth and early twentieth centuries. One must be very cautious, however, about speaking of the end of anything, especially ideology, and one also encounters in Protean man what I would call strong ideological hunger. He is starved for ideas and feelings that can give coherence to his world, though here too his taste is toward new combinations. And while he is by no means without yearning for the absolute, what he finds most acceptable are images of a more fragmentary nature than those of the ideologies of the past. And these images, limited and fleeting though they may be, can have enormous influence on his psychological life. Thus political and religious movements, as they confront Protean man, are likely to have much less difficulty convincing him to alter previous convictions than they do providing him with a set of beliefs which can command his allegiance for more than a brief experimental interlude. The problem is to build structures, to create boundaries, but not just any structures or any boundaries, and not just at any given historical moment. Here one must keep in mind Protean man's allergy to that which strikes him as inauthentic.

And bound up with his flux in emotions and beliefs is a profound inner sense of absurdity which finds expression in a tone of mockery. Absurdity and mockery are central to Protean man, and are related to a perception of surrounding activities and beliefs as strange and inappropriate. They stem from a breakdown of a fundamental kind in the relationship between inner and outer worlds—that is, in the sense of symbolic integrity—and are part of the pattern of psychohistorical dislocation I mentioned earlier. For if we view man as primarily a symbol-forming organism, we must recognize that he has constant need of a meaningful inner formulation of self and world, in which his actions, and even his impulses, have some kind of "fit" with the "outside" as he perceives it.

The sense of absurdity, of course, has a considerable modern tradition, and has been discussed by such writers as Camus as a function of man's spiritual homelessness and inability to find any meaning in traditional belief systems. But absurdity and mockery have taken much more extreme form in the post–World War II world, and have in fact become a prominent part of a universal life-style.

I suggested before that Protean man was not free of guilt. He indeed suffers from it considerably, but often without awareness of what is causing his suffering. For his is a form of hidden guilt: a vague but persistent kind of self-condemnation related to the symbolic disharmonies I have described, a sense of having no outlet for his loyalties and no symbolic structure for his achievements. This is the guilt of social breakdown, and it includes various forms of historical and racial guilt experienced by whole nations and peoples, both by the privileged and the abused. Rather than a clear feeling of evil or sinfulness, it takes the form of a nagging sense of unworthiness all the more troublesome for its lack of clear origin.

Protean man experiences similarly vague constellations of anxiety and resentment. These too have origin in symbolic impairments and are particularly tied in with suspicion of counterfeit nurturance. Often feeling himself uncared for, even abandoned, Protean man responds with diffuse fear and anger. But he can neither find a good cause for the former, nor a consistent target for the latter. He nonetheless cultivates his anger because he finds it more serviceable than anxiety, because there are plenty of targets of one kind or another beckoning, and because even moving targets are better than none. His difficulty is that focused indignation is as hard for him to sustain as is any single identification or conviction. In his discomforts and even his symptoms he experiences the same kind of formlessness, together with flexibility and search, that characterizes the rest of his psychological experience.

Involved in all of these patterns is a profound psychic struggle with the idea of change itself. For here too Protean man finds himself ambivalent in the extreme. He is profoundly attracted to the idea of making all things, including himself, totally new—to the "mode of transformation." But he is equally drawn to an image of a mythical past of perfect harmony and prescientific wholeness, to the "mode of restoration." Moreover, beneath his transformationism is nostalgia, and beneath his restorationism is his fascinated attraction to contemporary forms and symbols. Constantly balancing these elements midst the extraordinary, rapid change surrounding his own life, the nostalgia is pervasive, and can be one of his most explosive and dangerous emotions.

Following upon all that I have said are radical impairments to the symbolism of transition within the life cycle—the *rites de passage* surrounding birth, entry into adulthood, marriage, and death. Whatever rites remain seem shallow, inappropriate, fragmentary. Protean man cannot take them seriously, and often seeks to improvise new ones with whatever contemporary materials he has available, including cars and drugs.

As I suggested earlier, Protean man is left with two paths to symbolic immortality which he tries to cultivate, sometimes pleasurably and sometimes desperately: the natural mode (also under some threat) and the mode of "experiential transcendence," within which he not only embraces chemical aids to "expanded consciousness," but also the "community high" of group living and political action. And indeed all revolutions may be thought of, at bottom, as innovations in the struggle for immortality, as new combinations of old modes.

Three questions about Protean man, each rather fundamental, readily arise. Is Protean man always a *young* man? Is he really a *new* man, or merely a resurrection of a type familiar from the past? And midst his fluidity, what, if anything, remains stable? To which I would answer, very briefly, as follows. The fluctuating pattern I described is indeed most prominent in the young (late teens and early twenties), but for the rest of us to assume that we are totally immune from it would seem to me to be a great mistake. My contention, in fact, is that Protean man inhabits us all. We all live in contemporary society, and are all in greater or lesser degree exposed to the forces I have mentioned. Although the pattern is most characteristic of advanced, affluent societies, even those in non-affluent, economically backward societies are by no means free of them. And although men resembling Protean man have undoubtedly existed in earlier historical periods that were, like our own, notably "out of joint," the extremity of recent historical developments has rendered him a much more discrete and widespread entity. That is what permits us to stress his emergence. Concerning his stability, it is true that much within him must remain constant in order to make possible his psychological flux. I would include here certain enduring elements in the mother-child relationship, various consistencies in style (including elements of mockery and the sense of absurdity, approaches to individual and group relationships, and a generally aesthetic emphasis), as well as the stabilizing aspect of constant anticipation of change itself. The whole stability-change issue badly needs general psychological reevaluation, especially in regard to the kinds of significant change that can take place within a person while much else remains constant.

We may say then that young adults individually, and youth movements collectively, express most vividly the psychological themes of Protean man. But we may also say that Protean man's affinity for the young, his being metaphorically and psychologically so young in spirit, has to do with his never-ceasing quest for imagery of rebirth. He seeks such imagery of rebirth from all sources, from ideas, techniques, religions, and political systems, from mass movements and of course from drugs, or from special individuals of his own kind—that is, from fellow Protean voyagers—whom he sees as possessing that problematic gift of his namesake, the gift of prophecy. The dangers inherent in the quest seem hardly to require emphasis. What perhaps needs most to be kept in mind is the general principle that renewal on a large scale, wherever it may occur, is impossible to achieve without forays into danger, destruction, and negativity. The principle of death and rebirth is as valid psycho-historically as it is mythologically. And the direction of Protean man's prophecy lies in new, fluid, threatening, liberating, confusing, and revitalizing personal boundaries.

21

The Healthy, Happy Human Being
Wears Many Masks

KENNETH GERGEN

One of the leading exponents of postmodern psychology challenges the traditional doctrine that mental health requires a coherent sense of identity. He proposes instead a new exploration of the idea that every person carries the potential of many selves, capable of being realized in different social settings.

To thine own self be true, and it must follow, as the night the day, Thou canst not then be false to any man.   —POLONIUS TO LAERTES

HAMLET, SCENE I, ACT III

Polonius undoubtedly had good intentions; his counsel to his son seems eminently reasonable. It has a ring of validity and it fits our religious and moral values. But it is poor psychology. I think we are not apt to find a single, basic self to which we can be true.

I came to this belief after writing letters to close friends one evening. When I read over what I had written, I was first surprised, then alarmed. I came across as a completely different person in each letter: in one, I was morose, pouring out a philosophy of existential sorrow; in another I was a lusty realist; in a third I was a lighthearted jokester; and so on.

I had felt completely honest and authentic as I wrote each letter; at no time was I aware of putting on a particular style to please or impress a particular friend. And yet, a stranger reading those letters all together would have no idea who I am. This realization staggered me. Which letter, if any, portrayed the true me? Was there such an entity—or was I simply a chameleon, reflecting others' views of me?

Such questions I find are widespread in our culture. One young woman described the problem to her encounter group thus: "I feel like I'm contradictory . . . and people keep hitting me with the *you're-not-what-you-seem* issue, and it's really wearing me down . . . it's like I feel I can only give part here to one person and part there to another, but then I become a bunch of parcels. If I could just get all my reactions together . . ."

Her difficulties evoke Erik Erikson's classical description of identity diffusion: a state of bewilderment, typical of the young, at the lack of a firm sense of self. Other psychiatrists speak of self-alienation, a depressed feeling of estrangement from the masks of identity that society forces on the individual. Contemporary critics argue that rapid social and technological upheaval has created a crisis of identity: an individual no longer can develop and maintain a strong, integrated sense of personal identity. Writers from Alexander Pope to sociologist Erving Goffman have been alternately impressed and irritated at the use of masks in social life.

Such critics and psychologists have been working on two assumptions:

(1) that it is normal for a person to develop a firm and coherent sense of identity, and

(2) that it is good and healthy for him to do so, and pathological not to.

The first assumption underlies virtually all psychological research on the development of the self. Psychologists maintain that the child learns to identify himself positively (high self-esteem) or negatively (the inferiority complex); they have sought the origins of such feelings in different kinds of home environments and socialization styles. They believe that once the sense of self is fixed, it remains a stable feature of personality. Moreover, knowing a person's fixed level of self-esteem allows us to predict his actions: his neurotic or healthy behavior, his assertiveness in social relations, his academic performance, his generosity, and more.

The second assumption—that a unified sense of self is good and that inconsistency is bad—is so pervasive in our cultural traditions that it is virtually unquestioned. At the turn of the century William James said that the person with a divided sense of self had a "sick soul": he was to be pitied and redeemed. The psychologist Prescott Lecky argued that inconsistency of self was the very basis of neurotic behavior. And of course we are all apt to applaud the person of firm character who has self-integrity; we think of the inconsistent person as wishy-washy, undependable, a fake.

My research over the past few years has led me to question both of these assumptions very seriously. I doubt that a person normally develops a coherent sense of identity, and to the extent that he does, he may experience severe emotional distress. The long-term intimate relationship, so cherished in our society, is an unsuspected cause of this distress because it freezes and constricts identity.

My colleagues and I designed a series of studies to explore the shifting masks of identity, hoping to document the shifts in an empirically reliable way. We wanted to find the factors that influence the individual's choice of masks; we were interested in both outward appearances and inward feelings of personal identity. To what extent are we changeable, and in what conditions are we most likely to change? Do alterations in public identity create a nagging sense of self-alienation? How do we reconcile social-role-playing with a unified personality?

Our studies dealt with the influence of the other person, the situation, or the individual's motives. In each experiment, we would vary one of these three factors, holding the other factors constant. We would thus assess their impact on the subject's presentation of himself; and when the whole procedure was over, we explored the participant's feelings of self-alienation and sincerity.

William James believed that one's close friends mold his public identity: "a man has as many different social selves as there are distinct groups of persons about whose opinion he cares." Our research supports this Jamesian hypothesis, and goes further. One's identity will change markedly even in the presence of strangers.

For instance, in one experiment a woman co-worker whom we identified as a clinical trainee interviewed eighteen women college students. She asked each student a variety of questions about her background, then sixty questions about how she saw herself. Every time that the student gave a self-evaluation that was more positive than the norm, the interviewer showed subtle signs of approval: she nodded her head, smiled, occasionally spoke agreement. Conversely, she would disapprove of the student's negative self-evaluations: she would shake her head, frown, or speak disagreement. It became clear to the student that the trainee took a very positive view of her.

As a result of this procedure, the students' self-evaluation became progressively more positive. This increase was significantly greater than the minimal change that occurred in the control condition, where students received no feedback from the trainee.

This finding demonstrates that it is easy to modify the mask of identity, but it says little about underlying feelings. Did the young women think they were misleading the interviewer—telling her one thing while they secretly believed something else? To check on their private evaluations of themselves, after the interview we asked the students to undertake honest self-ratings that were not to be seen by the interviewer. We found significant increases in the self-esteem of students who had received the positive feedback; we found no such increases in the control condition. (We compared these self-ratings with those taken in other circumstances a month earlier.) One student in the experimental group told me later: "You know, it's very strange; I spent the rest of the day whistling and singing. Something about that interview really made me happy."

Our next experiment found that even this minimal amount of supportive reinforcement is not necessary to raise one's self-esteem. Sometimes another's outward characteristics are sufficient by themselves to change our self-concepts. Consider our response to the braggart, who spins glorious tales of success, and the whiner, who snivels and frets about his failures. My research with Barbara Wishnov suggests that these two types create entirely different identities in those around them.

Wishnov asked fifty-four pairs of young women college students to write descriptions of themselves. She explained that she would give the descriptions from one member to the other in each pair. Actually, instead, what she passed along to each was an evaluation that we had prepared in advance.

Each member of one group of students found herself reading the words of a braggart—a peer of impeccable character who described herself as being cheerful, intelligent and beautiful. She loved school, had had a marvelous childhood, and was optimistic about the future.

In contrast, each member of a second group read a description of a fellow student who might have been a dropout from psychotherapy: she was a whiner, unhappy, ugly, and intellectually dull; her childhood had been miserable; she hated school; and she was intensely fearful of the future.

The experimenter then asked each student to respond to this supposed partner by describing herself as honestly as possible in direct response to her.

Self-evaluations soared among the students who read positive evaluations of their peers; they found positive qualities in themselves that were nowhere in evidence in the self-appraisals they had made a month before; they hid negative characteristics. The braggart may produce a power imbalance that persons try to equalize by affirming their own virtues. It is as if they are saying: *You think you're so great; well, I'm pretty terrific too.*

The whiner produced strikingly different results in the students who read the negative evaluations. These young women responded by admitting to an entire array of shortcomings that they had not previously acknowledged. They adopted a mask that seemed to say: *I know what you mean; I've got problems too.* Even so, they resisted admitting that they were just as unfortunate as the whiner: perhaps they sought to avoid budding friendships based on misery. Thus they did not conceal the virtues they had claimed for themselves a month earlier.

Again we tried to explore beneath these masks. We asked the students a variety of questions after the interchange: *Is it possible that anything the other [young woman] said about herself may have influenced you in any way? How honest did you feel you could be with her? Do you feel that your self-evaluations were completely accurate?*

About 60 percent of the subjects said that they felt completely comfortable with the selves they had presented to the partner. The partner had had no effect, they replied, and their own self-evaluations were completely honest and accurate. Moreover, they did not differ at all from the 40 percent who had felt alienated from their self-presentations. The young women shifted their masks with little conscious awareness that they were doing so.

A third experiment showed that we can induce changes in the way one presents oneself simply by varying the physical appearance of the other person.

In an experiment at the University of Michigan, Stanley J. Morse and I sought male applicants for an interesting summer job that paid well. As each volunteer reported in, we seated him alone in a room with a long table, and gave him a battery of tests to fill out. Among them, of course, was a self-evaluation questionnaire. We explained that his responses on this questionnaire would have nothing to do with his chances for being hired, but that we needed his honest answers to construct a good test. As the applicant sat there working, we sent in a stooge—supposedly another applicant for the job.

In half of the cases, the stooge was our Mr. Clean. He was a striking figure: well-tailored business suit, gleaming shoes, and a smart attaché case, from which he took a dozen sharpened pencils and a book of Plato. The other half of the job applicants met our Mr. Dirty, who arrived with a torn sweat shirt, pants torn off at the knees, and a day's growth of beard. He had no pencils, only a battered copy of Harold Robbins' *The Carpetbaggers*. Neither stooge spoke to the real applicants as they worked on self-ratings.

We then compared the evaluations before and after the arrival of the stooge. Mr. Clean produced a sharp drop in self-esteem. Applicants suddenly felt sloppy, stupid and inferior by comparison; indeed, Mr. Clean was an intimidating character. But Mr. Dirty gave everyone a psychological lift. After his arrival, applicants felt more handsome, confident and optimistic. We might conclude that the slobs of the world do a great favor for those around them: they raise self-esteem.

The behavior and appearance of others inspire self-change, but the setting in which we encounter other persons also exerts an influence. For example, work situations consistently reward serious, steadfast, Calvinistic behavior. But for a person to act this way in all situations would be unfortunate, especially when the situation demands spontaneity and play. No one wants to live with the Protestant Ethic twenty-four hours a day; in this sense, the office door and the door to one's home serve as signals for self-transformation.

Freudian theory awakened us to the motives that underlie behavior; for instance, we have become aware of the self-gratifying aspects of even the most altruistic behavior. I think that we can apply this lesson to the study of public identity. If someone appears open, warm and accepting, we may ask why that person adopts such a mask. We may inquire what the cold and aloof individual hopes to attain with that appearance. We should not, however, conclude that the mask is a sure sign of the person's deep-seated character. When motives change, conviviality may turn to coolness, the open man may become guarded.

We studied the relationship between masks and motives in several experiments, most of them based on approval-seeking. Carl Rogers pointed out that the warm regard of others is vital to feelings of self-regard and hence to feelings of personal worth. So we asked: *How do individuals present themselves when they want to gain the approval of others?*

In experiments designed to answer this question, we varied the characteristics of the other in systematic ways. He might be senior to our subject in authority, or junior; open and revealing, or closed and remote; a stern taskmaster or an easy-going boss. When an individual seeks approval from this diverse range of personalities, he adopts wholly different masks or public identities. When he is not seeking approval, self-presentation is much different in character.

In subsequent research we found that persons can improve their feelings about themselves simply by thinking about their positive qualities. It is not necessary to act the role; fantasizing about how they would act is sufficient.

Taken together, our experiments document the remarkable flexibility of the self. We are made of soft plastic, and molded by social circumstances. But we should not conclude that all of our relationships are fake: subjects in our studies generally believed in the masks they wore. Once donned, mask becomes reality.

I do not want to imply that there are no central tendencies in one's concept of self. There are some lessons that we learn over and over, that remain consistent through life—sex-typing, for example. Men learn to view themselves as "masculine," women as "feminine." Some of us have been so rigorously trained to see ourselves as "inferior" or "superior" that we become trapped in these definitions. Often we cannot escape even when the self-concepts become inappropriate or unwanted.

But we have paid too much attention to such central tendencies, and have ignored the range and complexity of being. The individual has many potential selves. He carries with him the capacity to define himself, as warm or cold, dominant or submissive, sexy or plain. The social conditions around him help determine which of these options are evoked.

I believe we must abandon the assumption that normal development equips the individual with a coherent sense of identity. In the richness of human relations, a person receives varied messages about who he is. Parents, friends, lovers, teachers, kin, counselors, acquaintances all behave differently toward us; in each relationship we learn something new about ourselves and, as the relations change, so do the messages. The lessons are seldom connected and they are often inconsistent.

In this light, the value that society places on a coherent identity is unwarranted and possibly detrimental. It means that the heterosexual must worry over homosexual leanings, the husband or wife over fantasies of infidelity, the businessman over his drunken sprees, the commune dweller over his materialism. All of us are burdened by the code of coherence, which demands that we ask: *How can I be X if I am really Y, its opposite?* We should ask instead: *What is causing me to be X at this time?* We may be justifiably concerned with tendencies that disrupt our preferred modes of living and loving; but we should not be anxious, depressed or disgusted when we find a multitude of interests, potentials and selves.

Indeed, perhaps our true concern should be aroused when we become too comfortable with ourselves, too fixed in a specific identity. It may mean that our environment has become redundant—we are relating to the same others, we encounter the same situations over and over. Identity may become coherent in this fashion, but it may also become rigid and maladaptive. If a man can see himself only as powerful, he will feel pain when he recognizes moments of weakness. If a woman thinks of herself as active and lively, moments of quiet will be unbearable; if we define ourselves as weak and compliant we will cringe ineptly when we are challenged to lead.

The social structure encourages such one-dimensionality. We face career alternatives, and each decision constricts the possibilities. Our social relationships stabilize as do our professional commitments; eventually we find ourselves in routines that vary little from day to day.

Many of us seek refuge from the confining borders and pressures of careers in long-term intimate relationships. Here, we feel, we can be liberated: we can reveal our true selves, give and take spontaneously, be fully honest.

Unfortunately, salvation through intimacy usually is a false hope, based on Western romantic myth. Marriage, we are taught, soothes the soul, cures loneliness and frees the spirit. It is true that at the outset, love and intimacy provide an experience in personal growth. The loved one comes to see himself as passionate, poetic, vital, attractive, profound, intelligent, and utterly lovable. In the eyes of his beloved, the individual becomes all that he would like to be: he tries on new masks, acts out old fantasies. With the security of love, identity may flower anew.

I have had a broad range of experience with young married couples, and I observe that for most of them the myth of marriage dies quickly. In a matter of months they feel the pain of identity constriction; the role of mate becomes stabilized and rigid. I think that such stabilization occurs for at least three reasons:

(1) *The reliance of each spouse on the other for fulfillment of essential needs.* Interdependency fosters standardized behavior. And along with standardized behavior comes a limited identity.

(2) *Our general inability to tolerate inconsistencies in others.* We reward consistent identity in others and punish variations. This process eases interaction, makes it predictable, and greases the wheels of social discourse. In an intimate relationship, it also constricts identity.

(3) *Our inability to tolerate extreme emotional states for long periods of time.* The new identities that emerge in the early stage of a relationship depend in part on the emotional intensity of this period. But it is seldom that we can sustain such grand passion, or tolerate the anger and depression that are its inevitable counterparts. We weary of the emotional roller coaster, and replace passion with peace. It is difficult to restore intense feelings once we have quelled them, though some events may ignite them again temporarily.

This picture is depressing, I realize. But if we are aware of the process that limits identity, we can subvert it. We can broaden our experiences with others: the more unlike us they are, the more likely we are to be shaken from a rigid sense of identity. If each partner presents new demands, the stage is set for trying on new masks—and this in turn awakens new feelings about the self. Honest communication—*this is how I think you are now*—is essential. Once in the open, such images usually prove quite false; and as impressions are broken, expectations become more pliable and demands for consistency lose urgency. Finally, if playing a role does in fact lead to real changes in one's self-concept, we should learn to play more roles, to adopt any role that seems enjoyable—a baron, a princess, a secret agent, an Italian merchant— and, if the other is willing to play, a storehouse of novel self-images emerges.

The mask may be not the symbol of superficiality that we have thought it was, but the means of realizing our potential. Walt Whitman wrote: "Do I contradict myself? Very well then, I contradict myself. (I am large. I contain multitudes)."

22

The Death of the Self in a Postmodern World

CONNIE ZWEIG

The announcement that "the Self is dead" may have, for our time, the same kind of stunning, controversial effect that Nietzsche's famous "God is dead" had at the end of the last century. As we near the end of this one, different visions of the Self seem to be cropping up everywhere—even within psychological traditions such as the Jungian, in which the concept of the integrated Self once ruled with godlike certainty. Now, theorists in the Jungian lineage are wondering if there is any such thing as a stable Self at all.

Siddhartha Gautama the Buddha may have been the first deconstructionist. Born into the premodern world of Hindu India, in the sixth century B.C., he made the postmodern move of slaying the Self (or *Atman*) and positing the no-Self (*Anatman* or *Shunyata*). The *Atman* was viewed as an immanent bit of *Brahman,* the transcendent Self or creator, that lived within human beings. For Hindus, enlightenment, or self-realization, involved awakening the *Atman* to its own divine nature.

But for the Buddha, the Self was an illusion, a creation of Mind that is not innate to our spiritual makeup but is, instead, constructed out of our identification with experience in each moment, thus providing a sense of continuity in time and space. He believed that the Self as a concept and as an experience needs to be discarded for the attainment of freedom, which occurs by seeing through the layers of *maya* or illusion to the essential emptiness of all things. The no-Self of Buddhism, then, refers to this essential emptiness and to the idea that we give things substance or "reality" with our minds.

The search for the true nature of the Self has been one of the constant preoccupations of philosophers: Is there an essential part of human nature that is "higher," more evolved, even divine? Does it reside in an unchanging state of being, untouched by the process of becoming? Or is this simply a wish on our parts, a fantasy that enables us to feel solid, purposeful, and connected to something greater than ourselves? In the modern era, the theme was taken up by psychologists, who offered new models of the Self's inner structure, as well as therapies for curing its distresses and promoting its growth.

Today the very idea of the Self is under siege. In much the same way that Nietzsche's pronouncement that "God is dead" reverberated through the hearts and minds of thoughtful people in the early decades of this century, a parallel declaration of the death of the Self troubles our own time. The Self is being deconstructed, bit by bit, until it becomes transparent, like so many other beliefs in the postmodern age. This is reflected in the thinking of many contemporary psychologists, some of whom now doubt the existence of any constant Self that we can enshrine as either the observer or the observed.

THE SELF IN PSYCHOLOGY AND BEYOND

Sigmund Freud's concept of the Self was composed of three inseparable yet conflicted elements—Ego, Superego, and Id—with the Ego seen as the designated leader. In healthy self-development, the individual was supposed to tame some of the demands of the uncivilized Id and forge a strong, mature Ego. The motto of his therapy was: "Where Id was, there shall Ego be." Although the Freudian idea of the mind anticipated postmodern psychology to the extent of recognizing different parts, it was also strongly biased toward achieving an integrated, consistent personality.

Carl Jung also viewed the Self as the central organizing principle of development, but Jung—who had studied Eastern philosophy and traveled to India—brought other influences into his model of the psyche and told a much different story about the Self and the Ego. In mythology and dreams he found the recurring patterns or universal blueprints that he called archetypes. He posited the Self as the central archetype, around which the others (such as Anima/Animus and Shadow) revolved. He saw the Self as our source: In infancy, the Ego is in perfect union with the Self. And he saw it as our goal: With healthy growth—individuation—the Self is like the North point on the compass.

Jung's concept of the Self provides meaning, direction, order, and a sense of wholeness. Classical Jungians such as Edward Edinger view individual development along the Ego-Self axis: If the Ego is too separate from the Self, it may feel deprived and suffer depression. If the Ego is too closely identified with the Self, it may become inflated and suffer grandiosity. Because of its position in relation to the Self, the Ego is diminished during individuation. Thus Jung's dictum—in considerable contrast to Freud's—was: "Any victory for the Self is a defeat for the Ego."

Yet, despite the centrality of the idea of the Self to Jungian psychology, Jung knew that the Self was not a "thing" with substance. He called it the "dream of totality." He saw it as a psychic reality, not an objective one. But it became a key construct on which other parts of his theory hinged, and it is an attractive concept to those of us who seek a more spiritual psychology than Ego psychology. Experiences of the Self can be mystical experiences—full and expansive, reconciling opposites and generating meaning.

Today, under the influence of postmodernism and the ever-increasing absorption into Western culture of spiritual philosophies such as Buddhism, many psychologists in the Jungian tradition are taking a hard look at the Self and are seeing its complexity, its multifaceted nature.

According to analyst Charles Asher, Jung's Self has theological overtones, perhaps attributable to the influence of Jung's minister father. It is the God within, like a patriarchal ruler, always unattainable, "higher" and mightier than where we live our lives. It is static, unchanging. It resides within the psyche, the inner world—perhaps a reflection of Jung's own introversion—and does not enter into relations with others or with the natural world.

As a principle of order it is Apollonian, never Dionysian—can we experience the Jungian Self in a dance? As a single entity, center of the psychic universe, it is monotheistic or kinglike. It reminds me of the biblical admonition: "Thou shalt have no other gods before me."

Archetypal psychologist James Hillman has offered a provocative recasting of Jungian psychology. He has chased the Self from its throne and replaced it with a plural psyche—a panoply of Greek gods, each of whom has a distinct flavor, style, and shadow side. Among these are Hermes, Demeter, Dionysus, Aphrodite, Zeus, Athena, Artemis, and Pan.

For Hillman the essential building blocks of the psyche are not abstract, universal archetypes such as the Self, or symbols in a dream such as the Shadow, but rather fantasy-images that are concrete, particular, and real in the psychic realm of each individual. He suggests that we witness the images that arise—not interpret them, as Jung did. The images, he says, may lead to story, which may lead to myth. They are visitations from the mysterious realm of Soul. They are not to be "integrated" as disowned parts for the sake of the Self's greater good, but to be heard and respected.

Hillman has moved the focus of attention from Self to Soul. While Self suggests order, meaning and direction, Soul, in Hillman's usage, suggests deepening, intensity, underworld. While Self suggests moving toward wholeness, Soul suggests being in the moment. So he has dislocated the Self from the center of the psyche—in fact, with his idea of *anima mundi*, or world-soul, he has dislocated it from within the psyche altogether. This is a radical leap away from Jung, but quite compatible with the various contemporary thinkers of an eco-spiritual bent who link the human realm to the realm of nature and see healthy personal development as a deepening identification with Earth and all non-human life. Usually the eco-self is still posited in human terms, but phenomenologist Robert Romanyshyn offers a concept of "green consciousness" as a frequency band, seeking to eliminate this species bias. The ideal of eco-spirituality and eco-psychology is to attain a "non-anthropocentric" world.

Back in the human realm, many feminist psychologists are examining the *self-in-relation*, the idea that identity for women emerges in relationship with others—not a separate, heroic Ego as it may be for men who, in our culture, need to differentiate from their mothers. Such feminists believe that modern psychology (as developed by men) leaves out female subjectivity; its definitions of Self do not really apply to women. This is a cultural critique: Girls are raised to consider others, to consider context, and to be self-sacrificing. For this reason, their Egos may have different developmental needs, and the "Ego defeat" prescribed by Jung may not be such a good idea. Rather, they may need to become "somebody" before they try to become "nobody" by transcending the Ego.

SEEING THROUGH THE SELF

While the modern era was characterized by a war of paradigms, belief against belief, the postmodern era throws into question the nature of belief itself. "Seeing through belief" is, I think, not only an intellectual exercise but also a spiritual practice much like that proposed by the Buddha. While he suggested that Mind created structures that we then take to be "real," postmodern thinkers in a similar vein suggest that cultures create structures. Our beliefs, in this view, are socially constructed—designed for the purpose of building a consensual reality and enabling a society to function.

Such postmodern views could only emerge and be widely accepted in an era of globalization when we can see, each night on CNN, that there are as many realities as there are cultures—or, perhaps more accurately, as many as there are people. In this vast bazaar of realities, who or what is the True Self? Why would Jung be more correct in his view than an Islamic fundamentalist or an Estonian Slav or a Yoruba tribesman?

This relativizing of beliefs about the Self in our time goes far beyond a mere nod of the head to cultural pluralism: Many theorists are calling into question any idea of a Self as a stable, continuing entity apart from its own descriptions of being. As Jacques Lacan has said, "I am not a poet but a poem." Think about that, and consider the following elaboration of the thought by Paul Kugler, a contemporary Jungian:

> Today, it is the speaking Subject who declared God dead one hundred years ago whose very existence is now being called into question. No longer is the speaking subject unquestionably assumed to be the source of language and speech, existence and truth, autonomy and freedom, unity and wholeness, identity and individuality. The transcendence of Descartes' "cogito" is no longer so certain. The speaking subject appears to be not a

referent beyond the first person pronoun, but, rather, a fragmented entity produced by the act of speaking. Each time the first person pronoun is uttered it projects a different entity, a different perspective and identity. It is positioned in a different location.

This idea is not new. It is the same message about the true death of the Ego that the Buddha imparted to his followers 2,500 years ago, and that countless teachers in various spiritual traditions have handed down through the centuries. But it is a powerful, shattering idea to enter mainstream thinking in many disciplines—as it is now doing—at a time when we are being confronted with so much evidence of multiple realities, so many reasons to question commonplace assumptions. It raises basic questions about the phenomena that psychologists and psychotherapists used to talk about with the secure knowledge that they were discussing a stable entity: Who, then, is the subject of therapy? Who is the dreamer of dreams?

Amid the relativism forced upon us by the experiences of living in a global civilization and hearing the profound questions now being asked about the images of Self that have been so much a part of our heritage, we are all challenged to look again in the mirror and rethink our assumptions about who and what we are. We face the discomfort—and the depth—of living with uncertainty, paradox, ambiguity, and constant change. Perhaps these are the tools of postmodern literacy.

A final personal confession: I must admit, after all is said and done, that I still feel nostalgia for that good ol' self, and hope to glimpse the wizard behind the curtain one day.

23

Constructing Emancipatory Realities

MAUREEN O'HARA

*In her survey of the wide variety of feminist ideas currently making
their way in the world, Maureen O'Hara identifies a kind of postmodern feminism that is very much in the affirmative category—not
a sense of despair over the collapse of the modern era's beliefs, but
rather "an enormous sense of relief, hope and responsibility."*

*Her essay is, like that of bell hooks, a rejection of essentialism—
in this case, essentialist definitions of "female nature."*

The field of psychology is buzzing with new ways of thinking about concepts
such as "self" and "reality." Feminist theory and practice has, from the
beginning, been in the thick of such arguments, and for good reason. When
every "system of truth" we've ever known, from oldest myth to modern
medical science, has concluded that women are biologically, intellectually
and morally inferior, that we are at once dangerous and naturally nurturing,
that we are unsuitable for public office and should be protected and
subjugated—then you bet feminists have a stake in conversations about
"truth" and "reality"!

Contemporary feminist ideas about the nature of female reality fall into at least four different streams. One, more common among American feminists, takes the view that there is an essential female nature determined by and manifest through the female body, with its possible multiple orgasms, its internal sex organs, and its capacity for pregnancy, and milk-nursing. This line of argument sees female nature violently repressed and compromised by patriarchal and misogynistic societies that have prevented a woman from fully knowing herself, other women and womankind. Through practices, customs, taboos and restrictions that circumscribe every aspect of her life, she is pruned and doctored like a Bonzai tree so that by the time she is an adult she sees this as the natural state of affairs. She willingly perpetuates the process by cooperating with the pruning of the next generation—her daughters. The radical version of this line of thinking, exemplified by Mary Daly in *Gyn/Ecology,* leads to a separatist position, where women would remove themselves from all institutions currently created in man's image and, in order to rediscover their lost "sacred femininity," withdraw from all contact with men. They would create their own institutions, symbols, religions, mores and forms of government that more faithfully reflect "essential feminine consciousness." Another important voice in American feminist scholarship is Carol Gilligan. Her work on moral development and Mary Belenky's work on the relationship between the development of women's voice, self and mind suggest that in our sexist society, where women still do most of the caring for small children, there is an asymmetry in early childhood experiences of boys and girls: girls stay more connected, boys must separate to individuate. This leads to distinctly "women's ways of knowing"—a more connected, participatory sense of reality. Although in Gilligan's work the differences between men and women are attributed to "nurture" rather than "nature," they are seen as so profound (and until men and women share early childcare equally, inescapable) that if women are ever to become emancipated and achieve full equality with men, educational, legal, political and religious institutions will have to acknowledge that woman's ways of knowing are not second-rate versions of "real (read patriarchal) knowledge" but in fact speak to crucial aspects of human existence totally ignored by "male-stream" thinking.

Another major stream is the constructivist theory that comes from French feminists such as Julia Kristeva, Luce Irigary and Helene Cixous, who draw on both Lacanian psychoanalysis and Marxism to argue that even the deepest layers of our psyche—the symbols, the desires, the fundamental structure of our sense of self, what Daly argues is "nature"—are constructed by our minds as ways to account for what happens to women (because they have no phallus) in a misogynistic society.

The fourth important stream is close to the constructivist position (at least for the purpose of this discussion). It is made up of poststructuralists like Chris Weedon, who also argue that there is no such thing as "feminine nature." They say that our biology is not our destiny but our consciousness, mediated through symbolic language, which we derive from the culture we live in. If our culture feels that women are inferior then so we will experience our nature. If our culture sees us as brood mares then we ourselves will prize our reproductive natures rather than our minds or our athleticism. This line of thinking, drawing on the deconstructionist thought of Derrida, as well as Lacan, Foucault, Althusser and others, focuses on the way language creates experience rather than merely reports it. For poststructuralists, if we value our mothering it is not through biological imperatives but because patri-archal societies require that we voluntarily accept roles such as unpaid child-rearing and domestic work. To help solidify these work roles into aspects of identity, ideologies of "femininity" arise—what Betty Freidan termed "fem-inine mystique." These codes of conduct feel so basic to us that we experi-ence real anxiety if we try to go against them, thus reinforcing the belief that it is against our "nature" to want not to mother or have no sexual relations with men. This poststructuralist and constructivist line of discussion sees our nature as "man-made" and points to the way it shifts from discourse to discourse, from community to community and from era to era as evidence for the plasticity of "female nature." When patriarchal interests shift, as in a war when women are needed to work in the armaments factories, we are subjected to new propaganda urging us to downplay motherhood and promoting a new ideology of "womanhood" that makes heroines out of Rosie the Riveters and aviatrixes. When the thinned ranks of men come home from the battlefield the "cult of motherhood" is reintroduced to get women out of the jobs the men need and to replace the population deci-mated by the war.

There are, of course enormous implications for the therapist in these different positions. If you believe that a woman's meaninglessness and emptiness—her depression—stems from her alienation from primordial femininity, then your therapy will be geared toward separatism, casting off the artifices of "masculine consciousness" and reaffirming the "essential feminine." You will eschew activities associated with the "masculine" and cleave to those that are womanist. You will see intuition, feeling, magic, sensuality, dance, poetry and mysticism as facilitating your client's recovery of her "divine female nature"; you will view rationality, politics, education in established institutions, participation in established religions, law, heterosexual marriage, competition, business and so on as taking her away from her Self and, therefore, as contributing factors in the depression.

By contrast, therapy informed by a poststructuralist or constructivist position necessitates a heightened commitment to rationality and critical analysis of both the outer world of signs and language and inner subjectivity. It involves consciousness-raising activities to challenge even deeply felt identifications and pull apart cherished psychic structures with the view to realigning them with female emancipatory interests. Such a therapy has to be essentially activist, requiring women to get involved in the social, economic and political structures of society in order to transform them from exploitative forms to emancipatory forms, and, in the crucible of our community conversations about reality, to become, each of us, both an interpreter of culture and a maker of culture.

Within the humanistic psychology community there has been a clear preference for the "essential feminine" version of feminist psychology. I argue that this is a mistake, albeit one that is very easy to understand. The idea of ourselves as "goddesses" or "priestesses" is a deeply comforting antidote to the usual sense of insignificance most women experience in their daily lives. Nonetheless I think "goddess"-type language and affirmations of some inborn, biologically based "femininity" in fact only perpetuate ways of thinking about human realities that themselves justify attitudes and social practices that have disenfranchised women for millennia. When we look dispassionately at the newly emergent "goddess" stories we can hardly fail to recognize how they derive from myths about female nature that have been part of patriarchal societies since ancient times.

The constructivist position is a harder pill to swallow. Its arguments leave the question of biological contribution to consciousness veiled in mystery. It is not that our biology is irrelevant but that it serves as a lower boundary condition through which and upon which we must construct symbolic reality, both internal and social. The content of our lives—consciousness, the unconscious, experience, even "self"—is constructed from semantic and semiotic symbols we encounter in our interactive dialogue with the world.

Some people feel the poststructural position leads to despair. Derrida himself is often quoted as saying he is in despair. I am not. Interestingly it is not the feminist poststructuralists who cry out in angst but the white, European males! What I feel, and read in the work of feminist poststructuralists, is an enormous sense of relief, hope and responsibility. Far from despair, the idea that each of us recreates reality with each encounter fills me with wondrous hope, empowerment and community connection. If there is no absolute truth "out there" to create pristine "expert systems" that can somehow solve our problems mathematically; if I am who I am because you are who you are and we both are who we are because others are who *they* are; if we accept that when we enter into dialogue we *both* change; if it is true that we *co-create* reality, which in turn creates us—then we are called to a new kind of community. If I can make culture I must act responsibly. If I can only ever be part of the creation I must act humbly. I'd take that over a goddess any day!

24

The Postmodernization of Sex and Gender

WILLIAM SIMON

It is not only ideas about gender—about the differences or non-differences between males and females—that are changing in the general onslaught against the modern concept of identity. People are also (as you may have noticed) challenging traditional ideas about sexual behavior and about the meanings we attribute to it.

Gender is possibly the last enduring and universal master aspect of identity, one that has significance in virtually all sectors of social life. Gender has been used to define, explain and justify polarities such as active/passive, internal/external, and receptive/intrusive. In social science, it is used to make distinctions regarding group leadership: We speak of "task instrumental leadership," which implicitly corresponds to traditional idealizations of masculinity, and "socio-emotional leadership," which evokes feminine ideals of nurturance and comforting.

As the world changes in frequently unanticipated ways, the constancy of gender takes on a new relevance: It is an important part of the diminished resources available to many individuals for sustaining self-cohesion as they traverse complex and mobile lives. As a result, gender becomes the focal point of numerous, cross-cutting discourses. We place increasing emphasis on a quest for the ultimate "truth" of gender—a "truth" that might justify either complying with or resisting transformations within our current division of labor, a "truth" that might account for how a legacy of tradition could have eroded in use so quickly.

Ironically, the very imperative nature of current quests for the "truth" of gender appears to frustrate its realization. A quest for some seemingly permanent objective guide to human uses of gender tends to reveal little more than a history of historically specific human uses. The quest for a comprehensive species-wide "truth" only reveals a rapidly expanding pluralization of gender "truths."

The last few decades have seen dramatic modifications of gender rules in every area of social life: not only an essentially linear shift from an "old" to "the new," but also an explosion of pluralizations between and within the lives of men and women. It may seem simple to check boxes marked M or F, but our actual use of gender codes in interpersonal and intrapsychic behavior is far more complex and dynamic. *Gender identity* is not so much a thing as a continuing process of *negotiation*—not only between the individual and the world, but also between different constructions of the self. The negotiation does not occur on an empty stage, but within specific encounters between individuals.

That which is new is rarely equally new for all. What may be an identity-challenging threat for some becomes a self-confirming liberation for others and a comfortably unexciting everyday reality for still others. To hold that the self is a process of social construction does not mean that the effects are graciously pliable. For example, though I would like to think of myself as a committed feminist, I also know that having been raised in this culture my unmonitored feelings are full of embarrassingly sexist preferences.

Much of what has been said with reference to the social construction of gender and its implications for today's world can also be said of sexuality. Sexuality also comes to us shrouded with cultural and psychological significances accumulated over a history of past uses. It comes to us appearing to be a singular common thread that joins all of human history. It comes to us appearing to be a truth of nature that can be modified by social life only at its own peril. Though not as constant a presence as gender, it remains an oppressive presence. Its application to individuals—labels like heterosexual, homosexual, bisexual—tends to take on the appearance of some intrinsic biological imperative.

But sexual behavior, social responses to it, and public erotic cultures have been undergoing unprecedented changes. In less than three decades, premarital sex has gone from the margins of deviance to statistical normality and, in many ways, to almost full cultural acceptance. Marriage has lost its monopoly as the sole legitimate location for sexual behavior. Despite the panic provoked by the spread of HIV infection, homosexuality has entered the suburbs of respectability. And our cultural landscape is cluttered with eroticized images of remarkable variety and explicitness.

I will limit my discussion of this to three points:

First, even more than gender, considerations of sexuality invariably reveal the impoverishment of narrow behaviorism. For all the significance we attach to it, sexual behavior does little to signify by itself. (Who was it that observed that describing a sex act detail by detail was like trying to describe a meal bite by bite?) From the prepubescent Sambian males who ingest the semen of their postpubescent, unmarried fellow villagers (incidentally, generating very little that we might label as subsequent homosexuality) to the contemporary North American middle-class adolescents who may be the first in large numbers to engage in premarital sexual intercourse, sexual *behavior* by itself, appears mute, inarticulate.

It becomes articulate by being transformed into sexual *conduct*—that is, behavior given meaning, evaluated. The very behavior that is often viewed as a constant thread running through human history and as a powerful and primary drive may, in fact, be among the most meaning-dependent of all behaviors. It may be among the most dependent on extrinsic factors for its capacity to motivate or even—perhaps I should say, especially—its capacity to pleasure. It is clearly linked to the larger issue of gender, as can be seen in the association of sexual behavior with gender competence—currently among sexuality's most powerful aspects.

Rarely has a major category of behavior been so inarticulate with reference to motivations, phenomenological experience, or potential consequences. The one generalization about sexuality that can be stated with elegant simplicity is the observation that there are many more reasons for being sexual than there are ways of being sexual.

Second, in its very meaning-dependency, sexuality must reflect the broad changes taking place at both cultural and individual levels. We find, in Freud to Elias and Foucault, the idea that the Western experience has elaborated or enlarged the scope of private life—which suggests the growth of private (intrapsychic) sexual cultures that parallel but are not identical to public cultures. Few eras have ever assigned as much significance to sex or talked so much about it.

The personal or subjective aspect of sexuality, conceived as a universal and compelling drive, turns attempts to control or repress sexual behavior into advertisements for the possibility of resistance. Attributing sexual drives to all individuals turns its manifestations into measures of moral, gender and social competence. The policing of the sexual has encouraged a quality of self-scrutiny and reflexivity possibly unparalleled in human history—unparalleled both in its intensity and in the proportion of the population involved.

For many people, the sexual part of their lives will take on new and somewhat disruptive salience—disruptive in the sense that the metaphoric richness of the sexual may have to risk real-life tests, tests that involve the effort to bring one's fantasies into one's reality. Such efforts have commonly led either to crises or to an impoverishment of both fantasy and reality.

Third, sexuality reflects powerful pluralizing forces. Not only can we expect wider patterns of variation in the kinds of sexual activities we engage in, but even wider variations in how this component of existence resonates with other aspects of life. All at once, to know about an individual's sexual history—even to know it in great detail—is to know very little, to have little understanding of why it occurred or the meaning it will have for that person. Much of the effort of sex researchers and theoreticians has been dedicated to explaining different sexual outcomes, different kinds of sexual careers. Long before we have realized this goal, we may be confronted by a more challenging effort—that of understanding why persons engaged in very different sexual activities may actually share a great deal in common.

All change can be described as either evolutionary or revolutionary: evolutionary in the sense that all events presuppose long and complicated histories, without which they could not have happened; revolutionary in the sense that events happen when they do, in a specific point in space or time, and preclude all the other ways events might have worked out. History tends not only to not repeat itself, but to not repeat the opportunities it presents.

If I had to select two lines of development that can be seen as products of postmodernity, I would select psychology and pluralization—which may only be different highlights of the same emergent process. Psychology in the sense that the understanding of the individual as a constructive and creative center of action has been made more necessary by the conditions within which increasing numbers of persons live increasing portions of their lives. Pluralism in the sense that the varieties of humanity will fully resemble the current varieties of experience and lifestyles. As a result, few totalizing definitions or explanations will serve, though the temptation to seek and implement them will increase. Liberty and freedom have always been double-edged.

Change always risks alienation, and only the most naive or ideologically driven can imagine that the present upheaval of gender roles and/or sexual practices is either liberating or satisfying for all (or even most) individuals. And while this does not mean that the process of reformulating gender rules should be stopped or slowed (as if it could be), or that we may have to accept experimentation in areas of human interaction that we once thought to be established beyond question, it does require that the responses to this process of reformulation must be understood in all their diversity.

The changes implicit in this rewriting of gender rules and uses of sexuality—especially as they occur in all sectors of social life—touch and often threaten some of the deepest, most sensitive levels of selfhood. And there is little likelihood that there will be simple, uniform or comprehensive ways of understanding the potential for distress. Individuals will respond differently according to such variables as age, gender or social status—but rarely in uniform ways. Some will retreat by finding faith in unexamined absolutes or in the desire to return to imagined worlds of the past. Some will experience a continuing sense of panic. And for still others this landscape of change will simply be what the world is all about, an everyday reality.

If I retain a fair measure of optimism, it is because we are confronted with a rare opportunity. More than ever before we are being pushed toward a more holistic view of the individual. This holism does not arise out of some abstract belief, but because the practices of life require nothing less. And, while armed with hard-won current knowledge, diagnostic instruments and strategies of healing, we must at the same time learn to *listen* as if we have never heard before, because even that which is comfortably familiar may have different meanings and consequences in this new and continuously changing context.

25

Studying Consciousness
in the Postmodern Age

STANLEY KRIPPNER AND MICHAEL WINKLER

The emerging postmodern vision of the human personality calls for a new perspective toward consciousness—one that recognizes the enormous variety of ways that different peoples have sought to understand the workings of the mind. The approach advocated by Krippner and Winkler is not to abandon science in favor of primitive wisdom, but rather to use science to explore what it has previously ignored.

In 1992, Vaclav Havel, the playwright-turned-statesman, counseled, "We have to abandon the arrogant belief that the world is merely a puzzle to be solved, a machine with instructions for use waiting to be discovered, a body of information to be fed into a computer in the hope that, sooner or later, it will spit out a universal solution."[1] This proclamation could serve as a precept for the shift that science is making as it shifts from modernity to postmodernity. Nowhere is this mutation as apparent as in the field of consciousness studies—the disciplined inquiry into perception, cognition, emotion, and volition in all of their aspects and permutations.

In recent decades, consciousness studies have become a popular topic for the general populace as well as for social scientists, behavioral scientists, and neuroscientists. Yet consciousness remains somewhat of an enigma. Psychodynamic conceptions of how human activity is influenced by unconscious processes persist in psychiatric circles. Most psychological models of consciousness are derived from cognitive science, ranging from computer simulation of intelligence to parallel distributed memory and attentional processing. The neurosciences explain consciousness in terms of brain and central nervous system corollaries, with special attention to the neurotransmitters and their effects.

Each of these perspectives contend in the multitiered shopping center of competing models that characterizes the field of consciousness studies. These models vie for serious consideration, attempting to gain the attention of the powerful institutions that bestow research grants, foundation awards, academic appointments, and book contracts. Applied technologies of consciousness are purchased by consumers eager to reduce their stress levels, improve their sex life, cope with psychological or physical pain, patch up relationships, or obtain job promotions. These therapies, workshops, training sessions, and mechanical devices all reflect explicit or implicit models of what English speaking Westerners refer to as "consciousness," and illustrate the postmodern existence of multiple realities and worldviews.

Western science holds that what is available to perception "out there" is an orderly and systematic universe, potentially the same for everyone; thus, logical thought, rational problem-solving, and scientific investigation will ultimately secure universal agreement about its nature. The postmodern investigator realizes that human phenomena are altered when they are studied, especially if research participants are given feedback about the investigation and their role in it. Postmodern scientists understand that science is not value-free but both produces and reflects implicit or explicit values, especially when its findings become the basis for applied technology (e.g., atomic bombs, space satellites, electronic media). If modern science has a publicly stated value it is its quest for "certainty," a goal that postmodernists regard as futile because of their conviction that knowledge tends to be local rather than universal.

According to postmodernists, the most important human activities can barely be measured, much less predicted and controlled. Rather, the postmodern scientist strives to identify, describe, and understand these activities as deeply and as thoroughly as possible. "Truth" is a matter of perspective, and perspectives are a byproduct of social interchange or "discourse." One's language about the world operates as the lens that construes that world into something not simply "out there." It is an interactive process. The "observer" and the "observed" are in constant dialogue. Modernity tries to hold a mirror to nature, not realizing that language rests midway between nature and discourse. Postmodernity, to the contrary, asks the scientist to join this cultural discourse, hoping that it will yield new insights and novel interpretations. Consciousness studies are an integral part of this discourse because it frequently involves stepping out of one's milieu, culture, worldview, and thought processes in order to reflect upon them.

From a postmodern perspective, not only is the term "consciousness" socially constructed, but "conscious experience" is constructed differently in various times and places. People in each culture construct experience in terms of the categories provided by their own linguistic system, coming to terms with a "reality" that has been filtered through their language. Each culture has a specialized terminology regarding those aspects of consciousness important for its functioning and survival. Many writers have pointed out that Western culture describes inner experience primarily in psychopathological terms while traditional Eastern cultures have equally intricate vocabularies for describing altered states of consciousness and spiritual experiences. Furthermore, Western psychology equates "reality" with the world as perceived in the ordinary waking state, denying credibility to "realities" perceived in other types of awareness. Eastern perspectives, on the other hand, dismiss the physical world as an illusion and see "reality" as something that cannot be grasped in ordinary waking awareness. And, commenting on the Mexican Huichol tribe, Ptolemy Tompkins in his 1990 book, *This Tree Grows out of Hell*, remarks, "By our standards, all of Huichol life is a kind of well-organized hallucination, for the cosmos they believe and live in bears very little resemblance to the one that Western civilization wakes up to every morning."[2]

Tompkins also points out that Freud's image of the conscious ego as the external boundary of an invisible matrix of volatile psychic "energies" that feeds and informs it, resembles the shamanic model. But for the shaman, what Westerners would call "unconscious energies" were not blind but keenly intelligent, originating in the earth itself rather than in the neurons of the brain. Modern Western models of consciousness ignore the concept of the shaman's dreaming body, a body that is capable of moving into realms existing beneath the earth and in the sky.

Swami Radakrishna Radha observes that the Eastern equivalent of the Western "unconscious" is the process of "not being fully aware of one's true nature."[3] Indeed, Hindu and Buddhist texts are replete with discussions of conscious states and how to regulate them. The Tibetan Buddhist tradition contains thousands of volumes on conscious states, most of them dealing with meditative practices and experiences. The phenomenologies of these experiences are remarkably consistent across texts with a sophisticated language that beginning yogis are required to learn.

The Mayan model of consciousness was depicted by artists who showed how the world of everyday reality and the dreamworld sometimes overlapped, allowing beings from both realms to interact. In dreams and in waking visions, the Maya asked the deities to appear before them, thus remaining faithful to the shamanic tradition of visionary ecstasy that had bequeathed this vivid universe to them, a universe, so intense it could easily overwhelm them at any moment. Living in such a world has been compared by Tompkins to "living perennially in the first stages of waking consciousness that return after a particularly vivid dream, when for a moment 'dream' and 'reality' are confused."

In retrospect, students of consciousness in different eras and locations have used different terms and have focused on different aspects of the "consciousness project," but have posed similar questions: What is meant by "mind"? What techniques can be used to regulate, direct, and utilize consciousness? What are the different states, forms, and levels of consciousness? From the perspective of some postmodernists, these questions are self-referential and not worthy of serious discussion. From other postmodernist perspectives, there is no need to look for single answers to these questions, but a need to appreciate how these issues have been dealt with over the years and how various communities have used the resulting insights and technologies, e.g., meditation, dreamworking, visionary journeys. Indeed, this overview on the varieties of consciousness construction suggests that postmodernist proposals may stimulate valuable discourses on consciousness and theory, research and practice.

What would a postmodern approach to the mind/body problem look like? Perhaps one direction it would take is exemplified by the work of the anthropologist Charles Laughlin, summarized in *Scientific Explanation and the Life-world,* who proposes that the principle operating in the consciousness of most people moves toward an "effort after meaning" rather than an "effort after truth."[4] For Laughlin, the brain constantly imposes order on its experiences to enable people to lead purposive lives and pursue meaningful experiences. Ascertaining the "truth" of a belief is less important than the realization that the belief makes sense in relation to one's overall worldview. Laughlin's work focuses on the premise that consciousness and neurophysiology are two views of the same reality. This "two hands clapping" approach suggests that for every event in consciousness there is a corresponding and causally interrelated process in the organism's neurophysiology (i.e., "the other hand"). The two events jointly construct the "life-world" in each moment of consciousness. The resulting "conscious network" is a continuously changing field of intentional neural entrainments that may include any particular neural network one moment and disentrain it the next.

To Laughlin, the evidence is overwhelming that the networks comprising the cognized environment have their developmental origins in structures that are present before, at, or just after birth, the organization of which is largely determined genetically. The brain actively constructs a world of meaningful experience for itself and its structure is indelibly but flexibly engraved upon every moment of consciousness. Laughlin contends that acceptance of this position would encourage scientists to be less rigid in their claims, to observe anomalies that they have missed because of their rigidity, and to acknowledge that their vaunted theories become "truths" only if they are socially favored and culturally approved.

Postmodernists also have presented many reasons why theoreticians of consciousness can not glibly use such terms as "truth," "reality," and "self" without being challenged with such questions as "whose truth?" what reality?" "which self?" in "what time?" and in "what place?" Postmodernists can bring increased attention to the way philosophers and theoreticians of consciousness use language. Many terms will be deconstructed so completely that they will be found to be virtually useless in reasoned discourse; other terms will remain, but their usage will be marked by increased modesty and clarity.

Charles Tart has called for the development of "state-specific sciences" that are based on the perceptions, logics, and communications obtained when investigators are in altered states.[5] To some degree, forms of state-specific inquiries already exist in the form of various shamanic procedures, yogic practices, and meditative disciplines that foster the premise that "specific states" of consciousness will access alternate "realities." Tart's proposal is one of the most ambitious of the envisioned additions to research methodology, and it may demonstrate that the postmodern concept of "other realities" is a viable one. Moreover, this multiplicity of "states" and "realities" and the activities that would occur in them undermines modernism's promise of universal laws of behavior. The conjecture that there are multiple "realities" is mirrored by the emergence of a multiplicity of "human science" research methods, each with its champions, e.g., phenomenology, hermeneutics, participant/observation, psychohistory, systems inquiry.

Within the past decade a new form of systems inquiry has emerged that is beginning to demonstrate its utility in describing and understanding processes that undergo continuous change, growth, and evolution of a chaotic nature, such as weather patterns, ecological systems, and a whole array of phenomena that operate in a nonlinear fashion. Chaotic systems analysis may become an important method of inquiry in both the biological and behavioral sciences. Chaos methodology shifts emphasis from relationships of cause and effect to more interactive, multivariant approaches that stress the importance of defining patterns, form, self-organization, and adaptive qualities of complex processes. Although there exists a rampant debate among postmodernists about the usefulness of any scientific method employing mathematics, we contend that chaotic systems analysis provides a rich and elegant way of describing various psychological processes such as heartbeat rhythms and EEG brain wave patterns. If we are to entertain the notion that any disciplined scientific inquiry is yet another narrative that can provide useful information for our understanding of the world, chaotic systems analysis is an avenue that is likely to provide new and valuable ways of conceptualizing consciousness.

Postmodernists are suspicious of "metanarratives," "models," and "paradigms" because they may suppress differences in order to legitimate their own vision of reality. Postmodern psychologists recognize that even though personal accounts are largely culturally constructed, researchers can look for common themes in these "texts" both within a culture and cross-culturally. The results may provide information about the loading of local significance in these "texts" as well as what David Hufford has termed "core beliefs" ("humans have souls that leave the body," "there are threatening and frightening spirits") and the "core experiences" associated with them ("out-of-body" experiences, "demonic possession").[6] Highly unusual and vivid narrative reports emerge, in part, from these core experiences and form local folk traditions. Thus, postmodernity has helped to bring folklorists and their research methods into the field of consciousness studies.

Some postmodernists dismiss the distinction between mental states and the outside world as illusory. Kenneth Gergen asks, "Can one identify an 'inner state' not already prefigured in the public language? Can an American look inward and identify an emotion for which there is no English word?"[7] Language is a structure of reality in itself, which varies across cultures and provides distinct constructions of time/space and causality. Gergen also discusses the role of the media in constructing emotional and mental events, lamenting that "for many people film experiences provide the most emotionally wrenching experiences of the average week."

The term "postmodern" was first used in architecture and art, and just as art uses one or more types of media to portray as vividly as possible lived activity and experience, consciousness researchers use one or more investigative methods to identify, understand, and describe as accurately as possible lived activity and experience. Postmodernists also resemble artists in their use of narrative, their interest in symbol and metaphor, their attempt to incorporate intuition and feeling in their research, their attempt to close the gap between the person and the phenomenal world, and their appreciation that the persons who serve as research participants have identities that are embedded in a social-cultural context. Nor are the texts of postmodern writers and artists, in principle, governed by preestablished rules; following this exemplar, postmodern psychological researchers do not force metanarratives on their research participants' texts.

Postmodernity could contribute in several ways to creativity research. Creativity can be seen as the result of cultural and historical processes—and as a judgment that is made by observers (such as critics) that may change from one era to the next. Some postmodernists have deconstructed the terms "artists" and "authors"; others hold that the judgment of a person and his or her products (or texts) as "creative" involves mutual dialogues. Yet there are few research studies on group creativity, the cultural context of creativity, and the longevity of creativity judgments. Cultural psychologists such as Richard Shweder remind us that nothing human actually exists independent of humanity's involvement with it and interpretation of it.[8] As regards creativity and talent, Shweder suggests that a focus on gifted performers' "domain-specific knowledge" and "dedicated mastery" of a subject or process will yield a greater understanding than a study of their content-free logical or psychological test scores.

Modern psychology typically ignores what postmodernists refer to as "the other," including women and minority groups, members of other cultures and the natural environment, and what Rhea White refers to as "exceptional human experiences."[9] These experiences of "other" genders (such as gays and lesbians), lifestyles (such as cross-dressing), cultural activities (such as Native American ceremonies), and unusual "realities" (such as "leaving the body," recalling a "past life," seeing a "nature spirit") have been dismissed, ignored, ridiculed, and pathologized by modern psychologists. Nevertheless, narratives of lucid dreams, shamanic journeying, sexual "merging," firewalking, peak sports performance, and other exceptional human experiences demand attention and respect if the totality of human activity is to be appreciated.

From the standpoint of modernity, an individual observes and reflects on the world, transforming this consciousness experience into words that will express these perceptions and thoughts to others. For the postmodernist, language is a system unto itself, a social format that is shaped by a community of participants. However, the cultural agencies with power and authority not only influence how conscious events will be communicated but how they will be experienced. Again, modesty is required when researchers depend upon language to convey the experience of a life-changing vision, a dream that came true, an interpersonal adventure, an encounter with nature, a personal loss, a terminal illness, or any other exceptional human experience that is worth studying, albeit with tools that are not completely adequate.

The long-term effects of postmodern approaches to consciousness may move Western psychology from a perspective that recognizes the value of only a single "normal" state of consciousness to one that values multiple states; from one that sees human development as having a ceiling to one that

views such limitations as culturally determined; from the dismissal of exceptional human experiences as pathological or illusory to the appreciation of
their potential in illuminating neglected human capacities; from the devalu-
ing of non-Western psychologies as "primitive" or "quaint" to the honoring
of their richness and complexity; from ridiculing experiences of "union"
with the Earth and the cosmos to an awareness that this sensibility may well
be critical for the survival of the planet and its inhabitants. Postmodernity is,
itself, a story. And when other stories about consciousness emerge, let us
hope that the postmodernists will listen to them, encourage their voices to be
heard, and advocate that their tales be told.

26

Psychotherapy's Own Identity Crisis

MAUREEN O'HARA AND
WALTER TRUETT ANDERSON

Negotiating an identity—navigating through different commu-
nities, choosing among competing values and beliefs—is never easy.
Sometimes people turn for help to psychotherapists, but the "mental
health" field is not in the best of health. Although there are many
postmodern and constructivist explorers, the psychotherapy profession
as a whole is still presenting to the world a somewhat deceptive mask
of scientific certainty. In this article, a San Diego psychotherapist and
I survey the problems of therapy and of some clients of therapy. The
names have been changed, but the people are real.

Jerry feels overwhelmed, anxious, fragmented and confused. He disagrees
with people he used to agree with and aligns himself with people he used to
argue with. He questions his sense of reality and frequently asks himself what
it all means.

He has had all kinds of therapeutic and growth experiences: gestalt,
rebirthing, Jungian analysis, holotropic breathwork, bioenergentics, the
Course in Miracles, twelve-step recovery groups, Zen meditation, Ericksonian hypnosis. He has been to sweat lodges, to the Rajneesh ashram in
Poona, to the Wicca festival in Devon. He is in analysis again, this time with
a self-psychologist. Although he is endlessly on the lookout for new ideas and

experiences, he keeps saying that he wishes he could simplify his life. He talks about buying land in Oregon. He loved *Dances With Wolves*.

Jerry is like so many educated professionals who come in for psychotherapy these days. But he is not quite the typical client: He is a well-established psychotherapist. He conducts stress-reduction workshops nationwide; his current foray into self-psychology analysis is another attempt to find some conceptual coherence for his own work—and, of course, for his life.

Alec is also a client, but not a therapist. He's forty-two, single, and for most of his life has felt lonely and alienated. He's never cared much about politics, considers himself an agnostic, and has never found a hobby or interest he would want to pursue consistently. He says he doesn't think he really has a self at all. He's had two stints of psychotherapy; both ended inconclusively, leaving him still with chronic, low-grade depression.

Nowadays he's feeling a little better about himself. He has started attending a local meeting of Adult Children of Alcoholics. People at the meetings seem to understand and validate his pain; he's making friends there and believes he "belongs" for the first time since he left the military. But he confesses to his therapist that he feel "sort of squirrely" about it because he's not an adult child of an alcoholic. He is faking the pathological label in order to be accepted by the community, and he's not too sure he really buys their twelve-step ideology, either.

Then there's Beverly, who comes into therapy torn between two lifestyles and two identities. In the California city where she goes to college, she is a radical feminist; on visits to her Midwestern home town she is a nice, sweet, square, conservative girl. The therapist asks her when she feels most like herself. She says, "When I'm on the airplane."

All these people are shoppers in the great marketplace of realities that the contemporary Western world has become: here a religion, there an ideology, over there a lifestyle. They, and millions like them, browse among a vast array of possibilities and in the process change not only their beliefs but their beliefs about belief—their ideas about what truth is and where it is found. They change not only their identities (I'm a woman, I'm a Jew, I'm a Jungian, I'm a liberal, I'm a Libra) but their ideas about what identity means. Some enjoy the freedom that can be found in this, some try to escape from the freedom and some are nearly destroyed by it. Meanwhile, new products keep arriving at the marketplace. If old-time religion doesn't do the job for you, perhaps Deep Ecology will.

Prophets of modernism used to predict that, with progress, old beliefs would simply wither away. But that hasn't happened: Ancient traditions, from astrology to Zoroastrianism, are still around. Some contemporary prophets of neo-primitivism, fresh from a weekend of shamanistic drum beating, actually express their hope that the old beliefs will triumph and the modern ones will disappear. But that doesn't seem to be happening either; science and modernism are still alive and well. What does seem to be happening is that belief itself is changing. People do not so much believe as have beliefs. Look back over the brief anecdotes above—the stories of Jerry and Alec and Beverly—and you can see them moving through different belief systems, cultures, lifestyles, inhabiting them in rather tentative ways. You may disapprove of them for this, as they often disapprove of themselves, but it is hard to imagine a contemporary world in which people didn't or couldn't shop around among different realities.

Irony becomes an important survival strategy in such a world. Traditionally, irony was regarded as a mild form of sarcasm implying a disbelief in what appeared on the surface to be true. For philosophers, the supreme ironist was Socrates, the wise man who played at knowing nothing. Postmodern irony is a bit different. Today's ironists—in Richard Rorty's definition—"realize that anything can be made to look good or bad by being redescribed," and are "always aware that the terms in which they describe themselves are subject to change, always aware of the contingency and fragility of their final vocabularies, and thus of their selves."

For Beverly, the radical feminist–nice girl–airline passenger, this would mean that the rhetoric and agendas of the women at the university, the traditions of the folks at home and, for that matter, the rituals and mannerisms that go with airplane flight are all only vocabularies that work perfectly well in their contexts but do not have to be regarded as universal. Being an ironist also means—and this is the more frightening part—letting go of the idea of a True Self that is the same in all contexts.

In some ways, most of us already think that way. But in some ways we do not—or, when we think that way, we think we shouldn't be thinking that way.

Postmodernity does not mean that we have left the modern era behind. It is all around us and within us. Most of us slip back and forth like bilingual children between postmodern, constructivist modes of thought in which we regard reality as socially constructed, and modern, objectivist modes of thought in which we regard reality as something that is nonhuman yet *known* (or at least potentially knowable) with unshakable certainty through some approach to the truth—science, religion, history, psychotherapy. We cling to the hope that one or another of these approaches will explain everything for us and maybe even for everyone else as well. Both modern and postmodern, but never sure which, we also have hankerings for what we imagine were the simple joys of the premodern.

The profession of psychotherapy also stands with one foot in each world or, to stretch the metaphor, in all three. It is as pluralistic as any postmodern theorist could hope for, yet unwilling to confront the implications of its own pluralism, which is that none of its approaches can qualify as a universally acceptable body of knowledge of the human psyche. It has not only multiple realities but multiple approaches to reality—everything from science to myth. What it doesn't have is a way of making sense of this multiplicity and helping its clients make sense of it. Clients come into therapy looking for some certainty and guidelines because they are confused by the staggering variety of beliefs from which they may choose. But frequently the therapist is as confused as they are.

Most of Jerry's professional life has been spent pursuing the therapist's equivalent of the Holy Grail: a universally true psychological theory and practice in which he can find himself—his true self—mirrored. He has spent literally tens of thousands of dollars searching for an approach that he can trust unreservedly and that dependably meets the needs of his clients. Yet it seems to Jerry and to many others like him that the longer he searches for therapeutic certainty the farther away he gets from it. The plurality of choices becomes another problem, as serious as the problems that caused them to enter therapy in the first place.

Last fall a woman, a young social work student, attended the Ericksonian Institute's "Evolution of Psychotherapy" conference in Southern California, which brought together the leading proponents of most of the dominant therapeutic schools. Afterward, she said, "The Titans dazzled us with technical and theoretical brilliance, but they left the most interesting and scary issue untouched. If all these approaches are so different, and all of them are supposed to be 'true,' how can I believe in any of them?" Her question may seem a bit naive, but it is one the modern era never managed to answer. How does the profession of therapy maintain its claim to scientific legitimacy in the face of the growing recognition that all knowledge is relative?

One way is exemplified by the various guilds that serve as the profession's gatekeepers, inventing, refining and enforcing an array of procedures that give therapy the status of modern-style objective knowledge. All the licensing laws, the accreditation of training programs, the legitimizing bodies like the National Register with its standardized testing and treatment procedures (approved by medical insurance companies), the utilization of psychologists as expert witnesses in trials, the profession-wide agreement to use the categories described in the *Diagnostic and Statistical Manual of Mental Disorders*—all these serve to create the illusion of objective discourse. They delineate what is inside and what is outside the boundaries of psychological truth. They lend credibility to practitioners and to the profession itself, presumably making room for multiple approaches and fencing out the weirdos. At the same time, these gatekeepers are never able to state their criteria objectively and are continually fighting skirmishes at the boundaries of legitimacy.

This ideological disarray has been pointed out for decades by mavericks like Thomas Szasz, who recently summed up his case by calling the mental health system "a house of cards," held up by nothing more, or less, than popular as well as professional belief in the truth of its principles and the goodness of its practices. Szasz and others charge that this system, however shaky, is also a power structure representing the interests of the elites who maintain it. Similar critiques are stated by various groups including scientific skeptics and libertarians, New Age practitioners, feminists, minorities and political radicals. Many point out that several European countries, no less civilized than our own, get by without the huge legitimizing bureaucracy we seem to require; England, for example, has no licensing of psychologists.

Most seasoned psychotherapists spend their lives somewhere in the uncomfortable gap between the establishment and the mavericks, suspicious of the scientific claims of positivist biological or behavioral medicine, yet unwilling to throw all the legitimation procedures out the window and let anyone who feels like it hang out a shingle. They are likely to say, "You've got to have some standards," and to believe that the system, however flawed, protects the client against unscrupulous and/or incompetent practitioners. Therapists are particularly likely to believe this, of course, if they are viewing the system from the inside.

As one grows older it becomes easier to put postmodern (and ironic) quotation marks around the truths of therapy and definitions of mental health and sanity, and to accept them as socially constructed realities. But the therapist who attains to this level of sophistication, the closet ironist, may be reluctant to share his or her wisdom with patients, students, grant-making agencies, insurance company representatives or lawyers looking for expert witnesses.

Many therapists describe moments of absolute terror when the knowledge fails, when they are confronted with situations that they simply do not understand or know what to do about. The patient can confess, in the midst of therapy, to being utterly uncertain about anything, but the therapist (especially the young therapist who has not yet grown skeptical of what he or she was taught in school) often believes he or she has to *know* what to do.

For some, dealing with a therapeutic belief system that happens to conflict with their own simply becomes a matter of telling lies. Consider the experience of Mara, a postdoctoral intern who works in a battered women's shelter serving a largely Latino population. In a women's psychology supervision group, she admitted that she favors a supportive, compassionate mode of therapy and was routinely lying to her supervisor—a person she described as "a kick-ass existentialist who thinks support by the therapist is 'enabling' or 'co-dependent hand-holding.' " Although the supervisor was pleased with Mara's work on the basis of positive reports from clients and the agency, Mara was deeply distressed and was thinking about leaving the field even though her licensing examination was just four months away. She had her own rationale, as a feminist and a Mexican-American, for the way she worked with clients, but didn't know how to make it sound like a legitimate approach to therapy. She said, "I'm afraid that if I tell the truth about what I do I won't get my license, but if I do what they say I just can't live with myself. So I lie. But then what's the truth anyway? How do I know that I'm *not* enabling? Maybe it's all just meaningless bullshit."

Many people, both therapists and patients, encounter such dilemmas in their personal and professional lives. Some, perhaps most, avoid them as best they can, fearing that a hard look at their own uncertainty may turn into a glimpse of unimaginable psychic chaos. Some survive by fuzzying up the issues. Some survive by becoming True Believers in one system or another and arranging their lives in ways that protect them from too much exposure to other people's realities. But many are working toward another way of being.

They may not state their problems in the arcane language of postmodern intellectualism, but they often manage to be quite explicit about the problems. Some, like Alec, the counterfeit Adult Child of Alcoholics, can even explain how they come to terms with life in a world of multiple realities.

"I just try not to take the belief system, the twelve steps and all that, too seriously," he says. "Does it matter if it's not true in some absolute sense as long as it helps? Can't it be true for them and not be true for me as long as it works anyway?" Another closet ironist.

One therapy client, Nelli, has struggled desperately to create a coherent image of herself as a woman. She has been hospitalized four times after disastrous collapses of her self-image—two failed marriages, two severe crises in her professional career. She achieved a breakthrough of sorts in therapy recently when she said she had always imagined that, to be acceptable, her Self should have the balance and proportion of a Greek vase. Instead, she said with a slight smile and something approaching self-appreciation, "I'm more like a David Hockney photo-collage. If my glue doesn't hold, with creativity and a little help from my friends I can always stick myself together into some arrangement that feels right most of the time." In this she was not only saying something about who and what she is, but something about what a self is.

More often than not the ventures into postmodern thinking—Alec's way of dealing with the ACOA ideology, Nelli's way of dealing with the idea of the self—are expressed a bit apologetically. People are aware of having let go of something but not really confident of having found something with which to replace it. Neither they nor the culture nor the mental health establishment has a language for naming such small discoveries as explorations and triumphs. Such people present to their therapists, and to the profession itself, the challenge of learning how to live in a world that is not quite the same as the world in which therapy originated.

The bad news about postmodern life is the serious despair, emptiness and social disintegration that sometimes follow the disappearance of all certainties. The good news is the freedom it offers, the great wealth of opportunities to explore and create. The weakness of many of the texts of postmodern thought is that, for all their analytical brilliance, they tend to be rather abstract about the human experience involved. They are long on phrases such as Michel Foucault's advice to "prefer what is positive and multiple, differences over uniformity, flows over unities, mobile arrangements over systems," but short on practical ideas about how this is to be done. The task of therapists is to turn some of postmodernism's vague celebrations of multiplicity into lived experience.

PART FOUR

FAITH AND FREEDOM

The modern era was the age of science; it was also the age of what is sometimes called scientism—the naive acceptance of science as the source of absolute truth. Scientism—still going strong in some circles—is a kind of fundamentalism. If you set a true religious fundamentalist, say one of the "inerrantists" who believe that the Bible is the actual word of God, next to a fundamentalist of science who believes that the folks in lab jackets have all the right answers, the two will probably have plenty to argue about. But if you listen carefully you will note that, although they are literally worlds apart in terms of what they believe to be true, they are close together about how they believe it. They both see the truth as found or revealed—not made. They are what Richard Rorty would call metaphysicians. That deeper agreement is what makes them so violent in their difference.

Today the true believers on both sides are still going at it, but the ground is moving beneath their feet.

The world of science has never been as scientistic as many nonscientists thought it was, and it is becoming less so—more postmodern—all the time. The most powerful influence in science's postmodern turn was Thomas Kuhn's concept of paradigm shift, as presented in his book *The Structure of Scientific Revolutions*. It is a *constructivist* description of how science progresses. Kuhn showed that members of a scientific community periodically re-create the world to make room for new ideas and discoveries. In many ways, it shattered the scientistic image of steady, objective progress.

The term "paradigm shift" is overused these days—so much that I hesitate to use it here—and it is also misused. Kuhn used it in reference to what happens within specific scientific communities, meaning groups of people who share common knowledge and concerns. He was not talking about change within whole societies—much less within highly pluralistic ones—and it is an abuse of his ideas to use them in service of any proclamation that everybody is about to turn in one set of values and beliefs in favor of a new one. The picture is a lot more complicated than that, and this complexity is particularly evident in contemporary religious life.

It's obvious that some people are adopting new values and beliefs, but it's equally obvious that other people are holding on for dear life to the old values and beliefs that are institutionalized in traditional religions. And yet others are making themselves comfortable with the old ones (or somebody else's old ones) but doing it with a completely different style of belief. Nowadays people who say "I believe devoutly" seem to be looking over their own shoulders with the same postmodern self-consciousness that Umberto Eco talks about when he describes somebody saying "I love you madly."

There is a term commonly used by Roman Catholics that speaks volumes about what is going on today: "cafeteria Catholics." A cafeteria Catholic is someone who behaves within the faith as one might behave in one of those restaurants where the customer takes a tray, goes down along a counter, and selects the dishes that appeal to him or her at the moment—chooses what to eat and what not to eat. The conservative elders of the Church say this is no way to deal with the faith. The teachings are all of a piece and must be accepted as such—accepted and believed. But most contemporary Catholics—clergy as well as parishioners—feel free to pick and choose. They accept the general outlines of the faith and usually want to participate in the sacraments while they reject the doctrine of original sin and the prohibitions against birth control. And there are not only cafeteria Catholics, but cafeteria Protestants, cafeteria Jews, cafeteria Muslims, and cafeteria Native Americans—people of all kinds who make their own idiosyncratic decisions about what to believe, what rituals to observe.

As people's ideas about both science and religion change, so does the tension between the two. In some ways science and religion seem to be drawing father apart, in other ways they seem to be coming closer together. Listen to an argument between a Creationist and a hard-line Darwinian, and it sounds like the division is as sharp as it ever was. Listen, on the other hand, to various postmodern voices, and you will be told that the division is yet another socially constructed boundary that begins to fade in the light of contemporary thinking about cosmology, about the relationship between humanity and nature, about the frailties and greatness of individual scientists. Stephen Toulmin, for example, believes that "there is indeed room for scientists, philosophers, and theologians to sit down together and to reexamine in detail" some of the major issues of our time.[1]

This does not mean that science and religion are now sweetly merging together into a super-truth that is going to explain everything and satisfy everybody. I don't see any evidence of that happening. Rather, each of those traditions is taking on new meanings, each becoming part of a new post-modern consciousness that is able to draw on both traditions and on others as well.

27

Gifted Worldmakers

HOWARD GARDNER

All too frequently, the word "only" creeps into descriptions of how postmoderns view truth. In regard to science, for example, the great theories are "only" social constructions, "only" stories—the implication being that an act of creation is somehow inferior to an act of discovery. Howard Gardner argues that our greatest constructions, whether in science or art, are precious, extraordinary and indispensable—but never final.

"Out yonder," Albert Einstein once wrote, "is this huge world which exists independently of human beings and which stands before us like a great eternal riddle, at least partially accessible to our inspection and thinking. Nature has a character of such a well-designed puzzle."

Owing to Einstein's faith that this puzzle could be solved, we now have a much richer notion of the nature of physical reality. Yet some contemporary philosophers and scientists do not find it useful to posit a world out there waiting to be understood; they find it is pointless to speak about something the existence of which can never be proved. Others, while not doubting the existence of a world, believe in a multitude of equally acceptable ways of making sense of that world. Such critical thinkers raise disturbing questions for those who, like Einstein, believe in a world that can be explained. Yet the skeptics must themselves face a difficult issue: how can we ever know whether any theory or any work of art has greater merit than others that offer competing visions?

As Einstein saw it, all scientific thinking began with the data available to one's senses. But sense experiences were only a point of departure: one must be willing to play with the data, try out various patterns and combinations, let one's imagination wander freely. Complementing the data of experience were the concepts that previous generations of scientists had developed to describe the world. The challenge confronting every scientist was to reconcile new information from the senses with issues growing out of the conceptual frameworks handed down by others.

As a result of his own puzzling, Einstein arrived at an unexpected but tremendously powerful formulation. He was able to demonstrate that neither time nor space has an objective, independent existence. Movements, speeds, distances could only be defined relative to one another. But once these perspectives are taken into account, it was, he believed, possible to derive the fundamental laws of nature.

No sooner was the theory of relativity born, however, than some of Einstein's colleagues raised even more unsettling questions about the possibility of knowing the real world. Kurt Gödel demonstrated that certain mathematical problems that had engaged Einstein's interest could, in principle, never be solved. The Danish physicist Niels Bohr challenged a part of Einstein's theory by demonstrating that the images of both waves and particles were needed to depict the behavior of electrons. Werner Heisenberg, a German colleague, wrought the most serious damage with his indeterminacy principle, which established that one cannot at the same time determine where a particle is and how it is moving; the more accurately we observe its location, the less we are able to observe its momentum. These demonstrations, and indeed the whole area of quantum mechanics, clouded Einstein's lifelong quest for a solution to the puzzle of nature: a unified theory of physical reality.

While physicists were raising unsettling questions about the possibility of knowing the real world, prominent philosophers were also voicing increased skepticism. We can glimpse this shift in philosophical thinking by examining two approaches to visual perception. According to a naive, "real-istic" view, we see the world just as it is: it has an objective appearance and we are so designed as creatures that we can automatically "read" this world correctly. The contrasting, "constructivist" view, which has gained adher-ents over the past century, refuses to recognize an objective world apart from our own construal or interpretation. In this view, the individual, over time, constructs successive versions of the world—mental representations that are more like models or blueprints than like exact copies. In short, the naive realist believes that we know what we see; the constructivist believes that we see what we know.

Among contemporary philosophers, the individual who has applied the constructivist analysis most searchingly is Harvard philosopher Nelson Goodman. In his 1978 book, *Ways of Worldmaking,* Goodman wrote that the first philosophers accepted "the real world" as is; a subsequent genera-tion held that knowledge of the world must be sifted through certain categories inherent in our minds; and a new generation of thinkers embraces the view that our knowledge of reality is necessarily couched in one or another symbol system. From Goodman's perspective, it is misleading to speak of the world as it is, or even of a single world. It makes more sense to think of various versions of the world that individuals may entertain, var-ious characterizations of reality that might be presented in words, pic-tures, diagrams, logical propositions, or even musical compositions. Each of these symbol systems captures different kinds of information and hence presents different versions of reality. All we have, really, are such ver-sions; only through them do we gain access to what we casually term "our world."

At first blush, Goodman seems to defend a total relativism. He refuses to give any priority to a material world or to a description in terms of physics. In his view, physics—be it the variety put forth by Aristotle, Newton, or Einstein—is but one version of the world. And this version is not inherently superior to versions of the world fashioned by Homer, Shakespeare, or James Joyce. As scientific or artistic creators, we don't solve the jigsaw puzzle of reality. Rather, we build endless realities out of Lego.

But while Goodman refuses to consider one domain of knowledge inherently superior to another, or to compare a given physicist with a given poet, he does not embrace total relativism. Instead, using a homey but revealing analogy, he provides a suggestive way to think about how one version of the world might be better than another. Suppose a tailor is asked to produce a sample from a given bolt of cloth. Almost any piece cut from the bolt can be called a sample. But, Goodman points out, only a select number of those pieces would count as a *fair sample*. For example, in the illustration below, five segments of equivalent size have been cut from the same bolt. But only the one in the lower right panel can serve as a fair sample,

accurately reflecting the principal features of the entire bolt. Samples that omit the basic pattern altogether or present it at a misleading angle obviously cannot qualify as fair samples.

In Goodman's view, works of art can also be profitably viewed as samples. Just as certain fabric swatches accurately reflect the whole bolt, so may certain works of art accurately reflect, literally or metaphorically, important forms, feelings, affinities, and contrasts from the fabric of life. To put the matter perhaps too simply, versions of the world that strike us as being "fair" or "right" are those that seem to capture significant aspects of our own experience, perceptions, attitudes, and intuitions.

Goodman himself is reluctant to designate certain artists or works as inherently fairer than others. Yet his writings indicate the kinds of criteria he would employ. For example, we might apply his reasoning to explain why, of the many versions of the Last Supper painted in the Renaissance, Leonardo's famous work on the wall of a church in Milan was "the fairest of them all." Assuming that all of the artists were striving to capture the drama of the pivotal moment when Christ revealed that one of his disciples would betray him, we might examine their works in terms of the range of emotions explored, the extent to which the tensions have been captured, the care with which interpersonal dynamics are portrayed. In earlier versions, the disciples were typically aligned from left to right in a wooden manner, with practically no variation in expression. Leonardo, however, painted each with clear personality traits and definite facial expressions, talking, gesticulating, and eyeing one another—reflecting the drama of the moment.

To take a somewhat different example, consider the effect sometimes achieved by an artist whose vision is radically new. If after looking at a variety of Postimpressionist paintings, we see a Cézanne for the first time, we may begin to view the everyday world through fresh eyes. The artist may then be said to have fairly sampled the visual world—that is, to have created an experience that others ultimately recognize as an authentic version of reality. That the artist, in so doing, also *creates* reality is illustrated by a Picasso anecdote. When the artist unveiled his portrait of Gertrude Stein, an observer remarked that it did not much look like Miss Stein. "No matter," Picasso said. "It will."

Goodman would be the last to insist that standards of rightness are unchanging. Indeed, a continuing function of works of art is to alter the way we conceive of experience and hence to change our attitudes about what is important and what feels right. But that is only to say that our versions of the world also continue to change. Just as the never-innocent eye comes to see the world in ever-changing ways, so, too, do the versions that we construct further influence and change our conceptions, at least as long as we allow them to do so. While refusing to attribute a unique status to the physicist's (or the artist's) version of reality, Goodman does furnish us with ways of judging among the versions fashioned *within* each creative domain.

In a way reminiscent of Einstein, Goodman leads us to the very edge of relativism, only then to step back and to suggest certain criteria of fairness and rightness. But like Einstein, Goodman himself does not directly address a question of fundamental psychological importance: what enables certain individuals, for example a Newton or a Homer, to devise versions of the world that are powerfully appealing, that strike individuals as right, and that exert a lasting effect on the way we conceptualize reality? By combining insights from Einstein and Goodman, we may be able to "puzzle fairly" about the gift that enables a few geniuses to devise effective new versions of the world.

We have all heard about people who, very early in life, demonstrate an ability to penetrate the essence of a domain of experience; prodigies who, with remarkably little experience, can learn the rules of chess, mathematics, foreign languages, or music and can perform at an astonishingly high level. Based on exposure to a small sample of data, they produce powerful and robust generalizations about the field in which they are gifted. They seem "pretuned" to make telling discoveries.

I think Einstein had such powers in mind when he talked about the possibility of making sense of the world. He considered that he had this gift in physics, though not in mathematics. For it was in physics that he sensed what the important problems were and how to intuit "the depths of reality."

But the course of *scientific* progress suggests that no version of the world will be permanently entrenched, not even Einstein's. Every breakthrough paves the way for still further breakthroughs. Every intuition, no matter how deep, will ultimately be supplanted by other intuitions. Even though Einstein stood on the shoulders of giants and saw far, he was limited at the time of his major discoveries by his ignorance of certain experimental data and conceptual clarifications of the sort Gödel, Bohr, and Heisenberg eventually pointed out.

Such limitations affect other forms of understanding as well. Homer and Shakespeare saw far, and many aspects of their vision continue to speak to us today. And yet, in certain areas, for example, in knowledge of unconscious motivation or in the recognition of women as possessing a full range of human abilities, we find their world views deficient.

Another aspect of Einstein's thinking that can be challenged is the priority he gave to describing physical realities in the formulas of physics. As Goodman stresses, we can devise versions of the world in many symbol systems, thereby capturing many aspects of reality. It should prove possible to secure an indefinite number of equally significant versions of reality drawn from the full gamut of symbol systems.

Approaching the issue from a psychologist's perspective, it seems likely that individuals differ in the extent to which they can attain deep intuitions about these several domains of experience. Just as Einstein was especially gifted in detecting fair samples in the world of material reality, Mozart had an unrivaled flair for effective music; Rembrandt, for using pigment and light to create convincing visual versions of the world; Christ, Gandhi, and Martin Luther King, Jr., for articulating a social and political reality that made profound sense to their own generations and perhaps to generations to come. To be sure, not all powerful visions are well motivated or enduring. Alchemy and the phlogiston theory of combustion had an impact on the science of their respective epochs, but not a particularly productive one; Hitler and Stalin contrived powerful political visions that at one time seemed to speak to many people but are now seen as fundamentally flawed. Yet, if science is not simply superstition, it should prove possible over the long run to distinguish the sham and shallow versions of reality from the powerful and penetrating ones.

The gifts required to create such visions are obviously rare. They presuppose keen perceptual powers, exquisite sensory memory, an unerring ability to pick out essentials from accidents, a rigorous self-criticism, an unflagging pursuit of truth—and perhaps also the quiet faith of an Einstein. And yet, we can discover intimations of these powers in more modest forms throughout the rest of humanity; in the capacity of every schoolchild to think in terms of analogies; in the ability of adults of average intelligence to appreciate the novel perspectives of, say, a Darwin or a Picasso; in the human mind's ability to reconcile sense data with fundamental conceptual concerns. If only one in a million persons has the power to conceive a new scientific principle or a masterpiece of art, millions can at least appreciate such miracles of human creation. In that sense, Einstein's faith in the "harmony of all beings" proves well placed.

28

Scientists and Their Worldviews

THOMAS KUHN

Professor Kuhn's study of how scientific revolutions take place is one of the most important and influential philosophical works of our time, a masterful description of how truths are socially constructed within scientific communities. In his analysis, Kuhn drew on historical accounts of scientific discoveries. He also made use of psychological experiments: tests of a subject's ability to recognize an anomalous playing card such as a red six of spades and the gestalt experiments with drawings that could be "read" in two different ways—now it's a duck, now it's a rabbit. And he made it clear that his intent was not to trivialize scientific research or devalue its findings, but to place it in a human context.

Examining the record of past research from the vantage of contemporary historiography, the historian of science may be tempted to exclaim that when paradigms change, the world itself changes with them. Led by a new paradigm, scientists adopt new instruments and look in new places. Even more important, during revolutions scientists see new and different things when looking with familiar instruments in places they have looked before. It is rather as if the professional community had been suddenly transported to another planet where familiar objects are seen in a different light and are joined by unfamiliar ones as well. Of course, nothing of quite that sort does occur: there is no geographical transplantation; outside the laboratory everyday affairs usually continue as before. Nevertheless, paradigm changes do cause scientists to see the world of their research-engagement differently. In so far as their only recourse to that world is through what they see and do, we may want to say that after a revolution scientists are responding to a different world.

It is as elementary prototypes for these transformations of the scientist's world that the familiar demonstrations of a switch in visual gestalt prove so suggestive. What were ducks in the scientist's world before the revolution are rabbits afterwards. The man who first saw the exterior of the box from above later sees its interior from below. Transformations like these, though usually more gradual and almost always irreversible, are common concomitants of scientific training. Looking at a contour map, the student sees lines on paper, the cartographer a picture of a terrain. Looking at a bubble-chamber photograph, the student sees confused and broken lines, the physicist a record of familiar subnuclear events. Only after a number of such transformations of vision does the student become an inhabitant of the scientist's world, seeing what the scientist sees and responding as the scientist does. The world that the student then enters is not, however, fixed once and for all by the nature of the environment, on the one hand, and of science, on the other. Rather, it is determined jointly by the environment and the particular normal-scientific tradition that the student has been trained to pursue. Therefore, at times of revolution, when the normal-scientific tradition changes, the scientist's perception of his environment must be re-educated—in some familiar situations he must learn to see a new gestalt. After he has done so the world of his research will seem, here and there, incommensurable with the one he had inhabited before. That is another reason why schools guided by different paradigms are always slightly at cross-purposes.

In their most usual form, of course, gestalt experiments illustrate only the nature of perceptual transformations. They tell us nothing about the role of paradigms or of previously assimilated experience in the process of perception. But on that point there is a rich body of psychological literature, much of it stemming from the pioneering work of the Hanover Institute. An experimental subject who puts on goggles fitted with inverting lenses initially sees the entire world upside down. At the start his perceptual apparatus functions as it had been trained to function in the absence of the goggles, and the result is extreme disorientation, an acute personal crisis. But after the subject has begun to learn to deal with his new world, his entire visual field flips over, usually after an intervening period in which vision is simply confused. Thereafter, objects are again seen as they had been before the goggles were put on. The assimilation of a previously anomalous visual field has reacted upon and changed the field itself.[1] Literally as well as metaphorically, the man accustomed to inverting lenses has undergone a revolutionary transformation of vision.

The subjects of the anomalous playing-card experiment . . . experienced a quite similar transformation. Until taught by prolonged exposure that the universe contained anomalous cards, they saw only the types of cards for which previous experience had equipped them. Yet once experience had provided the requisite additional categories, they were able to see all anomalous cards on the first inspection long enough to permit any identification at all. Still other experiments demonstrate that the perceived size, color, and so on, of experimentally displayed objects also varies with the subject's previous training and experience.[2] Surveying the rich experimental literature from which these examples are drawn makes one suspect that something like a paradigm is prerequisite to perception itself. What a man sees depends both upon what he looks at and also upon what his previous visual-conceptual experience has taught him to see. In the absence of such training there can only be, in William James's phrase, "a bloomin' buzzin' confusion." . . .

The subject of a gestalt demonstration knows that his perception has shifted because he can make it shift back and forth repeatedly while he holds the same book or piece of paper in his hands. Aware that nothing in his environment has changed, he directs his attention increasingly not to the figure (duck or rabbit) but to the lines on the paper he is looking at. Ultimately he may even learn to see those lines without seeing either of the figures, and he may then say (what he could not legitimately have said earlier) that it is these lines that he really sees but that he sees them alternately *as* a duck and *as* a rabbit. By the same token, the subject of the anomalous card experiment knows (or, more accurately, can be persuaded) that his perception must have shifted because an external authority, the experimenter, assures him that regardless of what he *saw,* he was *looking at* a black five of hearts all the time. In both these cases, as in all similar psychological experiments, the effectiveness of the demonstration depends upon its being analyzable in this way. Unless there were an external standard with respect to which a switch of vision could be demonstrated, no conclusion about alternate perceptual possibilities could be drawn.

With scientific observation, however, the situation is exactly reversed. The scientist can have no recourse above or beyond what he sees with his eyes and instruments. If there were some higher authority by recourse to which his vision might be shown to have shifted, then that authority would itself become the source of his data, and the behavior of his vision would become a source of problems (as that of the experimental subject is for the psychologist). The same sorts of problems would arise if the scientist could switch back and forth like the subject of the gestalt experiments. The period during which light was "sometimes a wave and sometimes a particle" was a period of crisis—a period when something was wrong—and it ended only with the development of wave mechanics and the realization that light was a self-consistent entity different from both waves and particles. In the sciences, therefore, if perceptual switches accompany paradigm changes, we may not expect scientists to attest to these changes directly. Looking at the moon, the convert to Copernicanism does not say, "I used to see a planet, but now I see a satellite." That locution would imply a sense in which the Ptolemaic system had once been correct. Instead, a convert to the new astronomy says, "I once took the moon to be (or saw the moon as) a planet, but I was mistaken." That sort of statement does recur in the aftermath of scientific revolutions. If it ordinarily disguises a shift of scientific vision or some other mental transformation with the same effect, we may not expect direct testimony about that shift. Rather we must look for indirect and behavioral evidence that the scientist with a new paradigm sees differently from the way he had seen before.

Let us then return to the data and ask what sorts of transformations in the scientist's world the historian who believes in such changes can discover. Sir William Herschel's discovery of Uranus provides a first example and one that closely parallels the anomalous card experiment. On at least seventeen different occasions between 1690 and 1781, a number of astronomers, including several of Europe's most eminent observers, had seen a star in positions that we now suppose must have been occupied at the time by Uranus. One of the best observers in this group had actually seen the star on four successive nights in 1769 without noting the motion that could have suggested another identification. Herschel, when he first observed the same object twelve years later, did so with a much improved telescope of his own manufacture. As a result, he was able to notice an apparent disk-size that was at least unusual for stars. Something was awry, and he therefore postponed identification pending further scrutiny. That scrutiny disclosed Uranus' motion among the stars, and Herschel therefore announced that he had seen a new comet! Only several months later, after fruitless attempts to fit the observed motion to a cometary orbit, did Lexell suggest that the orbit was probably planetary.[3] When that suggestion was accepted, there were several fewer stars and one more planet in the world of the professional astronomer. A celestial body that had been observed off and on for almost a century was seen differently after 1781 because, like an anomalous playing card, it could no longer be fitted to the perceptual categories (star or comet) provided by the paradigm that had previously prevailed.

The shift of vision that enabled astronomers to see Uranus, the planet, does not, however, seem to have affected only the perception of that previously observed object. Its consequences were more far-reaching. Probably, though the evidence is equivocal, the minor paradigm change forced by Herschel helped to prepare astronomers for the rapid discovery, after 1801, of the numerous minor planets or asteroids. Because of their small size, these did not display the anomalous magnification that had alerted Herschel. Nevertheless, astronomers prepared to find additional planets were able, with standard instruments, to identify twenty of them in the first fifty years of the nineteenth century.[4] The history of astronomy provides many other examples of paradigm-induced changes in scientific perception, some of them even less equivocal. Can it conceivably be an accident, for example, that Western astronomers first saw change in the previously immutable heavens during the half-century after Copernicus' new paradigm was first proposed? The Chinese, whose cosmological beliefs did not preclude celestial change, had recorded the appearance of many new stars in the heavens at a much earlier date. Also, even without the aid of a telescope, the Chinese had systematically recorded the appearance of sunspots centuries before these were seen by Galileo and his contemporaries.[5] Nor were sunspots and a new star the only examples of celestial change to emerge in the heavens of Western astronomy immediately after Copernicus. Using traditional instruments, some as simple as a piece of thread, late sixteenth-century astronomers repeatedly discovered that comets wandered at will through the space previously reserved for immutable planets and stars.[6] The very ease and rapidity with which astronomers saw new things when looking at old objects with old instruments may make us wish to say that, after Copernicus, astronomers lived in a different world. In any case, their research responded as though that were the case.

The preceding examples are selected from astronomy because reports of celestial observation are frequently delivered in a vocabulary consisting of relatively pure observation terms. Only in such reports can we hope to find anything like a full parallelism between the observations of scientists and those of the psychologist's experimental subjects. But we need not insist on so full a parallelism, and we have much to gain by relaxing our standard. If we can be content with the everyday use of the verb "to see," we may quickly recognize that we have already encountered many other examples of the shifts in scientific perception that accompany paradigm change. The extended use of "perception" and of "seeing" will shortly require explicit defense, but let me first illustrate its application in practice. . . .

During the seventeenth century, when their research was guided by one or another effluvium theory, electricians repeatedly saw chaff particles rebound from, or fall off, the electrified bodies that had attracted them. At least that is what seventeenth-century observers said they saw, and we have no more reason to doubt their reports of perception than our own. Placed before the same apparatus, a modern observer would see electrostatic repulsion (rather than mechanical or gravitational rebounding), but historically, with one universally ignored exception, electrostatic repulsion was not seen as such until Hauksbee's large-scale apparatus had greatly magnified its effects. Repulsion after contact electrification was, however, only one of many new repulsive effects that Hauksbee saw. Through his researches, rather as in a gestalt switch, repulsion suddenly became *the* fundamental manifestation of electrification, and it was then attraction that needed to be explained.[7] The electrical phenomena visible in the early eighteenth century were both subtler and more varied than those seen by observers in the seventeenth century. Or again, after the assimilation of Franklin's paradigm, the electrician looking at a Leyden jar saw something different from what he had seen before. The device had become a condenser, for which neither the jar shape nor glass was required. Instead, the two conducting coatings—one of which had been no part of the original device—emerged to prominence. As both written discussions and pictorial representations gradually attest, two metal plates with a non-conductor between them had become the prototype for the class.[8] Simultaneously, other inductive effects received new descriptions, and still others were noted for the first time.

Shifts of this sort are not restricted to astronomy and electricity. We have already remarked some of the similar transformations of vision that can be drawn from the history of chemistry. Lavoisier, we said, saw oxygen where Priestley had seen dephlogisticated air and where others had seen nothing at all. In learning to see oxygen, however, Lavoisier also had to change his view of many other more familiar substances. He had, for example, to see a compound ore where Priestley and his contemporaries had seen an elementary earth, and there were other such changes besides. At the very least, as a result of discovering oxygen, Lavoisier saw nature differently. And in the absence of some recourse to that hypothetical fixed nature that he "saw differently," the principle of economy will urge us to say that after discovering oxygen Lavoisier worked in a different world.

I shall inquire in a moment about the possibility of avoiding this strange locution, but first we require an additional example of its use, this one deriving from one of the best known parts of the work of Galileo. Since remote antiquity most people have seen one or another heavy body swinging back and forth on a string or chain until it finally comes to rest. To the Aristotelians, who believed that a heavy body is moved by its own nature from a higher position to a state of natural rest at a lower one, the swinging body was simply falling with difficulty. Constrained by the chain, it could achieve rest at its low point only after a tortuous motion and a considerable time. Galileo, on the other hand, looking at the swinging body, saw a pendulum, a body that almost succeeded in repeating the same motion over and over again ad infinitum. And having seen that much, Galileo observed other properties of the pendulum as well and constructed many of the most significant and original parts of his new dynamics around them. From the properties of the pendulum, for example, Galileo derived his only full and sound arguments for the independence of weight and rate of fall, as well as for the relationship between vertical height and terminal velocity of motions down inclined planes.[9] All these natural phenomena he saw differently from the way they had been seen before.

Why did that shift of vision occur? Through Galileo's individual genius, of course. But note that genius does not here manifest itself in more accurate or objective observation of the swinging body. Descriptively, the Aristotelian perception is just as accurate. When Galileo reported that the pendulum's period was independent of amplitude for amplitudes as great as 90°, his view of the pendulum led him to see far more regularity than we can now discover there.[10] Rather, what seems to have been involved was the exploitation by genius of perceptual possibilities made available by a medieval paradigm shift. Galileo was not raised completely as an Aristotelian. On the contrary, he was trained to analyze motions in terms of the impetus theory, a late medieval paradigm which held that the continuing motion of a heavy body is due to an internal power implanted in it by the projector that initiated its motion. Jean Buridan and Nicole Oresme, the fourteenth-century scholastics who brought the impetus theory to its most perfect formulations, are the first men known to have seen in oscillatory motions any part of what Galileo saw there. Buridan describes the motion of a vibrating string as one in which impetus is first implanted when the string is struck; the impetus is next consumed in displacing the string against the resistance of its tension; tension then carries the string back, implanting increasing impetus until the mid-point of motion is reached; after that the impetus displaces the string in the opposite direction, again against the string's tension, and so on in a symmetric process that may continue indefinitely. Later in the century Oresme sketched a similar analysis of the swinging stone in what now appears as the first discussion of a pendulum.[11] His view is clearly very close to the one with which Galileo first approached the pendulum. At least in Oresme's case, and almost certainly in Galileo's as well, it was a view made possible by the transition from the original Aristotelian to the scholastic impetus paradigm for motion. Until that scholastic paradigm was invented, there were no pendulums, but only swinging stones, for the scientist to see. Pendulums were brought into existence by something very like a paradigm-induced gestalt switch.

Do we, however, really need to describe what separates Galileo from Aristotle, or Lavoisier from Priestley, as a transformation of vision? Did these men really *see* different things when *looking at* the same sorts of objects? Is there any legitimate sense in which we can say that they pursued their research in different worlds? Those questions can no longer be postponed, for there is obviously another and far more usual way to describe all of the historical examples outlined above. Many readers will surely want to say that what changes with a paradigm is only the scientist's interpretation of observations that themselves are fixed once and for all by the nature of the environment and of the perceptual apparatus. On this view, Priestley and Lavoisier both saw oxygen, but they interpreted their observations differently; Aristotle and Galileo both saw pendulums, but they differed in their interpretations of what they both had seen.

Let me say at once that this very usual view of what occurs when scientists change their minds about fundamental matters can be neither all wrong nor a mere mistake. Rather it is an essential part of a philosophical paradigm initiated by Descartes and developed at the same time as Newtonian dynamics. That paradigm has served both science and philosophy well. Its exploitation, like that of dynamics itself, has been fruitful of a fundamental understanding that perhaps could not have been achieved in another way. But as the example of Newtonian dynamics also indicates, even the most striking past success provides no guarantee that crisis can be indefinitely postponed. Today research in parts of philosophy, psychology, linguistics, and even art history, all converge to suggest that the traditional paradigm is somehow askew. That failure to fit is also made increasingly apparent by the historical study of science to which most of our attention is necessarily directed here.

None of these crisis-promoting subjects has yet produced a viable alternate to the traditional epistemological paradigm, but they do begin to suggest what some of that paradigm's characteristics will be. I am, for example, acutely aware of the difficulties created by saying that when Aristotle and Galileo looked at swinging stones, the first saw constrained fall, the second a pendulum. The same difficulties are presented in an even more fundamental form by the opening sentences of this section: though the world does not change with a change of paradigm, the scientist afterward works in a different world. Nevertheless, I am convinced that we must learn to make sense of statements that at least resemble these. What occurs during a scientific revolution is not fully reducible to a reinterpretation of individual and stable data. In the first place, the data are not unequivocally stable. A pendulum is not a falling stone, nor is oxygen dephlogisticated air. Consequently, the data that scientists collect from these diverse objects are, as we shall shortly see, themselves different. More important, the process by which either the individual or the community makes the transition from constrained fall to the pendulum or from dephlogisticated air to oxygen is not one that resembles interpretation. How could it do so in the absence of fixed data for the scientist to interpret? Rather than being an interpreter, the scientist who embraces a new paradigm is like the man wearing inverting lenses. Confronting the same constellation of objects as before and knowing that he does so, he nevertheless finds them transformed through and through in many of their details.

None of these remarks is intended to indicate that scientists do not characteristically interpret observations and data. On the contrary, Galileo interpreted observations on the pendulum, Aristotle observations on falling stones, Musschenbroek observations on a charge-filled bottle, and Franklin observations on a condenser. But each of these interpretations presupposed a paradigm. They were parts of normal science, an enterprise that, as we have already seen, aims to refine, extend, and articulate a paradigm that is already in existence. Section III provided many examples in which interpretation played a central role. Those examples typify the overwhelming majority of research. In each of them the scientist, by virtue of an accepted paradigm, knew what a datum was, what instruments might be used to retrieve it, and what concepts were relevant to its interpretation. Given a paradigm, interpretation of data is central to the enterprise that explores it.

But that interpretive enterprise—and this was the burden of the paragraph before last—can only articulate a paradigm, not correct it. Paradigms are not corrigible by normal science at all. Instead, as we have already seen, normal science ultimately leads only to the recognition of anomalies and to crises. And these are terminated, not by deliberation and interpretation, but by a relatively sudden and unstructured event like the gesalt switch. Scientists then often speak of the "scales falling from the eyes" or of the "lightning flash" that "inundates" a previously obscure puzzle, enabling its components to be seen in a new way that for the first time permits its solution. On other occasions the relevant illumination comes in sleep.[12] No ordinary sense of the term "interpretation" fits these flashes of intuition through which a new paradigm is born. Though such intuitions depend upon the experience, both anomalous and congruent, gained with the old paradigm, they are not logically or piecemeal linked to particular items of that experience as an interpretation would be. Instead, they gather up large portions of that experience and transform them to the rather different bundle of experience that will thereafter be linked piecemeal to the new paradigm but not to the old.

29

Anything Goes

PAUL FEYERABEND

Feyerabend claimed that his career as a writer on the philosophy of science began when his friend Imre Lakatos cornered him at a party and said: "Paul, you have such strange ideas. Why don't you write them down?" Acting on that suggestion, Feyerabend proceeded to write a series of books and papers expressing his provocative—and radically pluralistic—vision of how science should proceed. In the following ironically serious essay he proposes a single master-law to govern science—anything goes—and proceeds to make a case for "counterrules" and "counterinductive" reasoning. Plain old inductive reasoning means drawing conclusions that fit the facts. Feyerabend's alternative would be to draw an occasional conclusion, just for the hell of it, that doesn't fit the facts.

The idea of a fixed method, or of a fixed theory of rationality, rests on too naive a view of man and his social surroundings. To those who look at the rich material provided by history, and who are not intent on impoverishing it in order to please their lower instincts, their craving for intellectual security in the form of clarity, precision, "objectivity," "truth," it will become clear that there is only *one* principle that can be defended under *all* circumstances and in *all* stages of human development. It is the principle: *anything goes.*

This abstract principle must now be examined and explained in concrete detail. Examining the principle in concrete detail means tracing the consequences of "counterrules" which oppose familiar rules of the scientific enterprise. To see how this works, let us consider the rule that it is "experience," or the "facts," or "experimental results" which measure the success of our theories, that agreement between a theory and the "data" favours the theory (or leaves the situation unchanged) while disagreement endangers it, and perhaps even forces us to eliminate it. This rule is an important part of all theories of confirmation and corroboration. It is the essence of empiricism. The "counterrule" corresponding to it advises us to introduce and elaborate hypotheses which are inconsistent with well-established theories and/or well-established facts. It advises us to proceed *counterinductively.*

The counterinductive procedure gives rise to the following questions: Is counterinduction more reasonable than induction? Are there circumstances favouring its use? What are the arguments for it? What are the arguments against it? Is perhaps induction always preferable to counterinduction? And so on.

These questions will be answered in two steps. I shall first examine the counterrule that urges us to develop hypotheses inconsistent with accepted and highly confirmed *theories.* Later on I shall examine the counterrule that urges us to develop hypotheses inconsistent with well-established *facts.* The results may be summarized as follows.

In the first case it emerges that the evidence that might refute a theory can often be unearthed only with the help of an incompatible alternative: the advice (which goes back to Newton and which is still very popular today) to use alternatives only when refutations have already discredited the orthodox theory puts the cart before the horse. Also, some of the most important formal properties of a theory are found by contrast, and not by analysis. A scientist who wishes to maximize the empirical content of the views he holds and who wants to understand them as clearly as he possibly can must therefore introduce other views; that is, he must adopt a *pluralistic methodology.* He must compare ideas with other ideas rather than with "experience" and he must try to improve rather than discard the views that have failed in the competition. Proceeding in this way he will retain the theories of man and cosmos that are found in Genesis, or in the Pimander, he will elaborate them and use them to measure the success of evolution and other "modern" views. He may then discover that the theory of evolution is not as good as is generally assumed and that it must be supplemented, or entirely replaced, by an improved version of Genesis. Knowledge so conceived is not a series of self-consistent theories that converges towards an ideal view; it is not a gradual approach to the truth. It is rather an ever increasing *ocean of mutually incompatible (and perhaps even incommensurable) alternatives,* each single theory, each fairy tale, each myth that is part of the collection forcing the others into greater articulation and all of them contributing, via this process of competition, to the development of our consciousness. Nothing is ever settled, no view can ever be omitted from a comprehensive account. Plutarch, or Diogenes Laertius and not Dirac, or von Neumann are the models for presenting a knowledge of this kind in which the *history* of a science becomes an inseparable part of the science itself—it is essential for its further *development* as well as for giving *content* to the theories it contains at any particular moment. Experts and laymen, professionals and dilettanti, truthfreaks and liars—they all are invited to participate in the contest and to make their contribution to the enrichment of our culture. The task of the scientist, however, is no longer "to search for the truth," or "to praise god," or "to systematize observations," or "to improve predictions." These are but side effects of an activity to which his attention is now mainly directed and which is *"to make the weaker case the stronger"* as the sophists said, *and thereby to sustain the motion of the whole.*

The second "counterrule" which favours hypotheses inconsistent with *observations, facts and experimental results,* needs no special defence, for there is not a single interesting theory that agrees with all the known facts in its domain. The question is, therefore, not whether counterinductive theories should be *admitted* into science; the question is, rather, whether the *existing* discrepancies between theory and fact should be increased, or diminished, or what else should be done with them.

To answer this question it suffices to remember that observational reports, experimental results, "factual" statements, either *contain* theoretical assumptions or *assert* them by the manner in which they are used. Thus our habit of saying "the table is brown" when we view it under normal circumstances, with our senses in good order, but "the table seems to be brown" when either the lighting conditions are poor or when we feel unsure in our capacity of observation expresses the belief that there are familiar circumstances when our senses are capable of seeing the world "as it really is" and other, equally familiar circumstances, when they are deceived. It expresses the belief that some of our sensory impressions are veridical while others are not. We also take it for granted that the material medium between the object and us exerts no distorting influence, and that the physical entity that establishes the contact—light—carries a true picture. All these are abstract, and highly doubtful, assumptions which shape our view of the world without being accessible to a direct criticism. Usually, we are not even aware of them and we recognize their effects only when we encounter an entirely different cosmology: prejudices are found by contrast, not by analysis. The material which the *scientist* has at his disposal, his most sublime theories and his most sophisticated techniques included, is structured in exactly the same way. It again contains principles which are not known and which, if known, would be extremely hard to test. (As a result, a theory may clash with the evidence not because it is not correct, but because the evidence is contaminated.)

Now—how can we possibly examine something we are using all the time? How can we analyse the terms in which we habitually express our most simple and straightforward observations, and reveal their presuppositions? How can we discover the kind of world we presuppose when proceeding as we do?

The answer is clear: we cannot discover it from the *inside*. We need an *external* standard of criticism, we need a set of alternative assumptions or, as these assumptions will be quite general, constituting, as it were, an entire alternative world, *we need a dream-world in order to discover the features of the real world we think we inhabit* (and which may actually be just another dream-world). The first step in our criticism of familiar concepts and procedures, the first step in our criticism of "facts," must therefore be an attempt to break the circle. We must invent a new conceptual system that suspends, or clashes with the most carefully established observational results, confounds the most plausible theoretical principles, and introduces perceptions that cannot form part of the existing perceptual world. This step is again counterinductive. Counterinduction is, therefore, always reasonable and it has always a chance of success.

One might get the impression that I recommend a new methodology which replaces induction by counterinduction and uses a multiplicity of theories, metaphysical views, fairy-tales instead of the customary pair theory/observation. This impression would certainly be mistaken. My intention is not to replace one set of general rules by another such set: my intention is, rather, to convince the reader that *all methodologies, even the most obvious ones, have their limits.* The best way to show this is to demonstrate the limits and even the irrationality of some rules which she, or he, is likely to regard as basic. In the case of induction (including induction by falsification) this means demonstrating how well the counterinductive procedure can be supported by argument. Always remember that the demonstrations and the rhetorics used do not express any "deep convictions" of mine. They merely show how easy it is to lead people by the nose in a rational way.

30

Postmodernism and the World's Religions

HUSTON SMITH

Huston Smith, one of the leading philosopher-theologians of our time, is a friend of mine but not a friend of postmodernism. His critique mounts a strong case against some postmodern attitudes—particularly the tendency to regard worldviews as culturally based, politically dangerous, limited and always subject to revision. Smith says that worldviews—meaning "inclusive posits concerning the ultimate nature of things"—are necessary to human life, and that good ones exist. It is a challenge to postmodernism, and yet I think that the conclusion he comes to is, in a sense, postmodern in its willingness to contemplate a future with what he calls a "minimally articulated narrative of faith"—a minimally dogmatic statement of what the specific contents of anybody's worldview need to be.

In the wake of its Traditional and Modern periods, the Western world is now generally regarded as having become Postmodern. And as the entire world is still (at this stage) westernizing, I propose to think about religion's relation to postmodernism. Dr. Akbar S. Ahmed of the University of Cambridge has written a book titled *Postmodernism and Islam*,[1] but my statement differs from his in two respects. I shall not limit my remarks to postmodernism's relationship to Islam, and I shall give "postmodern" a different twist from the one he gives it. Because Dr. Ahmed approaches the subject sociologically, his book is really about postmodern*ity* as a life-style. Postmodern*ism*, by contrast, suggests an outlook: the basic sense of things that gave rise to postmodernity in the first place and now reflects its way of life.

Contrasts tend to throw things into relief, so I shall define postmodernism by contrasting it with the traditional and modern outlooks that preceded it, using epistemology as my point of entry.

Even today, when *traditional* peoples want to know where they are—when they wonder about the ultimate context in which their lives are set and which has the final say over them—they turn to their sacred texts; or in the case of oral, tribal peoples (what comes to the same thing), to the sacred myths that have been handed down to them by their ancestors. *Modernity* was born when a new source of knowledge was discovered, the scientific method. Because its controlled experiments enabled scientists to prove their hypotheses, and because those proven hypotheses had the power to change the material world dramatically, Westerners turned from revelation to science for the Big Picture. Intellectual historians tell us that by the nineteenth century Westerners were already more certain that atoms exist than they were confident of any of the distinctive things the Bible speaks of.

This much is straightforward, but it doesn't explain why Westerners aren't still modern rather than postmodern, for science continues to be the main support of the Western mind. By headcount, most Westerners probably *are* still modern, but I am thinking of frontier thinkers who chart the course that others follow. These thinkers have ceased to be modern because they have seen through the so-called scientific worldview, recognizing it to be not scien*tific* but scien*tistic*. They continue to honor science for what it tells us about nature, but as that is not all that exists, science cannot provide us with a worldview—not a valid one. The most it can show us is half of the world, the half where normative and intrinsic values, existential and ultimate meanings, teleologies, qualities, immaterial realities, and beings that are superior to us do not appear.

Where, then, do we now turn for an inclusive worldview? Postmodernism hasn't a clue. And this is its deepest definition. In placing postmodernism's "rejection of the view of the world as a universal totality" first in cataloguing its traits, Dr. Ahmed follows the now generally accepted definition of postmodernism that Jean-François Lyotard fixed in place a decade ago, in *The Postmodern Condition:* "incredulity toward metanarratives."[2] Having deserted revelation for science, the West has now abandoned the scientific worldview as well, leaving it without replacement. In this it mirrors the current stage of Western science which leaves *nature* unimaged.

An analogy can pull all this together. If we think of traditional peoples as looking out upon the world through the window of revelation (their received myths and sacred texts), the window that they turned to look through in the modern period (science) turned out to be stunted. It cuts off at the level of the human nose, which (metaphysically speaking) means that when we look through it our gaze slants downward and we see only things that are inferior to us. As for the postmodern window, it is boarded over and allows no inclusive view whatsoever. The current issue of *The University of Chicago Magazine* features on its cover a photograph of Richard Rorty announcing that "There is no Big Picture."

This conclusion admits of three versions that grow increasingly shrill. *Minimal,* descriptive postmodernism rests its case with the fact that today no accepted worldview exists. *Mainline,* doctrinal postmodernism goes on from there to argue for the permanence of this condition. Never again will we have a worldview of which we can be confident—we know too well how little the human mind can know. Members of this camp disagree as to whether reality *has* a deep structure to be known, but they agree that *if* it has, the human mind is incapable of knowing it. *Hardcore,* polemical postmodernism goes a step further by adding, "Good riddance." Worldviews oppress. They totalize, and in doing so marginalize minorities.

These three postmodern stances set the agenda for the rest of my paper, for I want to argue that the world's religions question the last two, and qualify importantly the first. Negatively, they deny that inclusive views necessarily and preponderantly oppress. Positively, they affirm that the human mind is made for such views, and that reliable ones already exist. Before I enter upon these constructive points, however, I want to take a quick look at recent French philosophy. For though it was mostly the unbridled historicism of German philosophers—Hegel, Nietzsche, and Heidegger—that paved the way for postmodernism, as our century closes, it is the French who have taken the lead. Jacques Derrida is the obvious candidate for being postmodernism's most redoubtable spokesman. His deconstruction is said already to be a mummy in Europe, but in America no one has been able to topple it from its pedestal where it presides, more or less, over the postmodern scene.

THE FRENCH CONNECTION

Derrida and Deconstruction

Dr. Ahmed rounded off his characterization of postmodernity by noting that it is "not given to plain and simple language," and deconstructionist prose reads like a caricature of that point. Derrida calls "stupid" the view that deconstruction "amounts to saying that there is nothing beyond language," but whose fault is this? He ensconces "*il n'y a pas de hors-texte*" (there is nothing outside the text) as the veritable motto of his movement.[3] Even sympathetic interpreters have trouble explaining that motto. John Caputo, for example, assures us that Derrida does not "trap us inside the 'chain of signifiers,' in linguistic-subjective idealism, unable to do anything but play vainly with linguistic strings"; but a page or two later he tells us that "there are no things themselves outside textual and contextual limits, no naked contact with being which somehow shakes loose of the coded system which makes notions like the 'things in themselves' possible to begin with and which enables speakers to refer to them." Small wonder satirists have a field day.

Derrida insists that contrary to its public image, deconstruction is an affirmative project,[4] for its essence consists of its "openness to the other."[5] John Caputo (whom I rely on as a helpful interpreter of Derrida) glosses that definition as follows:

> Derrida's thought is through and through a philosophy of "alterity," . . . a relentless attentiveness and sensitivity to the "other." [It] stands for a kind of hypersensitivity to many "others"; the other person, other species, "man's" other, the other of the West, of Europe, of Being, of the "classic," of philosophy, of reason, etc. (The list goes on.)[6]

This understanding of deconstruction helps to situate it in the context of postmodernism, for if postmodernism is "incredulity toward meta-narratives," Derrida's "openness to the other" fuels that incredulity. For metanarratives brook no alternatives, so that to side finally with "others" is to renounce worldviews.

Let's look, then, at "sensitivity to others" as deconstruction's hallmark. Advancing it as such makes the position attractive, immensely so, for if God is included among the "others," deconstruction (in this reading) sounds a lot like religion, for surely religion's object is to deliver us from narcissistic self-centeredness into the otherness of God and, through God, to other people. But does deconstruction help with that project? Its theological enthusiasts see in it "a rich and vigorous catalyst for religious thought [for being] an open ended call to let something new come; . . . an approach that lets faith function with an enhanced sense of advent, gladdened by the good news of alterity by which we are summoned."[7] But this sounds like using the Christian notion of Advent to bless modern enthusiasms for quantity, the thrill of novelty, and the prospect of progress—the more new arrivals the better. What if the newly welcomed guest turns out to be the Devil in disguise? Should Skinhead Nazis and the Ku Klux Klan be given the same hearing as widows and orphans? Our hearts invariably go out to the "others" that deconstructionists name, but do deconstructionist "skills" include ones for winnowing hard cases? A countless number of possible contrasts to or negations of the present situation exist.

I fear that in giving the space that I have to Derrida my wish to come to grips with at least one instance of postmodernism may have drawn me too far into his circle, for hand-to-hand combat seems not to avail against these philosophers. Dirks don't reach them; their minds are too agile. So before proceeding to the religious alternative to postmodernism, I shall step back a few paces, reach for a javelin, and aim it at the premises that postmodernism works from. For in Yogi Berra's aphorism, postmodern philosophers make the wrong mistake. Misjudging what our times require, they provide brilliant answers to the wrong question. To wit:

Already at the opening of this century Yeats was warning that things were falling apart, that the center didn't hold. Gertrude Stein followed him by pointing out that "in the twentieth century nothing is in agreement with anything else," and Ezra Pound saw man as "hurling himself at indomitable chaos." It is not surprising, therefore, that when in her last interview Rebecca West was asked to name the dominant mood of our time, she replied, "A desperate search for a pattern." The search is desperate because it seems pointless to look for a pattern when reality has become, in Roland Barth's vivid image, kaleidoscopic. With every tick of the clock the pieces of experience come down in new array.

This is what we are up against, *this* is what postmodernity is, and (ignoring E. M. Forster's credo, "Only connect") postmoderns think that more disconnections, more dismantlings and differences (and the increased fragmentation, distractions, and dispersions these produce) is what we need. If we could replay at fast speed a videotape of our century's social and conceptual earthquakes, we would see the deconstructionists scurrying around like madmen trying to spot places where a little more demolition and destabilization might prove useful.

In turning now to postmodernism's religious alternative, I shall continue to speak of it in the singular and simply assume what I argued in *Forgotten Truth;* namely, that a common metaphysical "spine" underlies the differences in the theologies that the world's great religions present.[8] Tackling in reverse order the three modes of postmodernism that I delineated earlier, I shall report as straightforwardly as I can the religious claim that people need worldviews, that reliable ones are possible, and that they already exist.

RELIGION'S RESPONSE TO POSTMODERNISM
1. Worldviews Are Needed

As religions *are* worldviews or metanarratives—inclusive posits concerning the ultimate nature of things—its custodians cannot accept polemical postmodernism's contention that on balance they oppress. George Will has observed that "the magic word of modernity is "society' "; and the present case bears him out, for it is almost entirely for their social repercussions that postmoderns fault worldviews. In applying that measuring rod, they simply assume (they do not argue) that religion does more harm than good. That this runs counter to social science functionalism, which holds that institutions don't survive unless they serve social needs, is conveniently overlooked, but the deeper point is that the vertical dimension—the way religion feeds the human soul in its inwardness and solitude—gets little attention.

When the personal and private dimension of life (which intersects the vertical) *is* validated, it is not difficult to see the function that worldviews serve. Minds require echoniches as much as organisms do, and the mind's echoniche is its worldview, its sense of the whole of things, however much or little that sense is articulated. Short of madness, there is *some* fit between the two, and we constantly try to improve the fit. Signs of a poor fit are the sense of meaninglessness, alienation, and in acute cases anxiety, which postmodernity knows so well. The proof of a good fit is that life and the world make sense. When the fit feels perfect, the energies of the cosmos pour into the believer and empower him to a startling degree. He knows that he belongs, and this produces an inner wholeness that is strong for being consonant with the wholeness of the All. The very notion of an All is a red flag to deconstructionists for seeming to disallow alterity; and in a sense it does disallow it, for, being whole, God cannot be exclusive. But as God's inclusiveness is unique in including all the "otherness" there is—God's infinity is all-possibility—alterity is allowed as much room as it can logically have.

One would think that postmodern theologians, at least, would honor this sense of ultimate belonging that religion bestows. Heirs, though, to modernity, they too have adopted "society" as their point of reference, allowing social considerations to upstage ontological ones. Both absolutism and relativism have bright and shadow sides. The virtue of the Absolute is the power it offers the soul; its danger is the fanaticism into which the power can narrow. In the case of relativism, *its* virtue is tolearance, and nihilism is its danger. Where social considerations predominate it is the dark side of absolutism (fanaticism) and the bright side of relativism (tolerance) that are noticed, these being their social components. In both cases, the vertical dimensions—which would reverse our estimates of the two—are underplayed if not ignored.

II. Worldviews Are Possible

In proceeding from the need for worldviews to their possibility, I have in mind of course the possibility of *valid* worldviews, not castles in the air. The religious claim that the human mind has access to such views challenges *mainline* postmodernism in the way its preceding claim—that worldviews are needed—challenged postmodernism's polemical stance.

Mainline postmodernism takes its stand on human finitude, arguing that as finite minds are no match for the infinite, there can be no fit between the two. What gets overlooked in this disjunction is the subtlety that finitude admits of: its degrees, modes, and paradoxes. With its *fana, anatta,* and *maya,* religion ultimately denies that finitude, as such, exists. Postmodernism cannot comprehend that, any more than it can comprehend the other side of the paradox: that finitude hosts the Atman, Buddha-nature, *imago dei,* Uncreated Intellect, and Universal Man. God alone exists, and everything that exists is God.

These are difficult concepts, so I reach for analogies. A wisp of spray is not the ocean, but the two are identically water. Or if we imagine an infinite lump of clay that tapers into tentacles and then into filaments that dwindle toward nothingness, the final tips of those filaments are still clay. To the religious spirit, such thoughts can serve as powerful springboards in suggesting our connectedness to God. Which connectedness—this is the point at hand—has epistemic implications.

The components of postmodern epistemology that work most heavily to obscure the realization that there can be valid overviews are two: perspectivalism carried to the point of absurdity; and a mundane, run-of-the-mill conception of knowledge.

Perspectivalism becomes absurd when the obvious fact that we look at the world from different places, hence different angles, is transformed into the dogma that we therefore cannot know things as they actually are. For Kant, it was our human angle (the categories of the mind) that prevents us from knowing "things in themselves"; and when psychological, cultural, temporal, and linguistic filters are added to this generic, anthropological one, we get constructivism, cultural relativism, historicism, and cultural-linguistic holism. What dogmatic perspectivalism in all these modes overlooks is that to recognize that perspectives are such requires knowing to some extent the wholes that demote them to the status of parts. Without *this* recognition, each "take" (as they say in movie making) would be accepted as the thing in itself. Visually, we need only move around the room to get a sense of the whole that shows our perspectives to be no more than such; but the mind is a dexterous instrument and can put itself "in other peoples' shoes," as we say. When the shoes belong to strangers, we transcend cultural relativism; when they are removed in time we transcend all-or-nothing historicism. When this is pointed out to postmoderns they again burlesque, charging their informants with claiming to be able to climb out of their skins, or (in the case of time) hopping a helicopter for past epochs. Both images are self-serving by pointing their spatial analogies in the wrong direction. The alternative to perspectivalism is not to get out of oneself or one's times, but to go into oneself until one reaches things that are time*less* and elude space altogether.

Unencumbered by run-of-the-mill epistemology and perspectivalism gone haywire, religions accept their worldviews as their absolutes, which is to say, as true. That word is no more acceptable to postmoderns than "all" is; Wittgenstein prefigured the entire shift from modernity to postmodernity when he characterized his turn from his early to his late period as a shift from truth to meaning. Here again the postmodern preoccupation with social matters obtrudes, for the fanatical impulse to cram truth down other people's throats leads postmoderns to back off from truth in general, especially if it is capitalized. In doing so they overlook the fact that truth is falliblism's prerequisite, not its alternative. Where there is no *via* (way, truth) to de*via*te from, mistakes have no meaning.[9]

III. Valid Worldviews Exist

Working my way backwards through postmodernism's three versions, I come lastly to its minimal claim which simply reports that we have no believable worldview today. "We have no maps, and we don't know how to make them," is the way one of the authors of *The Good Society* states the point.[10]

Whereas the two stronger versions of postmodernism need to be challenged for interfering with the human spirit, this minimalist position, being at root a description, poses no real problem. The description can, though, be qualified somewhat. In saying that we have no maps, the "we" in the minimalist's assertion refers to Western intellectuals. Peoples whose minds have not been reshaped by modernity and its sequel continue to live by the maps of their revelations.

Prone to assume that maps must be believed fanatically if they are to be believed at all, polemical postmoderns condemn religions for fomenting disharmony. But it is useful here to refer back for a last time to Dr. Ahmed's characterizations of postmodernity, which include its being "paired with ethno-religious fundamentalism." Postmoderns overlook that pairing. They do not perceive the extent to which their styles of thought (with the dangers of relativism and nihilism they conceal) have *produced* fundamentalism; which fundamentalism is the breeding ground for the fanaticism and intolerance they rightly deplore.

If mainline and polemical postmodernism were to subside, the obsession with life's social dimension that they saddled us with would relax and we would find ourselves able to think ontologically again. An important consequence of this would be that we would then perceive how much religious outlooks have in common. For one thing, they all situate the manifest, visible world within a larger, invisible whole. This is of particular interest at the moment because currently science does the same. Dark matter doesn't impact any of science's detectors, and the current recipe for the universe is, "70 parts cold dark matter, about 30 parts hot dark matter, and just a pinch for all the rest—the matter detectable to scientific instruments."[11] The further unanimous claim of religious cosmologies, though, finds no echo in science, for (being a value judgment) it is beyond science's reach. Not only is the invisible real; regions of it are more real and of greater worth than the visible, material world.

The inclusive, presiding paradigm for traditional cosmologies is the Great Chain of Being, composed of links ranging in hierarchical order from meager existents up to the *ens perfectissimum;* and the foremost student of that concept, Arthur Lovejoy, reported that "most educated persons everywhere accepted [it] without question down to late in the eighteenth century."[12] To that endorsement, Ken Wilber has recently added that the Great Chain of Being is "so overwhelmingly widespread . . . that it is either the single greatest intellectual error ever to appear in humankind's history—an error so colossally widespread as to literally stagger the mind—or it is the single most accurate reflection of reality yet to appear."[13]

CONCLUSION

To propose that religions cash in their theological metanarratives for metaphysical similarities they share would be as absurd as to urge people to peel off their flesh so the similarities of their skeletons could come to light. But if the warfare between science and religion, and now postmodernism and religion, could wind down, religions might find themselves coexisting relatively happily within a minimally articulated metanarrative of faith that encompasses them all in the way the eight current models of the quantum world share the context of what quantum physicists in general agree on. Or in the way in which, in the modern period, competing scientific theories shared the metanarrative of the scientific worldview.

Were this to happen, the atmosphere would be more salubrious, for I know no one who thinks that the postmodern view of the self and its world are nobler than the ones that the world's religions proclaim. Postmoderns acquiesce to their stunted views, not because they like them, but because they think that reason and history now force them upon us.

It has been the burden of my remarks that this is not the case.

31

Religio-Secular Society

MARTIN MARTY

Are religious truths superior to scientific truths or vice versa? Martin Marty—in an interview with Nathan Gardels, editor of New Perspectives Quarterly—*says that's the wrong question, and that instead of agonizing over any such limiting either-or proposition we should cultivate a healthy ability to be open to different modes of experience.*

NPQ   The Japanese philosopher Takeshi Umehara argues that the collapse of Marxism, "a side current of modernity," was the precursor to the collapse of secular liberalism, "modernity's main current." Both, he argues, excommunicated the "other world, the world of the spirit" through their materialist philosophy. Both, as a result, are now failing.

Even foreign policy intellectuals like Zbigniew Brzezinski are beginning to argue that unless America and the West regain their spiritual vigor, they will fade on the world scene.

Do you agree?

MARTIN MARTY   Of course, Marxism promised an inevitable future utopia that could be tested on this earth. The Marxist-economic model failed, and when the political systems of the Soviet bloc came under pressure to deliver, we discovered there was nothing inside. They imploded.

Liberal societies are not sufficiently integrated as a system to implode in the same way in the face of crisis. What is true is a growing acknowledgment that the three pillars of secular liberalism—rationality as a mode of thinking, the constitutional republic and individualism—are of themselves spiritually sterile, which does not mean they should, or can be torn down. It only means that they alone cannot prop up a civilization; they answer wonderfully to the practical side of life, but do nothing for the passional side of life.

I am a Christian, but I think in secular rational ways all the time. If I am ill, I don't want Mormon brain surgery, I don't want Baptist blood transfusions and I don't want Lutheran proctology. I just want the job done. This mode or rationality isn't fortified too much by a heavy philosophy, but is likely to stay with us for many dimensions of life simply because it works too well.

The establishment of a constitutional republic—in effect the official privatizing of religion—has been able to keep the peace while unleashing in America a religious explosion, making this country the most religious of any advanced industrialized nation. Swirling all about this public/private division of religion are religious arguments affecting every major public debate, from the civil rights movement to abortion.

So, there is really a tremendous amount of this spiritual vitality going on, but it all has to follow the rules of the game using modes of reasoning not based upon one's particular revelation.

In the course of practical life we mix the religious and the rational in all that we do. If you are faced with the medial ethics question of "should we pull the plug on grandma?" what resources do you call upon?

You don't ask a philosopher to come in and lecture on Aristotle or Mills about the greatest good for the greatest number. You ask "what does my good doctor say, what does my rabbi say, what does my family say?" You ask a different range of questions that have to do with different dimensions. You employ intuition, tradition, community, memory, hope and affection. You ask, "Who is grandma, what does she mean to us, what are her thoughts and wishes?"

That mix of modes of experience—including the religious dimension—which are brought to bear in the challenges we face in life, is very vital, more than the culture knows. I don't think we want to try to impose on this realm a single metaphysic which presumes to have an answer for all things in all times and for all people.

When Zbigniew Brzezinski and others worry about the moral fabric of America and call for a social renewal, perhaps they tend a little too much toward the theocratic view of the need for a single spiritual system.

Our nation's spirituality is too particularized, so individualized, that you could almost say that the last twenty years of explosive spiritual revival in America has had almost no social consequences. Outside the anti-abortion activists, people are finding their own way. But as far as the fabric of the culture is concerned, it is about as decisive as whether you like Bartok or rock music. Individuals are on their own quest.

So, amid the pillars of secularism, people go to synagogue, they go to church, they go to co-dependency groups and affirm the existence of a higher power for which liberal culture has no vocabulary. When we are replenished in our spirit, we go back into the liberal culture, changing it bit by bit. Already liberal culture has been transformed into something quite different than that envisioned by the *philosophes* of the Enlightenment.

A lot of foundations are threatened in Western civilization; a lot of walls are sagging. I know many roofs that can cave in. But there is a lot of remodeling, annexing and improvisation going on autonomously throughout the culture. I do not think it is possible in the pluralist West that the alternative to our sagging civilization can be some kind of spiritual recovery based on the voluntary acceptance of a single metaphysic, be it Christian republicanism or "secular enlightenment" or what have you.

As usual, the elites in the mass media, academia, entertainment and commerce are only now catching on to what has been happening in most of the culture for decades. Then they try to codify in a film or systematize it in a program.

If we do try to turn all that autonomous improvisation into a system, then we will surely shortcut this "organic" spiritual renovation and invite the kind of fate that put the Marxist system in the trashbin of history.

NPQ But the concern of those whom you suspect of having theocratic, systematizing proclivities is not so much that they want a single metaphysic; they just object to a menu of metaphysics where there is no hierarchy of values, where everything that comes along is just as good as the next. It is only a matter of choice.

If liberal society needs a moral order, how can a relative, plural, decentralized array of spiritual choices provide it?

MARTY Pluralism can be exaggerated so much that the overlappages are forgotten. I'm not saying that a Buddhist is going to become a Christian. But I am not an "utter pluralist" who believes we all must just exist out there because distinct philosophies legitimate our beliefs. In America, we are a society of spiritual as well as political coalitions.

I am thus a civic pluralist who believes that we can draw on Aristotle's aggregates or Madison's pluralities for what they bring to the larger pattern, all the while honoring those pluralities and giving people some measure of identity and trust.

Also, as an historian, I do not think that the kind of cohesive moral order so many now harken back to ever existed in the systemic way they wish to remember.

Moral orders hang together in a different way. People know there are things, as Katharine Hepburn used to put it, that "you shouldn't oughta do." You shouldn't oughta put graffitti on walls, or vandalize, or abuse drugs.

But the "shouldn't oughtas" don't arise from a formal metaphysic. They emerge from a common life that is informally nurtured.

First in this mesh of relations is a *common devotion to place.* When you settle on a plot of earth, you consecrate it. You are attached to those you live with. A *common time* is another link in the mesh. The earth belongs to the living, but when we think of our grandchildren, we import their future time into ours and adopt the generational ethic of being environmentally aware. A *common story* means we share the same myths and reference points. You can point to many mythical points of reference in our society today—for example, the recent launching of the space shuttle Challenger with men and women right out of central casting for a plural society (Protestant, Catholic, Jew, black, white, Buddhist) says it all about who we are.

Then there are *common propositions,* the closest to a metaphysic, and, in American society, *common constitutionalism.* We agree, for example, that certain truths are "self-evident," such as individual freedom, and we agree to abide by a common set of rules applied equally to all.

And finally there is *common affection* in the sense of affectivity or attachment. You may fight all the time at the family reunion about who will get grandma's silver, but you are fighting with your own kin and wouldn't miss the reunion for anything.

All of these things are the locus of moral order, and they are infused with the values brought to them by religious faith.

My theology—the Augustinian-Calvin-Lutheran tradition—does not believe that everything good that happens in the world, and it is our mission to build the City of God, has to be done in the name of God. In *Christianity and the Encounter with World Religions,* Paul Tillich wrote that "in the depth of every living religion there is a point at which the religion itself loses its importance, a point at which it breaks through its particularity, elevating it to spiritual freedom and with it to a vision of the *spiritual presence in other expressions* as the ultimate meaning of man's existence."

It is through that spiritual presence that religious awakening in the West will influence and transform liberal culture.

NPQ All these less-than-universal commonalities don't however seem to counterbalance the all-embracing assault of consumer society and the invasion of the media into the places and affections of which you speak.

The stories are different, but the message is coherent in the "permissive cornucopia," as Brzezinski calls it, of the mass culture.

All the private spiritualism and the particular commonalities would seem to add up, in Leo Strauss's phrase, to "retail sanity, but wholesale madness."

MARTY I can match anybody in hyperbole about the terrible problems we face. But they have to be addressed piecemeal, not systematically. That is the way our culture works.

We are not innocent about these things any more. Whoever has written a book about how to solve the whole problem is today forgotten and unread. Arnold Toynbee towered over other historians with his power of synthesis. But today we read the pragmatists instead. Both political parties now appreciate Eisenhower.

NPQ The British writer Bryan Appleyard calls for a "post-scientific" society in which science is put in its proper place in a pecking order beneath religion and faith. Science and the secular liberal society it has spawned with its rational principles, he says, has left us marooned on barren sands.

You have spoken of a "religio-secular" society where the two coexist. How does your view fit with Appleyard's?

MARTY As I indicated earlier when talking about brain surgery, I think there are many domains of the scientific method that will survive any cultural shift, and for which there is no special reason to bring in issues of the transcendent, the spiritual, faith, the supernatural or the spooky.

I do think that sacral aura of science, and its priesthood of scientists, has faded as the ultimate authority in our lives. This is true from psychoanalysis to physics. There is no doubt the claims of science which appealed to the Promethean impulse in humans are more and more suspect.

Far from rendering man more divine, each pushing back of limits makes us aware of greater limits. Each conquest of distance reveals greater distance. Behind the light we have found a black hole.

As a result, the passional side of human nature is reclaiming its space.

I think "coexistence" is too cool a word to describe the relationship between science and religion in our age. The collapse of one in the face of the other, which seems to be Appleyard's approach, is too strong.

Perhaps Paul Tillich's idea of *correlation* would be better. In a religio-secular society there would be a certain symbiosis where the religious and the scientific *modes of experience* live off of each other, interacting.

The concept of *modes of experience* is critical to understanding the emergent religio-secular culture that I see. We all as individuals live many roles. A student may wear a *dashiki* to class, but he wears a cap and gown to graduation. We are citizen, father, cook, sufferer. When the minister says "dearly beloved" to his wife, to his children, to a couple getting married, to his congregation he means something different each time, though all these meanings come from a single core.

As a biblical scholar I analyze Romans Chapter 8 for its rhetoric, its grammar and for its location in the Greco-Roman discourse and the biography of Paul. The mode of experience I employ here is no different than that of an atheist scholar.

Then, I walk into a sanctuary where faith beckons to faith. In the midst of my own ambiguities and doubts, as a believer I am drawn to that text which says love is stronger than death, that you won't be overwhelmed. I can't prove it, but I believe it.

Then I could come home, as I did a dozen years ago, to learn that my wife had terminal cancer. Then that text spoke to me in a very different mode.

These modes of experience aren't contradictory. Though they come from separate universes of discourse, a person can hold them all in an integrated personality and not be schizophrenic. We possess all these modes in good faith and move about among them.

This is as true for civilizations as it is for individuals. Modes of experience do overlap, they cross boundaries and they can't be boxed off. Civilizations are not pure, thoroughly cogent and untouched by other modes of experience.

This comingling of modes of experience is unsettling to fundamentalists. For them, there can be only one mode and one meaning. For them, everyone of good faith and moderate intelligence would have to agree to the same meaning of the Qur'an or the Bible because it can only be seen one way. If you don't agree it is because of the devil, bad faith, chosen ignorance or willful resistance.

Fundamentalists worldwide are "non-hermeneutical." They believe that the meaning of a text was sealed when God or Allah gave it verbatim to the apostles or Muhammad. There is no room for interpretation based upon the modes of experience you bring to the text.

NPQ A thesis: The more modes of experience we come into contact with through global communications and the postmodern ubiquity of the consumerist media, the more fundamentalism will build as a backlash.

Do you see that dynamic?

MARTY Yes, but we must stick close to the facts.

A good part of the militant Islamic reaction in a place like Algeria today is due to the failure of the secular, nominally Muslim military regime to deliver on the economic goods. They created a void for someone to say compellingly: "Allah did not intend for you to spend your life in poverty and listlessness. He intended a better life for you; join our movement and you will have that life."

The Iranian revolution led by Ayatollah Khomeini against the modernizing Shah was a clear example of your thesis. Iranian parents saw their child being lured away from the righteous path by the Western media and technology. The parents, who know they can never realize the materialist aspirations promoted by Western advertising, tell her that modernity is evil and corrosive. They fear a blowing wind will take this tender, frail plant of their daughter's mentality away. So, they build a greenhouse out of Qur'anic passages to shelter their seedling.

The morally corrosive forms of modernity have had a similar effect in America, especially among those who have begun to rise in the economic system but then stalled out economically.

The signals on television undercut parental intentions for a four-year-old; the signals of pluralism which reduces overt religion in the classroom comes as an assault on what the parents want for the fourteen-year-old; the assault of relativism on solid values around us, the fact that nobody can come up with peer standards, confuses the twenty-four-year-old parent.

In all three instances, the parents and the young adults hear something like what the Muslim hears from Allah: God didn't intend for you to be this bereft, this marooned, this beleaguered.

What they hear is what those Iranians susceptible to Khomeini's message heard: God intended you to be a special people, a holy nation. You are supposed to be exalted individuals, the redeemed ones. You are supposed to be chosen by the covenant. Yet, here you are, overwhelmed by public schools, Hollywood and the cultural elites, MTV promiscuity and the Supreme Court.

The difference between fundamentalism and mere traditionalism or orthodoxy is that the fundamentalist fights back. These are not the Amish who withdraw into the countryside and let the world pass by. The fundamentalist must engage that world at the devil's domain, the domain of the Great Satan.

NPQ . . . a figurative *jihad*.

MARTY Yes, in the sense that the struggle against the devil is being turned over to God, the agent of apocalypse, who will settle all accounts in the end.

NPQ Though the Enlightenment worldview has been humbled in the many ways we have discussed, its lasting legacy of the free individual, is codified in the notion of universal human rights.

Isn't even the concept of human rights in conflict not just with fundamentalist Islam but with the avowedly religious civilization built upon submission to Allah, not individual liberation; fusion of temporal and spiritual realms; sovereignty of God, not the people; and rule of the Word, not reason?

MARTY   Theocracy and the concept of human rights as outlined by the United Nations, the Geneva Accords and the Helsinki Accords cannot be reconciled. Islamic definitions of human rights have glorious things to say about the rights of believers, and precious little about the infidel and nonbeliever or minority.

Many orthodox Muslims, of course, are moderate about human rights. But Islam never formally separated church and state, to use Western lingo in their context. Even when they did so tactically, they never separated religion and regime *theologically*. As a result, it is much easier for fundamentalists to seize their cultures than it would be in the West.

The West, however, must be cautious in its claim to universalism. A Buddhist of good will says to us, "OK, if the West wants to be universal, then it must give up the dogmatism and monotheism of Judeo-Christianity. . . ."

For myself, a good side of me, as a Christian believer, remains with the Enlightenment. Every time I see someone emerge from a sacred bath in the Ganges with dysentery, I am reminded of my secular commitments.

32

The Opening of the American Mind

ARTHUR SCHLESINGER, JR.

Professor Schlesinger—who has both written American history and helped make it—appears to share Martin Marty's confidence that contemporary society is not disappearing into a spiritual black hole. He is more concerned about the political and intellectual effects of absolutism, in either its secular or religious guises. And he believes that we have adequate resources—in our institutions and national character—to protect us against it. The American mind, he reminds us, "is by nature and tradition skeptical, irreverent, pluralistic and relativistic."

Little is more surprising these days than the revival of blasphemy as a crime. A secular age had presumably relegated blasphemy—irreverence toward things sacred—to the realm of obsolete offenses. No American has been convicted for blasphemy since Abner Kneeland in Massachusetts a century and a half ago (for what was deemed a "scandalous, impious, obscene, blasphemous and profane libel of and concerning God"); and the last prosecution, in Maryland twenty years ago, was dismissed by an appellate court as a violation of the First Amendment.

But a secular age, when it creates its own absolutes, may well secularize blasphemy too. Consider the deplorable role the Pledge of Allegiance to the flag played in a recent Presidential campaign; or the cries of outrage provoked by the Supreme Court decision in *Texas v. Johnson*, holding that punishment for the political burning of an American flag breached the Constitution; or the demonstrations protesting the "desecration" of the flag at the Art Institute of Chicago.

The very word "desecration" implies that the American flag is sanctified, an object of worship. We are witnessing the rise of what Charles Fried, Ronald Reagan's solicitor general, calls the "doctrine of civil blasphemy." Whether religious or secular in guise, all forms of blasphemy have in common that there are things so sacred that they must be protected by the arm of the state from irreverence and challenge—that absolutes of truth and virtue exist and that those who scoff are to be punished.

It is this belief in absolutes, I would hazard, that is the great enemy today of the life of the mind. This may seem a rash proposition. The fashion of the time is to denounce relativism as the root of all evil. But history suggests that the damage done to humanity by the relativist is far less than the damage done by the absolutist—by the fellow who, as Mr. Dooley once put it, "does what he thinks th' Lord wud do if He only knew th' facts in th' case."

Let me not be misunderstood lest I be taken for a blasphemer myself and thereby subject to the usual dire penalties. I hold religion in high regard. As Chesterton once said, the trouble when people stop believing in God is not that they thereafter believe in nothing; it is that they thereafter believe in anything. I agree with Tocqueville that religion has an indispensable social function: "How is it possible that society should escape destruction if the moral tie is not strengthened in proportion as the political tie is relaxed?" I also sympathize with Tocqueville who, André Jardin, his most recent biographer, tells us, went to his death an unbeliever.

It would hardly seem necessary to insist on the perils of moral absolutism in our own tawdry age. By their fruits ye shall know them. It is as illogical to indict organized religion because of Jimmy Swaggart and the Bakkers as Paul Johnson is to indict the intelligentsia because of the messy private lives of selected intellectuals; but the moral absolutists who are presently applauding

Paul Johnson's cheap book *Intellectuals* might well be invited to apply the same methodology to their own trade. As the great theologian Reinhold Niebuhr said, "The worst corruption is a corrupt religion"—and organized religion, like all powerful institutions, lends itself to corruption. Absolutism, whether in religious or secular form, becomes a haven for racketeers.

As a historian, I confess to a certain amusement when I hear the Judeo-Christian tradition praised as the source of our concern for human rights. In fact, the great religious ages were notable for their indifference to human rights in the contemporary sense. They were notorious not only for acquiescence in poverty, inequality, exploitation and oppression but for enthusiastic justifications of slavery, persecution, abandonment of small children, torture, genocide.

Religion enshrined and vindicated hierarchy, authority and inequality and had no compunction about murdering heretics and blasphemers. Till the end of the eighteenth century, torture was normal investigative procedure in the Roman Catholic church as well as in most European states. In Protestant America in the early nineteenth century, as Larry Hise points out in his book *Pro-Slavery: A History of the Defense of Slavery in America, 1701–1840,* men of the cloth "wrote almost half of all the defenses of slavery published in America"; an appendix lists 275 ministers of the Gospel who piously proclaimed the Christian virtue of a system in which one man owned another as private property to be used as he pleased.

Human rights is not a religious idea. It is a secular idea, the product of the last four centuries of Western history.

It was the age of equality that brought about the disappearance of such religious appurtenances as the auto-da-fé 'and burning at the stake, the abolition of torture and of public executions, the emancipation of the slaves. Only later, as religion itself began to succumb to the humanitarian ethic and to view the Kingdom of God as attainable within history, could the claim be made that the Judeo-Christian tradition commanded the pursuit of happiness in this world. The basic human rights documents—the American Declaration of Independence and the French Declaration of the Rights of Man—were written by political, not by religious, leaders. And the revival of absolutism in the twentieth century, whether in ecclesiastical or secular form, has brought with it the revival of torture, of slaughter and of other monstrous violations of human rights.

Take a look at the world around us today. Most of the organized killing now going on is the consequence of absolutism: Protestants and Catholics killing each other in Ireland; Muslims and Jews killing each other in the Middle East; Sunnites and Shiites killing each other in the Persian Gulf; Buddhists and Hindus killing each other in Ceylon; Hindus and Sikhs killing each other in India; Christians and Muslims killing each other in Armenia and Azerbaijan; Buddhists and Communists killing each other in Tibet. "We have," as Swift said, "just enough religion to make us hate, but not enough to make us love." The Santa Barbara Peace Resource Center, reporting on the thirty-two wars in progress around the planet in 1988, found that twenty-five had "a significant ethnic, racial or religious dimension." And when religious religion is not the cause, then the totalitarian social religions of our age inspire mass slaughter.

It is natural enough, I suppose, if you believe you have privileged access to absolute truth, to want to rid the world of those who insist on divergent truths of their own. But I am not sure that it is a useful principle on which to build a society. Yet, as I noted earlier, the prevailing fashion is, or was a year or two ago, to hold relativism responsible for the ills of our age. A key document, of course, is Allan Bloom's best-seller of a couple of years back, *The Closing of the American Mind.* Indeed, one cannot but regard the very popularity of that murky and pretentious book as the best evidence for Mr. Bloom's argument about the degradation of American culture. It is another of those half-read best-sellers, like Charles Reich's murky and pretentious *Greening of America* seventeen years before, that plucks a momentary nerve, materializes fashionably on coffee tables, is rarely read all the way through and is soon forgotten.

Now one may easily share Mr. Bloom's impatience with many features of higher education in the United States. I too lament the incoherence in the curriculums, the proliferation of idiotic courses, the shameful capitulation to factional demands and requisitions, the decay of intellectual standards. For better or for worse, in my view, we inherit an American experience, as America inherits a Western experience; and solid learning must begin with our own origins and traditions. The bonds of cohesion in our society are sufficiently fragile, or so it seems to me, that we should not strain them by excessive worship at artificial shrines of ethnicity, bilingualism, global cultural base-touching and the like. Let us take pride in our own distinctive inheritance as other countries take pride in their distinctive inheritances; and let us understand that no culture can hope to ingest other cultures all at once, certainly not before it ingests its own.

But a belief in solid learning, rigorous standards, intellectual coherence, the virtue of elites is a different thing from a faith in absolutes. It is odd that Professor Bloom spends 400 pages laying down the law about the American mind and never once mentions the two greatest and most characteristic American thinkers, Emerson and William James. Once can see why he declined the confrontation: it is because he would have had to concede the fact that the American mind is by nature and tradition skeptical, irreverent, pluralistic and relativistic.

Nor does relativism necessarily regard all claims to truth as equal or believe that judgment is no more than the expression of personal preference. For our relative values are not matters of whim and happenstance. History has given them to us. They are anchored in our national experience, in our great national documents, in our national heroes, in our folkways, traditions, standards. Some of these values seem to us so self-evident that even relativists think they have, or ought to have, universal application: the right to life, liberty and the pursuit of happiness, for example; the duty to treat persons as ends in themselves; the prohibition of slavery, torture, genocide. People with a different history will have different values. But we believe that our own are better for us. They work for us; and, for that reason, we live and die by them.

At least this is what great Americans have always believed. "Deep-seated preferences," as Justice Holmes put it, "cannot be argued about . . . and therefore, when differences are sufficiently far-reaching, we try to kill the other man rather than let him have his way. But that is perfectly consistent with admitting that, so far as it appears, his grounds are just as good as ours."

Once Justice Holmes and Judge Learned Hand discussed these questions on a long train ride. Learned Hand gave as his view that "opinions are at best provisional hypotheses, incompletely tested. The more they are tested . . . the more assurance we may assume, but they are never absolutes. So we must be tolerant of opposite opinions." Holmes wondered whether Hand might not be carrying his tolerance to dangerous lengths. "You say," Hand wrote Holmes later, "that I strike at the sacred right to kill the other fellow when he disagrees. The horrible possibility silenced me when you said it. Now, I say, 'Not at all, kill him for the love of Christ and in the name of God, but always remember that he may be the saint and you the devil.' "

These "deep-seated preferences" are what Holmes called his "Can't Helps"—"When I say that a thing is true, I mean that I cannot help believing it . . . But . . . I do not venture to assume that my inabilities in the way of thought are inabilities of the universe. I therefore define truth as the system of my limitations, and leave absolute truth for those who are better equipped." He adds: "Certitude is not the test of certainty. We have been cock-sure of many things that were not so."

Absolutism is abstract, monistic, deductive, ahistorical, solemn, and it is intimately bound up with deference to authority. Relativism is concrete, pluralistic, inductive, historical, skeptical and intimately bound up with deference to experience. Absolutism teaches by rote; relativism by experiment. "I respect faith," that forgotten wit Wilson Mizener once said, "but doubt is what gets you an education."

I would even hazard the proposition that relativism comports far more than absolutism with the deepest and darkest teachings of religion. For what we have learned from Augustine, from Calvin, from Jonathan Edwards, is not man's capacity to grasp the absolute but quite the contrary: the frailty of man, the estrangement of man from God, the absolute distance between mortals and divinity—and the arrogance of those who suppose they are doing what the Lord would do if He only knew the facts in the case. That is why Reinhold Niebuhr acknowledged such an affinity with William James—far more, I would warrant, than he would have found with Allan Bloom.

When it came to worldly affairs, Niebuhr was a relativist, not because he disbelieved in the absolute, but precisely because he believed in the absoluteness of the absolute—because he recognized that for finite mortals the infinite thinker was inaccessible, unfathomable, unattainable. Nothing was more dangerous, in Niebuhr's view, than for frail and erring humans to forget the inevitable "contradiction between divine and human purposes." "Religion," he wrote, "is so frequently a source of confusion in political life, and so frequently dangerous to democracy, precisely because it introduces absolutes into the realm of relative values." He particularly detested "the fanaticism of all good men, who do not know that they are not as good as they esteem themselves," and he warned against "the depth of evil to which individuals and communities may sink . . . when they try to play the role of God to history."

Niebuhr accepted, as James did, "the limits of all human striving, the fragmentariness of all human wisdom, the precariousness of all historic configurations of power, and the mixture of good and evil in all human virtue." His outlook is as far away from Mr. Bloom's simple-minded absolutism as one can imagine. It represents, in my view, the real power of religious insight as well as the far more faithful expression of the American mind.

I would summon one more American, the greatest of them all, as a last witness in the case for relativism against absolutes. In his Second Inaugural, Lincoln noted that both sides in the Civil War "read the same Bible, and pray to the same God; and each invokes His aid against the other. . . . the prayers of both could not be answered; that of neither has been answered fully. The Almighty has His own purposes." Replying thereafter to a congratulatory letter from Thurlow Weed, Lincoln doubted that such sentiments would be "immediately popular. Men are not flattered by being shown that there has been a difference of purpose between the Almighty and them. To deny it, however, in this case, is to deny that there is a God governing the world."

The Almighty has His own purposes: this is the reverberant answer to those who tell us that we must live by absolutes. Relativism is the American way. As that most quintessential of American historians, George Bancroft, wrote in another connection, "The feud between the capitalist and laborer, the house of Have and the house of Want, is as old as social union, and can never be entirely quieted; but he who will act with moderation, prefer fact to theory, and remember that every thing in this world is relative and not absolute, will see that the violence of the contest may be stilled."

The mystic prophets of the absolute cannot save us. Sustained by our history and traditions, we must save ourselves, at whatever risk of heresy or blasphemy. We can find solace in the memorable representation of the human struggle against the absolute in the finest scene in the greatest of American novels. I refer of course to the scene when Huckleberry Finn decides that the "plain hand of Providence" requires him to tell Miss Watson where her runaway slave Jim is to be found. Huck writes his letter of betrayal to Miss Watson and feels "all washed clean of sin for the first time I had ever felt so in my life, and I knowed I could pray now." He sits there for a while thinking "how good it was all this happened so, and how near I come to being lost and going to hell."

Then Huck begins to think about Jim and the rush of the great river and the talking and the singing and the laughing and friendship. "Then I happened to look around and see that paper. . . . I took it up, and held it in my hand. I was a-trembling because I'd got to decide, forever, betwixt two things, and I knowed it. I studied a minute, sort of holding my breath, and then says to myself: 'All right, then, I'll *go* to hell'—and tore it up."

That, if I may say so, is what America is all about.

33

The Search for Meaning
in a Global Civilization

VÁCLAV HAVEL

The postmodern world is a global civilization, and a civilization needs to have a few unifying truths and deeper values if it is to function. How are these to be found—or made? Václav Havel, searching for answers to what most people see as a religious question, finds some on the frontiers of science.

There are thinkers who claim that if the modern age began with the discovery of America, it also ended in America. This is said to have occurred in the year 1969, when America sent the first men to the moon. From this historical moment, they say, a new age in the life of humanity can be dated.

I think there are good reasons for suggesting that the modern age has ended. Today, many things indicate that we are going through a transitional period, when it seems that something is on the way out and something else is painfully being born. It is as if something were crumbling, decaying and exhausting itself, while something else, still indistinct, were arising from the rubble.

Periods of history when values undergo a fundamental shift are certainly not unprecedented. This happened in the Hellenistic period, when from the ruins of the classical world the Middle Ages were gradually born. It happened during the Renaissance, which opened the way to the modern era. The distinguishing features of such transitional periods are a mixing and blending of cultures, and a plurality or parallelism of intellectual and spiritual worlds. These are periods when all consistent value systems collapse, when cultures distant in time and space are discovered or rediscovered. They are periods when there is a tendency to quote, to imitate and to amplify, rather than to state with authority or integrate. New meaning is gradually born from the encounter, or the intersection, of many different elements.

Today, this state of mind or of the human world is called postmodernism. For me, a symbol of that state is a Bedouin mounted on a camel and clad in traditional robes under which he is wearing jeans, with a transistor radio in his hands and an ad for Coca-Cola on the camel's back. I am not ridiculing this, nor am I shedding an intellectual tear over the commercial expansion of the West that destroys alien cultures. I see it rather as a typical expression of this multicultural era, a signal that an amalgamation of cultures is taking place. I see it as proof that something is happening, something is being born, that we are in a phase when one age is succeeding another, when everything is possible. Yes, everything is possible because our civilization does not have its own unified style, its own spirit, its own aesthetic.

This is related to the crisis, or to the transformation, of science as the basis of the modern conception of the world.

The dizzying development of this science, with its unconditional faith in objective reality and its complete dependency on general and rationally knowable laws, led to the birth of modern technological civilization. It is the first civilization in the history of the human race that spans the entire globe and firmly binds together all human societies, submitting them to a common global destiny. It was this science that enabled man, for the first time, to see Earth from space with his own eyes, that is, to see it as another star in the sky.

At the same time, however, the relationship to the world that modern science fostered and shaped now appears to have exhausted its potential. It is increasingly clear that, strangely, the relationship is missing something. It fails to connect with the most intrinsic nature of reality, and with natural human experience. It is now more of a source of disintegration and doubt than a source of integration and meaning. It produces what amounts to a state of schizophrenia: Man as an observer is becoming completely alienated from himself as a being. Classical modern science described only the surface of things, a single dimension of reality. And the more dogmatically science treated it as the only dimension, as the very essence of reality, the more misleading it became. Today, for instance, we may know immeasurably more about the universe than our ancestors did, and yet, it increasingly seems they knew something more essential about it than we do, something that escapes us. The same thing is true of nature and of ourselves. The more thoroughly all our organs and their functions, their internal structure and the biochemical reactions that take place within them are described, the more we seem to fail to grasp the spirit, purpose and meaning of the system that they create together and that we experience as our unique "self."

And thus today we find ourselves in a paradoxical situation. We enjoy all the achievements of modern civilization that have made our physical existence on this earth easier in so many important ways. Yet we do not know exactly what to do with ourselves, where to turn. The world of our experiences seems chaotic, disconnected, confusing. There appear to be no integrating forces, no unified meaning, no true inner understanding of phenomena in our experience of the world. Experts can explain anything in the objective world to us, yet we understand our own lives less and less. In short, we live in the post-modern world, where everything is possible and almost nothing is certain.

This state of affairs has its social and political consequences. The single planetary civilization to which we all belong confronts us with global challenges. We stand helpless before them because our civilization has essentially globalized only the surface of our lives. But our inner self continues to have a life of its own. And the fewer answers the era of rational knowledge provides to the basic questions of human Being, the more deeply it would seem that people, behind its back as it were, cling to the ancient certainties of their tribe. Because of this, individual cultures, increasingly lumped together by contemporary civilization, are realizing with new urgency their own inner autonomy and the inner differences of others. Cultural conflicts are increasing and are understandably more dangerous today than at any other time in history. The end of the era of rationalism has been catastrophic: Armed with the same supermodern weapons, often from the same suppliers, and followed by television cameras, the members of various tribal cults are at war with one another. By day, we work with statistics; in the evening, we consult astrologers and frighten ourselves with thrillers about vampires. The abyss between the rational and the spiritual, the external and the internal, the objective and the subjective, the technical and the moral, the universal and the unique constantly grows deeper.

Politicians are rightly worried by the problem of finding the key to ensure the survival of a civilization that is global and at the same time clearly multicultural; how generally respected mechanisms of peaceful coexistence can be set up, and on what set of principles they are to be established.

These questions have been highlighted with particular urgency by the two most important political events in the second half of the twentieth century: the collapse of colonial hegemony and the fall of communism. The artificial world order of the past decades has collapsed and a new, more just order has not yet emerged. The central political task of the final years of this century, then, is the creation of a new model of coexistence among the various cultures, peoples, races and religious spheres within a single interconnected civilization. This task is all the more urgent because other threats to contemporary humanity brought about by one-dimensional development of civilization are growing more serious all the time.

Many believe this task can be accomplished through technical means. That is, they believe it can be accomplished through the invention of new organizational, political and diplomatic instruments. Yes, it is clearly necessary to invent organizational structures appropriate to the present multicultural age. But such efforts are doomed to failure if they do not grow out of something deeper, out of generally held values.

This, too, is well-known. And in searching for the most natural source for the creation of a new world order, we usually look to an area that is the traditional foundation of modern justice and a great achievement of the modern age: to a set of values that—among other things—were first declared in Philadelphia. I am referring to respect for the unique human being and his or her liberties and inalienable rights, and the principle that all power derives from the people. I am, in short, referring to the fundamental ideas of modern democracy.

I feel more and more strongly that even these ideas are not enough, that we must go farther and deeper. The point is that the solution they offer is still, as it were, modern, derived from the climate of the Enlightenment and from a view of man and his relation to the world that has been characteristic of the Euro-American sphere for the last two centuries. Today, however, we are in a different place and facing a different situation, one to which classically modern solutions in themselves do not give a satisfactory response. After all, the very principle of inalienable human rights, conferred on man by the Creator, grew out of the typically modern notion that man—as a being capable of knowing nature and the world—was the pinnacle of creation and lord of the world. This modern anthropocentrism inevitably meant that He who allegedly endowed man with his inalienable rights began to disappear from the world: He was so far beyond the grasp of modern science that he was gradually pushed into a sphere of privacy of sorts, if not directly into a sphere of private fancy—that is, to a place where public obligations no longer apply. The existence of a higher authority than man himself simply began to get in the way of human aspirations.

The idea of human rights and freedoms must be an integral part of any meaningful world order. Yet I think it must be anchored in a different place, and in a different way, than has been the case so far. If it is to be more than just a slogan mocked by half the world, it cannot be expressed in the language of a departing era, and it must not be mere froth floating on the subsiding waters of faith in a purely scientific relationship to the world.

Paradoxically, inspiration for the renewal of this lost integrity can once again be found in science. In a science that is new—let us say post-modern—a science producing ideas that in a certain sense allow it to transcend its own limits. I will give two examples.

The first is the Anthropic Cosmological Principle. Its authors and adherents have pointed out that from the countless possible courses of its evolution, the universe took the only one that enabled life to emerge. This is not yet proof that the aim of the universe has always been that it should one day see itself through our eyes. But how else can this matter be explained?

I think the Anthropic Cosmological Principle brings us to an idea perhaps as old as humanity itself: that we are not at all just an accidental anomaly, the microscopic caprice of a tiny particle whirling in the endless depths of the universe. Instead, we are mysteriously connected to the entire universe, we are mirrored in it, just as the entire evolution of the universe is mirrored in us. Until recently it might have seemed that we were an unhappy bit of mildew on a heavenly body whirling in space among many that have no mildew on them at all. This was something that classical science could explain. Yet the moment it begins to appear that we are deeply connected to the entire universe, science reaches the outer limits of its powers. Because it is founded on the search for universal laws, it cannot deal with singularity, that is, with uniqueness. The universe is a unique event and a unique story, and so far we are the unique point of that story. But unique events and stories are the domain of poetry, not science. With the formulation of the Anthropic Cosmological Principle, science has found itself on the border between formula and story, between science and myth. In that, however, science has paradoxically returned, in a roundabout way, to man, and offers him—in new clothing—his lost integrity. It does so by anchoring him once more in the cosmos.

The second example is the Gaia Hypothesis. This theory brings together proof that the dense network of mutual interactions between the organic and inorganic portions of the Earth's surface form a single system, a kind of mega-organism, a living planet—Gaia—named after an ancient goddess who is recognizable as an archetype of the Earth Mother in perhaps all religions. According to the Gaia Hypothesis we are parts of a greater whole. Our destiny is not dependent merely on what we do for ourselves but also on what we do for Gaia as a whole. If we endanger her, she will dispense with us in the interests of a higher value—that is, life itself.

What makes the Anthropic Principle and the Gaia Hypothesis so inspiring? One simple thing: Both remind us, in modern language, of what we have long suspected, of what we have long projected into our forgotten myths and what perhaps has always lain dormant within us as archetypes. That is, the awareness of our being anchored in the Earth and the universe, the awareness that we are not here alone nor for ourselves alone, but that we are an integral part of higher, mysterious entities against whom it is not advisable to blaspheme. This forgotten awareness is encoded in all religions. All cultures anticipate it in various forms. It is one of the things that form the basis of man's understanding of himself, of his place in the world, and ultimately of the world as such.

A modern philosopher once said: "Only a God can save us now."

Yes, the only real hope of people today is probably a renewal of our certainty that we are rooted in the Earth and, at the same time, the cosmos.

This awareness endows us with the capacity for self-transcendence. Politicians at international forums may reiterate a thousand times that the basis of
the new world order must be universal respect for human rights, but it will
mean nothing as long as this imperative does not derive from the respect of
the miracle of Being, the miracle of the universe, the miracle of nature, the
miracle of our own existence. Only someone who submits to the authority of
the universal order and of creation, who values the right to be a part of it and
a participant in it, can genuinely value himself and his neighbors, and thus
honor their rights as well.

It logically follows that, in today's multicultural world, the truly reliable path to coexistence, to peaceful coexistence and creative cooperation,
must start from what is at the root of all cultures and what lies infinitely
deeper in human hearts and minds than political opinion, convictions,
antipathies or sympathies: It must be rooted in self-transcendence. Transcendence as a hand reached out to those close to us, to foreigners, to the
human community, to all living creatures, to nature, to the universe; transcendence as a deeply and joyously experienced need to be in harmony even
with what we ourselves are not, what we do not understand, what seems
distant from us in time and space, but with which we are nevertheless
mysteriously linked because, together with us, all this constitutes a single
world. Transcendence as the only real alternative to extinction.

Epilogue:
The End and Beginning of Enlightenment

We began this book with a brief memorial service for the Enlightenment project, whose demise is so often used to mark the start of the postmodern era.

I think it's correct that the Enlightenment has long since lost its vitality—and yet, as far as a lot of people are concerned, the old project is alive and well. You can still find plenty of hardy rationalists in relentless pursuit of objective and universally acceptable explanations for everything. Meanwhile, for others, the Enlightenment era is just beginning: People in many places are only now taking up science and secular rationality, entering the edifice of modern thought by the front door just as so many other people are exiting by the back—or, as some see it, jumping out the window—into postmodernity. That's another facet of the pluralism of our time: For a brief, strange moment in human history, premodernity, modernity and post-modernity coexist.

And, to make the picture even more complex, postmodernity has its own kind of Enlightenment project.

People often miss this completely. Dazzled by that devilish word "deconstruction," they dismiss postmodern thought as simply nihilistic, having no purpose other than to undermine all worldviews, derail all quests for common ground. But it is much more than that: It is an attempt to map out a much larger landscape of the mind, and to locate a deeper commonality. If you look back through the selections in this book, you will see that most of them are exercises in construction as well as deconstruction.

In the very first selection, for example, Steinar Kvale includes "an expansion of rationality" in his list of the themes of postmodernity. And what he means by this isn't just an expansion of objective, scientistic thought, but rather an expansion of the *definition* of rationality. This theme is picked up later by Feyerabend, with his "anything goes" approach to science; and by Krippner and Winkler with their vision of many, many models of human consciousness that need to be taken into account in the construction of worldviews. These models aren't necessarily equal—any more than the various items in a toolbox are—but they may all be useful, and we do not have to be limited to a single one.

The postmodern verdict on the Enlightenment project is that it was a brilliant, ambitious effort, but that its field of vision was limited. Its leaders thought the task of building a universal human culture upon a foundation of rational thought would be easier than it has turned out to be. The universe now seems, if not infinite, at least infinitely complex and mysterious. Our eternal truths now appear to be inseparable from the cultures that created them and the languages in which they are stated. The human mind now appears to be anything but a neat thinking machine that—when properly operated—poses right questions and prints out right answers. It begins to look like the individual mind is pluralistic all by itself, naturally predisposed to function in many modes.

The quest for universal understanding—and the work of creating a global culture—goes on. But the scale changes, and the perspective shifts. What's happening now is in many ways similar to what happened a few centuries ago when people were exploring the planet: They kept discovering they lived in a wider world and re-drawing their maps. If you read a history of that adventure—Daniel Boorstin's *The Discoverers* is a wonderful example—you can see an ongoing process, cycles of deconstruction and reconstruction.[1] The world that had once been flat became round, and then it became larger, and old worldviews were discarded regularly. People invented new structures of reality to help them comprehend the world; the art of mapmaking made great strides during this period, and the fictitious lines of latitude and longitude became as important to navigators as the oceans and the winds. The world changed, and changed again. Some of the explorers—like the scientists in Thomas Kuhn's account—"adopted new instruments and looked in new places," and some of them—quoting Kuhn again—"saw new and different things when looking with familiar instruments in places they had looked before."

What is it that people are discovering now?

Ernest Becker said people are discovering "the fictitious nature of the action world," developing eyes to see that "flimsy canopy" that hangs over human life. Others say people are discovering the symbolic universe, the socially constructed nature of reality—or, simply, culture. People are constructing maps that enable them to find something new and different about the powerful symbolic structures that shape our lives: We are beginning to see all manner of things—values and beliefs, rituals, ideas about childhood and death, traditions, interpretations of history, rituals, ethnicity, even the idea of culture—as inventions. This discovery itself, now being made by people all over the world, becomes a part of our common ground. It is central to an emerging understanding of the human condition, and also a central part of a new global culture which is, in a sense, a culture about cultures.

The familiar pieces of our cultural furniture don't go away when we see them as inventions. We don't need them less or love them less. Whether they are invented or not, we could not live without them, because these are the kinds of animals we are. That does not change—but something *has* changed. The world around us has become a more human world. It is no longer what Berger and Luckmann called "a strange facticity, an *opus alienum*" over which we have no control.

The visible—sometimes funny, sometimes frightening—signs of this change are the things that people do as they begin taking control of their symbolic environments: playing with rituals and myths, revising religious doctrines, putting on hard-rock yoiking concerts, hanging Santa on the cross.

I am generalizing loosely about this discovery as if it were a single process or a direct result of conscious deliberation. And of course it isn't that at all: People react in all manner of ways to the postmodern condition. Most of them discover it not by studying philosophy but merely by taking in the multitudinous messages of our turbulent time—or by observing that a lot of other people are doing a lot of funny things with culture and apparently getting away with it.

Nobody makes the discovery all at once. There are some cultural realities that most of us readily accept as social constructions, and some that we don't care to see that way at all. The metaphor of the "onion peel" quality of beliefs—an old favorite of social psychologists—is useful here: It's fairly easy to peel away the outer layers but hard to get at the core. It doesn't take a great effort, for example, for most contemporary people to recognize that gender roles are socially constructed—however much they may dislike the idea. It's a bit more difficult to put more fundamental concepts such as ethnicity in that category—difficult, but still within reach if you follow the arguments of Werner Sollors and bell hooks.

The going gets tough when we come to the idea of the self. The proposition that the self is an illusion, a socially constructed reality—that there are quite different ways of thinking about personal identity—seems to contradict plain common sense. And even people who accept the idea in the abstract still don't necessarily *get* it in a way that makes any difference in how they experience daily life.

The concept of the self is not only close to the core of our personal beliefs; it also approaches the core—the secret heart—of postmodern thought. It is the point at which it becomes most apparent that there is a very strong similarity between the ideas of postmodern intellectuals and those that have been running through spiritual teachings for centuries. That other, much older, Enlightenment project—the one that we associate with the Buddhists and the Sufis—was also built around a radically different notion of personal identity, a quest for liberation from the ego. You can see the connection clearly enough in some of the quotations in Connie Zweig's article: Jacques Lacan's "I am not a poet but a poem" could be an aphorism from Zen. Paul Kugler's challenge to the permanence of any referent beyond the first person pronoun, his assertion that "each time the first person pronoun is uttered, it projects a different entity, a different perspective and identity," has a similarly Zen-like flavor. It also sounds a lot like Heraclitus talking psychology.

So—as several of the contributors to this book have pointed out—the basic ideas of postmodern thought are not new. For centuries, philosophers have been individually discovering the symbolic environment, and spiritual teachers have been instructing their followers in the path of liberation from the self—encouraging them to reconstruct identity. But other aspects of postmodernity—the mass media, the proliferation of discourses, all the cultural mixing and improvising, the pace of globalization—*are* new. So is the powerful influence of postmodern thought in different fields ranging from anthropology and architecture to psychology and religion. All these things are coming together in a way that has not happened before. What we are seeing now is the emergence into the foreground—into the center of our personal and public lives—of an ancient minor theme. As this becomes a part of general public discourse, it also calls for some rethinking of ideas about the course of history—about such things as progress.

The Enlightenment project—the European one—was wrapped up with a concept of progress that at times amounted to a virtual religion. The cult of progress was born in the middle of the eighteenth century, when the young French philosopher Turgot gave a public lecture at the Sorbonne declaring that humankind "advances ever, though slowly, towards greater perfection." His ideas had an electrifying impact on the Western world, and were picked up by many other revolutionaries and intellectuals who preached the doctrine of linear, onward-and-upward improvement in the human condition with increasing scientific knowledge.[2]

The postmodern Enlightenment project has its own concept of progress. It's not so explicit or linear, surely not so simple—but it's there. It is really more a concept of cultural evolution, based on the belief that the whole human race is involved in a huge learning process. This process is difficult, painful, and conflicted; it can't be reduced to things simply getting better. The postmodern Enlightenment project involves learning about learning, discovering something new about our own reality. It is, for many, a discovery full of hope. Ernest Becker described it as "one of the great, liberating breakthroughs of all time," and I don't think anybody ever accused the man who wrote *The Denial of Death* of being a Pollyanna.

So, as it turns out, we have not one Enlightenment project, but three: a Western one based on rational thought, an Eastern one based on seeing through the illusion of the Self, and a postmodern one based on the concept of socially constructed reality. And despite their many differences, they share the common goal of liberation. Jean-Jacques Rousseau made the famous revolutionary pronouncement that "men are born free, and everywhere they are in chains." A couple of centuries later that still holds truth for us, but now we see that the strongest chains are symbolic ones, mind-forged manacles.

We are making progress—toward a world in which the human species has taken possession of the symbolic skills that made it human, and in which people are no longer enslaved by their abstractions. No utopian that I know of has yet described such a world; we have no map of this larger historical space through which we are moving. So some confusion is unavoidable. We don't know precisely where we are or where we are going.

But then neither did Columbus, and, as Saul Bellow once pointed out, that didn't prove there was no America.[3]

NOTES

INTRODUCTION: WHAT'S GOING ON HERE?

1. Richard Shweder, "Why Do Men Barbecue? and Other Postmodern Ironies of Growing Up in the Decade of Ethnicity." *Daedalus,* Journal of the American Academy of Arts and Sciences, Winter 1993, Volume 122, Number 1.

2. John Rockwell, "For the Lapps, a Hesitant Cultural Flowering," *The New York Times,* Dec. 11, 1993, p. 13.

3. Trish Donnally, "Divine Inspiration: The Religious Look," *San Francisco Chronicle,* April 23, 1993, p. D3.

4. Gabrielle Sandor, "The 'Other' Americans," *American Demographics,* June 1994, pp. 36–42.

5. Stephen Toulmin, *The Return to Cosmology: Postmodern Science and the Theology of Nature* (Berkeley: University of California Press, 1985), p. 254. (Italics in original.)

6. David Harvey, *The Condition of Postmodernity: An Enquiry into the Origins of Cultural Change* (Cambridge: Basil Blackwell, 1989), p. 27.

7. Jean-Francois Lyotard, *The Postmodern Condition: A Report on Knowledge,* trans. Geoff Bennington and Brian Massumi (Minneapolis: University of Minnestota Press, 1984), p. xxiv.

8. Richard Rorty, *Contingency, Irony, and Solidarty* (New York: Cambridge University Press, 1989), p. 3.

9. Rorty, op. cit. pp. 4–5.

10. Kenneth J. Gergen, *The Saturated Self: Dilemmas of Identity in Contemporary Life* (New York: Basic Books, 1991).

INTRODUCTION TO PART ONE

1. Theodosius Dobzhansky, *The Biological Basis of Human Freedom* (New York: Columbia University Press, 1956), pp. 26, 27. Dobszhansky's formulation is still valid, although current thinking is more likely to regard other species as having rudimentary cultures based on various kinds of nonverbal communication. Another fading boundary.

2. Clifford Geertz, *The Interpretation of Cultures* (New York: Basic Books, 1973), p. 49.

3. Jim Collins, *Uncommon Cultures: Popular Culture and Post-Modernism* (New York: Routledge, 1989).

1. THEMES OF POSTMODERNITY

1. Richard Rorty, *Philosophy and the Mirror of Nature* (Princeton: Princeton University Press, 1979).

2. Humberto Maturana, "Reality: The Quest for Objectivity or the Search for the Compelling Argument," *Irish Journal of Psychology,* 9: 25–83.

3. Kenneth Gergen, *The Saturated Self* (New York: Basic Books, 1991).

4. Jean Baudrillard, *Selected Works,* ed. M. Poster (Cambridge: Polity Press, 1988).

5. Jurgen Habermas, *Legitimation Crisis* (Boston: Beacon Press, 1975).

6. Richard Rorty, "Habermas and Lyotard on Postmodernity," in R. J. Bernstein, ed., *Habermas and Modernity* (Oxford: Blackwell, 1985), p. 164.

7. M. Salner, "Validity in Human Science Research," in Steinar Kvale, ed., *Issues of Validity in Quantitative Research.* Lund: Studentenlitteratur, pp. 47–71.

8. Jean-Francois Lyotard, *The Postmodern Condition: A Report on Knowledge* (Manchester: Manchester University Press, 1984), p. 27.

9. H. O. Peitgen and P. E. Richter, *The Beauty of Fractals* (Berlin: Springer, 1986).

10. Robert Venturi, Denise Scott Brown, and Steven Izenour, *Learning from Las Vegas* (Cambridge: MIT Press, 1977).

2. WHAT IS POST-MODERNISM?

1. Jencks, *The Language of Post-Modern Architecture* (London: Academy Editions, 1991), p. 23.

2. Charles Newman, *The Post-Modern Aura: The Act of Fiction in an Age of Inflation,* with a preface by Gerald Graff (Evanston, IL: Northwestern University Press, 1985).

3. Leslie Fiedler, "The New Mutants" (1965) in *The Collected Essays of Leslie Fiedler,* Vol. II (New York: Stein and Day, 1970), and *A Fiedler Reader* (Stein and Day, 1977), pp. 189–210.

4. Andreas Huyssen, "Mapping the Postmodern," *New German Critique,* No. 33, Fall 1984, devoted to *Modernity and Postmodernity* (Milwaukee: University of Wisconsin, 1984).

5. Ihab Hassan, "The Question of Postmodernism," in Harry R. Garvin, ed., *Romanticism, Modernism, Postmodernism* (Lewisberg, Toronto and London: Bucknell University Press, 1980), pp. 117–26.

6. Mark C. Taylor, *ERRING: A Postmodern A/Theology* (University of Chicago Press, 1984).

7. John Barth, "The Literature of Replentishment: Postmodernism Fiction," *The Atlantic,* January 1980, pp. 65–71, and Umberto Eco, "Postmodernism, Irony, the Enjoyable," in *Postscript to the Name of the Rose* (New York: Harcourt, Brace Jo-

vanovich, 1984), first published in Italian, 1983. Eco's *The Name of the Rose* became, of course, a best-selling version of the kind of Post-Modern fiction that Barth and Eco describe in their theoretical writing.

8. Barth, op. cit, p. 70.

6. STRATEGIES OF POWER

1. Michel Foucault, *The Archaeology of Knowledge*, trans. A. S. London (New York: Pantheon, 1972), p. 17.

2. "Les intellectuels et le pouvoir," *L'Arc* (issue on Gilles Deleuze) 49 (March 1972), pp. 3–10.

7. THE IDEA OF PLURALISM

1. Quoted in Ernst von Glazersfeld, "An Introduction to Radical Constructivism," in Paul Watzlawick, ed., *The Invented Reality* (New York: W. W. Norton, 1984), p. 27.

2. Isaiah Berlin, *The Crooked Timber of Humanity* (New York: Knopf, 1991), p. 59.

9. THE IDEA OF ETHNICITY

1. Hayden White, "Foucault Decoded: Notes from the Underground" (1973), in *Tropics of Discourse: Essays in Cultural Criticism* (Baltimore and London: Johns Hopkins University Press, 1982), p. 252.

2. Hayden White, "The Fictions of Factual Representation" (1976), in *Tropics of Discourse*, p. 122.

3. "Introduction: Partial Truths," James Clifford and George E. Marcus, eds., *Writing Culture: The Poetics and Politics of Ethnography* (Berkeley: University of California Press, 1986), pp. 5–6.

4. Michael J. Fischer, "Ethnicity and the Post-Modern Arts of Memory," in *Writing Culture*, p. 195.

5. Benedict Anderson, *Imagined Communities: Reflections of the Origins and Spread of Nationalism* (London: Verso, 1985), p. 62.

6. Eric Hobsbawm and Terrence Ranger, eds., *The Invention of Tradition* (Cambridge: Cambridge University Press, 1983).

7. W. Lloyd Warner and Paul S. Lunt, *The Social Life of a Modern Community* (New Haven: Yale University Press, 1941).

8. "Story in Harlem Slang," in *Spunk: The Selected Stories of Zora Neale Hurston*, Bob Callahan, ed. (Berkeley: Turtle Island, 1985), pp. 83, 88.

9. Hamilton Holt, ed., *The Life Stories of Undistinguished Americans as Told by Themselves* (New York: James Pott & Co., 1906), p. 289.

10. Henry W. Grady, "In Plain Black and White: A Reply to Mr. Cable," *Century Magazine* 29 (1885), p. 911.

11. Charles W. Chesnutt, "Race Prejudice: Its Causes and Its Cures: An Address Delivered before the Boston Historical and Literary Association," *Alexander's Magazine*, 1 (July 1905), p. 25.

INTRODUCTION TO PART TWO

1. Karl Marx and Friedrich Engels, *The Communist Manifesto*.

2. Benjamin Whorf, *Language, Thought and Reality* (New York: Wiley, 1956), p. 214.

10. SANTA CLAUS ON THE CROSS

1. J. L. Hanna, "Issues in Supporting School Diversity: Academics, Social Relations and the Arts" (Washington, D.C.: Office of Educational Research and Improvement, United States Department of Education, 1991).

2. *New York Times*, 8 April 1991.

3. Roger M. Keesing, "Exotic Readings of Cultural Texts," *Current Anthropology* 30 (1989), pp. 459–69.

4. Ernest Gellner, *Relativism and the Social Sciences* (Cambridge: Cambridge University Press, 1985).

5. McKim Marriott, "Constructing an Indian Ethnosociology," *Contributions to Indian Sociology* 23 (1989): 1–39. The source is also available in McKim Marriott, ed., *India Through Hindu Categories* (Newbury Park, CA: Sage Publications, 1990).

13. THE PLAY OF SUBSTITUTION

1. Jean-Jacques Rousseau, *Confessions, Book XII* (Paris: Pleiade), p. 227.

17. AFFIRMATIVES AND SKEPTICS

1. D. Crane, *Invisible Colleges* (University of Chicago Press, 1972).

2. Ihab Hassan, *The Postmodern Turn* (Columbus: Ohio State University Press, 1987), p. 167.

3. Mike Featherstone, "In Pursuit of the Postmodern: An Introduction." *Theory, Culture and Society* 5 (1988) (2–3), p. 207.

4. See Jean Baudrillard, *Les strategies fatales* (Paris: Bernard Grasset, 1983); and Klaus Scherpe, "Dramatization and De-dramatization of 'The End': The Apocalyptic Consciousness of Modernity and Post-modernity," *Cultural Critique*, no. 5 (Winter 1986–87), pp. 95–129.

5. Todd Gitlin, "Postmodernism: Roots and Politics," *Dissent* (Winter 1989), pp. 100–108.

6. Matei Calinescu, *Five Faces of Modernity* (Durham, NC: Duke University Press, 1987), p. 305.

7. Jacques Derrida, *Marges* (Paris: Editions de Minut, 1978), p. 292.

8. Scherpe, op. cit.

9. Fergus M. Bordewich, "Colorado's Thriving Cults," *The New York Times Magazine*, May 1, 1988, pp. 37–43; Manfred Frank, *Was Ist Neostrukturalismus?* (Frankfurt: Suhrkamp Verlag, 1983), p. 405; Charles Levin and Arthur Kroker, "Baudrillard's Challenge," *Canadian Journal of Political and Social Theory*, 8 (1984), pp. 15–16.

18. FOUR DIFFERENT WAYS TO BE ABSOLUTELY RIGHT

1. Abraham Maslow, "Self-Actualizing People," in G. B. Levitas, ed., *The World of Psychology*, vol. 2 (New York: George Braziller, 1963), p. 548. I don't mean to classify Maslow as a postmodern psychologist; his view of the self was much more neo-romantic.

2. Allan Bloom, *The Closing of the American Mind: How Higher Education Has Failed Democracy and Impoverished the Souls of Today's Students* (New York: Simon & Schuster, 1987), pp. 320–22.

3. Kenneth Gergen, *The Saturated Self: Dilemmas of Identity in Contemporary Life* (New York: Basic Books, 1991), p. 147.

INTRODUCTION TO PART THREE

1. Sami Ma'ari, quoted in Kenneth Gergen, *The Saturated Self* (New York: Basic Books, 1991), p. 155.

2. Steinar Kvale, introduction to his anthology *Psychology and Postmodernism* (Newbury Park, CA: Sage, 1992), p. 15.

3. Gergen, op. cit. p. 147.

4. Kvale, op. cit. p. 31.

22. THE DEATH OF THE SELF IN A POSTMODERN WORLD

Recommended Reading

Anderson, Walter Truett. *Reality Isn't What It Used to Be.* (San Francisco: Harper-Collins, 1990).

Asher, Charles (1993). "The Communitarian Self as (God) Ultimate Reality: 9.5 Theses." In *Spring*, 54.

Edinger, Edward. *Ego and Archetype* (Boston: Shambhala, 1992).

Hillman, James. *Re-visioning Psychology* (New York: Harper and Row, 1975).

Jung, Carl. *Collected Works.* Vol. 9, Part II (Princeton, NJ: Princeton University Press).

Macy, Joanna. *World as Lover, World as Self* (Berkeley: Parallax Press, 1991).

Miller, Jean Baker. *Toward a New Psychology of Women* (Boston: Beacon Press, 1986).

Ponce, Charles. *The Archetype of the Unconscious and the Transfiguration of Therapy* (Berkeley: North Atlantic Books, 1990).

Romanyshyn, Robert. "Egos, Angels, and the Colors of Nature." Unpublished paper delivered at Pacifica Graduate Institute, Carpinteria, CA. Cassette available.

Samuels, Andrew. *The Plural Psyche* (London: Routledge, Kegan, Paul, 1993).

Watkins, Mary. "From Individualism to the Interdependent Self: Changing the Paradigm of Self in Psychotherapy." Unpublished paper delivered at Pacifica Graduate Institute, Carpinteria, CA. Cassette available.

23. CONSTRUCTING EMANCIPATORY REALITIES

Recommended Reading

Belenky, Mary, et al., *Women's Ways of Knowing* (New York: Basic Books, 1986).

Gilligan, Carol, et al., eds., *Mapping the Moral Domain: A Contribution to Women's Thinking in Psychological Theory and Education* (Cambridge, MA: Harvard University Press, 1988).

Evelyn Fox Keller, *Reflections on Gender and Science* (New Haven: Yale University Press, 1985).

Toril Moi, ed., *French Feminist Thought: A Reader* (Oxford: Basil Blackwell, 1987).

Chris Weedon, *Feminist Practice and Poststructuralist Theory* (Oxford: Basil Blackwell, 1987).

25. STUDYING CONSCIOUSNESS IN THE POSTMODERN AGE

1. Václav Havel, "The End of the Modern Era," *The New York Times*, March 1992, p. E15.

2. Ptolemy Tomkins, *This Tree Grows out of Hell: Mesoamerica and the Search for the Natural Body* (San Francisco: HarperCollins, 1990).

3. Radakrishna Radha, *Realities of the Dreaming Mind* (Spokane, WA: Timeless Books, 1994).

4. Charles D. Laughlin, *Scientific Explanation and the Life-world: A Biogenetic Structural Theory of Meaning and Causation* (Sausalito, CA: Institute of Noetic Sciences, 1992).

5. Charles Tart, *States of Consciousness* (New York: E. P. Dutton, 1975).

6. D. J. Hufford, *The Terror that Comes in the Night* (Philadelphia: University of Pennsylvania Press, 1982).

7. Kenneth Gergen, *The Saturated Self: Dilemmas of Identity in Contemporary Life* (New York: Basic Books, 1990).

8. Richard Shweder, "Cultural Psychology: What Is It?" in J. W. Stigler, R. A. Shweder and F. G. Herdt, eds., *Cultural Psychology: Essays on Comparative Human Development* (New York: Cambridge University Press, 1990), pp. 1–43.

9. Rhea White, "Feminist Science, Postmodern Views, and Exceptional Human Experience," in *Exceptional Human Experience*, 9 (1991), pp. 2–10.

INTRODUCTION TO PART FOUR

1. Stephen Toulmin, *The Return to Cosmology* (Berkeley: University of California Press, 1982), p. 268.

28. SCIENTISTS AND THEIR WORLDVIEWS

1. The original experiments were by George M. Stratton, "Vision without Inversion of the Retinal Image," *Psychological Review,* IV (1897), pp. 341–60, 463–81. A more up-to-date review is provided by Harvey A. Carr, *An Introduction to Space Perception* (New York, 1935), pp. 18–57.

2. For example, see Albert H. Hastorf, "The Influence of Suggestion on the Relationship between Stimulus Size and Perceived Distance," *Journal of Psychology,* XXIX (1950), pp. 195–217; and Jerome S. Bruner, Leo Postman, and John Rodrigues, "Expectations and the Perception of Color," *American Journal of Psychology,* LXIV (1951), pp. 216–27.

3. Peter Doig, *A Concise History of Astronomy* (London, 1950), pp. 115–16.

4. Rudolph Wolf, *Geschichte der Astronomie* (Munich, 1877), pp. 513–15, 683–93.

5. Joseph Needham, *Science and Civilization in China,* III (Cambridge, MA: Harvard University Press, 1959), pp. 423–29, 434–36.

6. T. S. Kuhn, *The Copernican Revolution* (Cambridge, MA: Harvard University Press, 1957), pp. 206–9.

7. Duane Roller and Duane H. D. Roller, *The Development of the Concept of Electric Charge* (Cambridge, MA: Harvard University Press, 1954), pp. 21–29.

8. See the discussion in T. S. Kuhn, *The Structure of Scientific Revolutions* (Chicago: University of Chicago Press, 1970), Section VII, and the literature to which the reference there cited in footnote 9 will lead.

9. Galileo Galilei, *Dialogues concerning Two New Sciences,* trans. H. Crew and A. de Salvio (Evanston, IL, 1946), pp. 80–81, 162–66.

10. Ibid., pp. 91–94, 244.

11. M. Clagett, *The Science of Mechanics in the Middle Ages* (Madison, WI, 1959), pp. 537–38, 570.

12. Jacques Hadamard, *Subconscient intuition, et logique dans la recherche scientifique Conférence faite au Palais de la Découverte le 8 Décembre 1945* [Alencon, n.d.], pp. 7–8. A much fuller account, though one exclusively restricted to mathematical innovations, is the same author's *The Psychology of Invention in the Mathematical Field* (Princeton, 1949).

30. POSTMODERNISM AND THE WORLD'S RELIGIONS

1. Akbar S. Ahmed, *Postmodernism and Islam* (London and New York: Routledge, 1992).

2. Jean-Francois Lyotard, *The Postmodern Condition: A Report on Knowledge* (Minneapolis: University of Minnesota Press, 1984), pp. xxiv, 3ff.

3. Jacques Derrida, *Of Grammatology,* trans. Gayatri Chakravorty Spivak (Baltimore: The Johns Hopkins University Press, 1977).

4. Jacques Derrida, "A Number of Yes," trans. Brian Holmes, *Oui Parle* 2 (1988), pp. 120–33.

5. In Richard Kearney, *Dialogues with Contemporary Continental Thinkers* (Manchester: Manchester University Press, 1984), p. 124.

6. John Caputo, "Good News about Alterity: Derrida and Theology," in *Faith and Philosophy*, p. 453.

7. Caputo, op. cit., p. 454, 457.

8. Huston Smith, *Forgotten Truth: The Common Vision of the World's Religions* (San Francisco: Harper, 1976/1992).

9. Robert Kane's *Through the Moral Maze: Searching for Absolute Values in a Pluralistic World* (New York: Paragon House, 1994) makes this point convincingly.

10. Richard Madsen, one of the authors of *The Good Society*, Robert Bellah et al. (New York: Knopf, 1991).

11. *San Francisco Chronicle*, October 1, 1992, p. A16.

12. Arthur Lovejoy, *The Great Chain of Being* (Cambridge: Harvard University Press, 1936), p. 59. Ernst Cassirer corroborates Lovejoy on this point: "The most important legacy of ancient speculation was the concept and general picture of a graduated cosmos." *Individual and Cosmos in Renaissance Philosophy*, p. 9.

13. Ken Wilber, "The Great Chain of Being," *Journal of Humanistic Psychology*, vol. 33, no. 3 (Summer 1993), p. 53.

EPILOGUE

1. Daniel Boorstin, *The Discoverers: A History of Man's Search to Know His World and Himself* (New York: Random House, 1983).

2. Robert Nisbet, *History of the Idea of Progress* (New York: Basic Books, 1980).

3. Saul Bellow, *The Adventures of Augie March* (New York: Viking, 1953), p. 504.

PERMISSIONS

"Themes of Postmodernity," by Steinvar Kvale. Excerpted from the essay "Postmodern Psychology: A Contradiction in Terms?" in his anthology *Psychology and Postmodernism,* published by SAGE Publications, Inc. The essay first published in *The Humanistic Psychologist,* 18(1) 1990, special issue on Psychology and Postmodernity, © the Editorial Committee of the Division of Humanistic Psychology. Reproduced by permission of the author and *The Humanistic Psychologist.*

"What is Post-Modernism?" by Charles Jencks. From his book *What Is Post-Modernism?,* published in New York by St. Martin's Press and in London by Academy Editions. Reprinted with permission of the author and Academy Group Limited.

"'I Love You Madly,' He Said Self-consciously," by Umberto Eco. Excerpt from *Postscript to The Name of the Rose,* copyright © 1983 by Umberto Eco, English translation, copyright © 1984 by Harcourt Brace & Company, reprinted by permission of the publisher.

"The Fragile Fiction," by Ernest Becker. Reprinted with the permission of The Free Press, an imprint of Simon & Schuster, from *The Birth and Death of Meaning,* by Ernest Becker. Copyright © 1962, 1971 by The Free Press.

"The Dehumanized World," by Peter L. Berger and Thomas Luckmann. From *The Social Construction of Reality: A Treatise in the Sociology of Knowledge,* by Peter L. Berger and Thomas Luckmann. Copyright © 1966 by Peter L. Berger and Thomas Luckmann. Used by permission of Doubleday, a division of Bantam Doubleday Dell Publishing Group, Inc.

"Strategies of Power," by Michel Foucault. Reprinted from Lawrence Kritzman, ed. *Michel Foucault: Politics, Philosophy, Culture* (1988), by permission of the publisher, Routledge, New York; Lawrence Kritzman; and *L'Express* magazine.

"The Idea of Pluralism," by Isaiah Berlin. From *The Crooked Timber of Humanity,* by Isaiah Berlin. Copyright © 1991 by Isaiah Berlin. Reprinted by permission of Alfred A. Knopf, Inc.

"The Idea of Culture," by Roy Wagner. From his book *The Invention of Culture,* published by the University of Chicago Press. Copyright © 1975, 1981 by Roy Wagner. Used by permission.

CONTRIBUTORS

JEAN BAUDRILLARD, French social critic and sociologist, is author of the highly acclaimed *America* and *Cool Memories.*

ERNEST BECKER (1924–1974) taught at the University of California, Berkeley, San Francisco State University, and Simon Fraser University in Canada. He won the Pulitzer Prize for general nonfiction in 1974 for his book *The Denial of Death.*

PETER L. BERGER, a leading theorist and scholar of the sociology of knowledge, is director of the Institute for the Study of Economic Culture at Boston University.

SIR ISAIAH BERLIN, historian of ideas and political philosopher, has won many awards for his writing and his work in defense of civil liberties. He is a fellow of All Souls College, Oxford, and a former president of the British Academy.

JACQUES DERRIDA, best known as the originator of the "deconstruction" school of literary criticism, is professor of the history of philosophy at the École Normale Supérieure in Paris.

UMBERTO ECO is a world-famous specialist in semiotics, as well as author of the best-selling novel *The Name of the Rose,* philosopher, historian, and freewheeling critic of literature and popular culture. He teaches at the University of Bologna and lives in Milan.

PAUL FEYERABEND (1924–1994) was professor of philosophy at the University of California, Berkeley, and is regarded as one of the most brilliantly controversial critics of science and scientific method.

MICHEL FOUCAULT (1926–1984) wrote *Madness and Civilization: A History of Instanity in the Age of Reason; Discipline and Punish: The Birth of the Prison;* and the three-volume *History of Sexuality.*

HOWARD GARDNER is professor of education at the Harvard Graduate School of Education, and co-director of Project Zero, an institute concerned with educational reform. His forthcoming book is entitled *Leading Minds.*

KENNETH J. GERGEN is professor of psychology at Swarthmore and a leading exponent of postmodern/constructivist psychology. His most recent book is *The Saturated Self: Dilemmas of Identity in Contemporary Life.*

VÁCLAV HAVEL is a playwright and president of the Czech Republic. In 1994 he was awarded the Philadelphia Liberty Medal.

BELL HOOKS, professor at Oberlin College, has written numerous books on racism and gender, as well as essays, plays, novels, short stories, and poems. She regularly contributes a bimonthly column, "Sisters of the Yam," to *Z* magazine.

JAMES DAVISON HUNTER is professor of sociology and religious studies at the University of Virginia.

CHARLES JENCKS is one of the leading definers of post-modernity (he prefers the hyphen), and an internationally renowned architect. He lives in the United Kingdom and teaches part-time at the University of California, Los Angeles.

STEPHEN KATZ teaches sociology at Trent University, Peterborough, Ontario. His essay "How to Speak and Write Postmodern," reprinted in this volume, was a classic on the Internet, where it first appeared. Copyright © 1995.

STANLEY KRIPPNER teaches at the Saybrook Institute in San Francisco. He edited the New Consciousness Reader *Dreamtime and Dreamwork* and has done extensive research and writing in parapsychology and consciousness studies.

THOMAS KUHN is the Laurence S. Rockefeller Professor of Philosophy at the Massachusetts Institute of Technology. His work on paradigm shifts in science is regarded as one of this century's most important contributions to Western philosophy.

STEINER KVALE is professor of educational psychology and director of the Centre for Qualitative Research at the Institute of Psychology, Aarhus University, Denmark. He is a noted international authority on postmodernism and psychology.

ROBERT JAY LIFTON is professor of psychiatry and psychology at the City University of New York, and author of many books, including landmark studies of the psychology of brainwashing in China, and of the psychological aftereffects of Hiroshima.

THOMAS LUCKMANN, who has taught at Hobart College, the New School for Social Research, and the University of Frankfurt, is now professor emeritus at the University of Constance.

MARTIN MARTY, one of America's most eminent theologians, is professor of theology at the School of Divinity at the University of Chicago and senior editor of

Christian Century. He recently co-directed the Fundamentalism Project of the American Academy of Arts and Sciences.

MAUREEN O'HARA is a psychotherapist, feminist scholar, and past president of the Association for Humanistic Psychology. She is currently working on research projects concerned with the relationship between social contexts and individual psyches.

RICHARD RORTY, University Professor of Humanities at the University of Virginia, is one of the most provocative and influential thinkers of our time. He has been described as "the most interesting philosopher in the world today."

PAULINE MARIE ROSENAU is professor of political science at the University of Quebec, Montreal, and author of *When Marxists Do Research.* She formerly wrote under the name Pauline Vallaincourt.

ARTHUR SCHLESINGER, JR., a Pulitzer Prize–winning historian, and senior adviser to President John F. Kennedy in the 1960s, is now professor of humanities at the City University of New York.

RICHARD SHWEDER is a cultural anthropologist, chair of the Committee on Human Development at the University of Chicago, and a recipient of numerous honors including the American Association for the Advancement of Science's socio-psychological award. His latest book is entitled *Why Do Men Barbecue? and Other Recipes for Cultural Psychology.*

WILLIAM SIMON is professor of sociology at the University of Houston, Central Campus, and author of *Postmodern Sexualities.*

HUSTON SMITH is emeritus professor of philosophy and religion, Syracuse University, and visiting professor of religious studies at the University of California, Berkeley. His books include *The World's Religions, Forgotten Truth,* and *Beyond the Post-Modern Mind.*

WERNER SOLLORS is professor of American literature and Afro-American studies at Harvard University. His most recent book is entitled *Neither Black nor White and Yet Both.*

ERNEST STERNBERG teaches in the School of Architecture and Planning at the State University of New York at Buffalo. He is currently at work on a book on the economy of icons, a project for which he received the research award of the Rollo May Center for Humanistic Studies in 1993.

ROY WAGNER is professor of anthropology at the University of Virginia. His books include *Symbols that Stand for Themselves, The Curse of Souw,* and *Habu: The Innovation of Meaning in Daribi Religion.*

MICHAEL WINKLER, a graduate student in psychology at the University of North Carolina at Asheville, has conducted research on mood cycles and is currently engaged in cross-cultural dream studies in South America. He has presented his work at international conferences in Chile and Greece.

CONNIE ZWEIG, former executive editor at Jeremy P. Tarcher, Inc., is editor of the collected volumes *Meeting the Shadow: The Hidden Power of the Dark Side of Human Nature* and *To Be a Woman: The Birth of the Conscious Feminine.*

ABOUT THE EDITOR

Walt Anderson's previous books include *Reality Isn't What It Used to Be*, *To Govern Evolution*, *Rethinking Liberalism*, *The Upstart Spring* and *Open Secrets*. A longtime resident of the San Francisco Bay area, he is a fellow of the Meridian Institute, an international network of scholars and practitioners concerned with issues of governance, learning, leadership and the future. He writes regularly for the Pacific News Service and currently serves as president of the American division of the World Academy of Art and Science.